*f*P

A Radical Line

*From the Labor Movement to the Weather
Underground, One Family's
Century of Conscience*

—

THAI JONES

FREE PRESS
NEW YORK   LONDON
TORONTO   SYDNEY

*f*P

FREE PRESS

A Division of Simon & Schuster, Inc.
1230 Avenue of the Americas
New York, NY 10020

FREE PRESS and colophon are
trademarks of Simon & Schuster, Inc.

For information about special discounts for bulk purchases,
please contact Simon & Schuster Special Sales:
1-800-456-6798 or business@simonandschuster.com

All photos are courtesy of the author.

Manufactured in the United States of America

1   3   5   7   9   10   8   6   4   2

Library of Congress Cataloging-in-Publication Data
Jones, Thai.
A radical line: from the labor movement to the Weather Underground,
one family's century of conscience/Thai Jones.
p. cm.
Includes bibliographical references and index.
1. Radicalism—United States—History—20th century. 2. Jones, Thai, 1977——Family.
3. Jones family. I. Title.

HN90.R3J66 2004
335.43'092'273—dc22
[B]   2004053217

ISBN 0-7432-5027-3

For Albert and Millie, Annie and Artie

CONTENTS

Prologue   3

CHAPTER 1   Cobblestones   15

CHAPTER 2   L'Enfant Jones   33

CHAPTER 3   *Konspiratsia*   50

CHAPTER 4   The Other Cheek   69

CHAPTER 5   The Committees   90

CHAPTER 6   Breakaway   120

CHAPTER 7   Class Struggle   146

CHAPTER 8   Days of Rage   173

CHAPTER 9   In the Forest   210

CHAPTER 10 The Bust   244

Afterword   283

Notes   289

Sources   301

Acknowledgments   307

Index   309

A Radical Line

*T*o me, we seemed like a normal family—no, a terrific family. I was four years old in October 1981, a kid in day care with dinosaurs roaming the brain. My father, who went by the name John Maynard, worked as a printer in Manhattan. My mother, whom I knew as Sally, was a secretary.

We lived in an apartment in the Bronx. Of our many homes, this one was the best. It had a sunken living room where my father and I had built models of the Titanic and the Empire State Building. At the end of a long hallway there was a miniature bedroom all for me. My name was Timmy Maynard.

On a Friday night, we had eaten a steaming spaghetti dinner and were watching the World Series on TV when the telephone rang. In all the months we had lived there, the phone in that apartment had never rung once. We stared at it. My father got off the bed and picked it up.

"Is this Mr. Maynard?" a hard voice asked over the line.

"Yes," my father said.

"This is Lawrence Wack. I'm a special agent with the Federal Bureau of Investigation. I want you to know that we have your apartment surrounded, that we have men on the rooftops of neighboring buildings, and that in thirty seconds there is going to be a knock on your front door. You are to follow the instructions of the officer at the door."

My father cupped the receiver in his palm, turned to my mother, and mouthed the words, "We're busted." She gathered me up and sat me on her lap.

"Timmy," she said in a voice meant to be soothing, "something really bad is about to happen. But it's going to be okay. Police are going to come and take us away. You're going to stay with some friends and we'll all be together again real soon."

In the living room, my father was starting to negotiate. "You've got your bust," he told Agent Wack, "but I want to say two things. Number one, we do not intend to resist the arrest, and number two, there's a child in the apartment."

Battering on the door ended conversation. Officers were beating it with their gloved fists and rifle butts. My father opened up to a flood of them dressed in full riot gear, carrying shotguns and M-16s, and expecting trouble. They washed into the apartment and spread from room to room, keeping their eyes sighted down their gun barrels until they felt secure. They tore through closets and searched under the bed, tossing away hand-stitched quilts, upending heaps of my Matchbox cars and Lego blocks.

Impelled at rifle point, my father was forced into the hallway and told to crawl its length. The old ladies on the floor peeked through their chained doors in horror as he scuttled across the oyster-cracker tiles. My mother was arguing with the police. For the moment, everyone had forgotten me.

I walked down the hallway to my bedroom and closed myself in. There had to be something I could do to help my parents. I made a fast survey of my possessions: a cowboy outfit, a coloring book, a stuffed Tyrannosaurus. I opened the drawer of my little desk and picked up my child's scissors. The ends were rounded, and the blades were covered by blue plastic guards.

Bouncing them in my hand and snipping at the air, I considered putting on the cowboy hat and charging into the hallway with scissors blazing to defeat these men who had come to hurt our family. Even then, I knew it was a battle against long odds. But I didn't realize it was a question that many in my family had already faced. They had chosen to fight.

For me, the decision was easy to make. I returned the scissors and closed the drawer. I went out to the hallway where my father was manacled, slid my small fingers around the cold cuffs into his palm, and stood with him in the corridor holding hands.

This is my earliest memory.

PROLOGUE

Name: Eleanor E. Raskin
Alias: Eleanor E. Stein
FBI Number: 47 593 H
Date of Birth: 3/16/46
Marital Status: Married
Height: 5'7"
Weight: 140
Eyes: Brown
Hair: Brown
Scars, marks and peculiarities: Wears glasses

My mother could hear the sirens as she walked down Eighth Street around noon on March 6, 1970. Emergency vehicles were approaching from several directions, and the noise rose in key and cadence. Taxis on Sixth Avenue edged away from the center lane. Some on the sidewalks paused to watch when, at the zenith of sound, the convoy of fire trucks blurred past. Visions of red and chrome, their helmeted drivers pressed the horns furiously at anything too slow to move aside. Then the alarm was clanging farther uptown, and the shocking sensory attack diminished as quickly as it had appeared. Eleanor had hardly bothered to look up.

She had lived in the city since girlhood, and no day had passed without its accompanying soundtrack of fire trucks, squad cars, and ambulances. She no longer even wondered where they went. Never once, until this moment, had the sirens wailed for her.

In one week, Eleanor would be twenty-four years old. In the previous six months, she had been arrested, quit law school and left her husband to help the Weathermen. The Vietnam War, which had begun when she was in high school, was about to spread into Cambodia. Most Americans opposed the fighting, but nothing they had done in a decade of dissent had affected the government's policies in any discernible way. The avenues of protest had been exhausted, and all that remained was grief or anger.

The Weathermen had chosen rage to the exclusion of all else. They trained themselves in the art of people's war and tested one another by attacking their weaknesses in all-night criticism sessions. Eleanor survived mostly on brown rice and a Vietnamese fish sauce called *nuoc mam*. She shared an undecorated apartment with half a dozen others and slept on a bare mattress flung across the floor. No sacrifice could be enough to prove that she and her comrades had shed their comfortably middle-class instincts and morphed into pure, stone-cold revolutionaries.

Yet her mother lived only a few blocks away and had a view overlooking Central Park. Even though Eleanor was supposed to be in hiding, she bumped into her friends all the time. She was never farther than a short walk or a taxi fare from her old life. She thought she could resume it at any time, and nothing she had seen led her to believe her choices were irrevocable.

Beyond her view, the fire trucks had turned onto West Eleventh Street. On a normal afternoon, it would be one of the quietest blocks in Greenwich Village. Now, black smoke rose above the three-story townhouses. Nearly twenty rescue vehicles plugged the narrow street, and police stood at both ends ordering drivers to go around. Firemen in turnout coats bellowed instructions as the pressurized water smacked against the crumbling brick walls of number eighteen. It had been one of the most valuable homes in the row. Neighbors had often watched the Wilkerson family's tuxedoed guests glide into the double drawing room for formal parties or listened to the murmur of afternoon teas served in the backyard. Now, before it could collapse on its own and damage its neighbors, a wrecking ball was called in to punch through its facade.

The explosion had come from the basement and punched through the sixteen-inch walls, leaving gaps big enough to drive a truck through and smashing glass in windows across the street. Immediately after the blast, two women in their twenties—Cathlyn Wilkerson and Kathy Boudin—both long-time members of Students for a Democratic Society, had emerged from the spreading flames. They were dazed, scraped and nearly naked. A neighbor clothed them and offered to let them rest. But when the police arrived to take their statements, the women had already fled.

It was hours later, back in her uptown apartment, that Eleanor learned about the accident. She realized that she had been in the general area at the time. She had been going to a meeting, having no idea that a Weatherman cell was operating in the neighborhood. She wondered if anyone was dead. Then she remembered the sirens and passing fire trucks and shivered at the recollection: that's how close she had come.

FBI agents would be on Eleventh Street by now. They would be swarming over the rubble and sniffing for a scent to trace. Anyone who had known the two missing women would be picked up. Eleanor realized she had to leave her apartment and find a place to stay for the night, somewhere the FBI would never think to find her. Around the country, hundreds of others were doing the same thing: disappearing from their lives.

At a friend's house near Columbia University, she watched the evening news. West Eleventh Street had been completely blocked off, and floodlights threw strange shadows across the abscess where the house had been. The first body had been found—a young man in blue jeans crushed beneath the fallen beams. Police had already abandoned their early suspicion of a gas leak. They recognized that the damage profile fit the pattern for a dynamite explosion.

That night Eleanor dreamed she was trapped inside a burning building.

The next morning was Saturday. Eleanor threw off the lamb's wool coat that served as a blanket and rose from the deflated pillows of the sofa. Brushing her tangled hair into near-submission, she zipped up her knee-high snakeskin boots. She had abandoned her family and her law career, but she had been unable to do without her wardrobe. Putting on the coat, she quietly opened the apartment door and slipped out.

"This is the end," she whispered to herself.

"This is the end," she repeated, walking down Broadway. And indeed the morning light looked eerie and apocalyptic. In a few hours, New York would find itself directly in the path of a total eclipse of the sun. No one could predict how the City would react to noontime darkness, and extra police had been called in to maintain order.

Descending into the 116th Street subway station, Eleanor scanned the crowd for suspicious faces. She knew that any of these strangers on the platform could be following her. They would be trained in stealth while she had no training at all. They would have ways to avoid detection while she relied on nerves and fear. She rode the train to Penn Station. There she squeezed through the sliding doors, climbed the ringing metal stairs, strode quickly to a northbound platform, and boarded an uptown subway car. She got off this second train at Columbus Circle, one of the busiest stops in the system, and then zig-zagged through midtown, walking in fits and starts, turning often, until she felt certain she was alone.

The image of nonchalance, Eleanor entered the Mayflower Hotel lobby and took a left. There, in a little out-of-the-way nook, was her row of pay telephones. In all the city, the Mayflower's phones were the most private and offered the widest choice of escape routes. She entered the last booth and shut the wood-and-glass door. At precisely 9:00 A.M., the phone started ringing. Eleanor picked up the receiver.

The voice on the line spoke vaguely but was all business. "I need to ask you to do me a favor. A mutual friend needs to take a vacation," it said. "Can you help?"

"Okay," Eleanor said. "What can I do?"

"You'll be in charge of wardrobe," it said. One of the women who had fled the explosion was trying to leave the city. By the next morning, her face would be in the pages of each edition of every newspaper. Eleanor's job was to find a disguise.

"Where should our friend meet you?" the voice asked.

"Have her come up to momma's house," replied Eleanor.

From the hotel, she walked downtown to Lord & Taylor's department store on Thirty-Ninth Street and Fifth Avenue. She brushed past the window displays for midi-skirts, which hung somewhere between the repressed hemlines of the Fifties and the outrageous minis of the Sixties. The police were looking for a hippie, and Eleanor planned to remove any traces of radical chic from the fugitive. She picked out several polyester ensembles and gaudy, bright lipstick. In the millinery department, she bought several wigs, choosing curly and frumpy models that could never be associated with the woman police were seeking.

Eleanor paid with her mother's charge account, signing "Annie Stein" on the receipt.

Outside, pedestrians stood still in the streets, staring at the sky. The eclipse had started. By early afternoon, the sun was 96 percent obscured, and the day was reduced to twilight. Fearing chaos, the police department had mobilized its Special Events Squad, but New Yorkers took it in stride, pausing for a few minutes to investigate the spectacle and then placidly getting back to business. Eleanor hardly noticed. With shopping bags in both hands, she went uptown to her mother's apartment on 100th Street.

> Name: Annie Stein
> Born: New York City
> Height: 5'7"
> Weight: 150–155
> Hair: Black, graying
> Eyes: Greenish brown, deep set
> Eyebrows: Black
> Characteristics: Thin face, prominent nose

Peculiarities: Husky voice. Domineering, does not lose nerve.

Annie had celebrated her fifty-seventh birthday a few days before the townhouse explosion. For thirty-seven of those years, she had been under FBI surveillance. Her hair had grayed in that time, and she trapped it in a tightly wrapped bun. Her husband, Arthur Stein, had been dead for a decade, and she was finally adjusting to life without him. She wore house dresses, unstylish flats, and big glasses, and looked like any of the other Upper West Side widows who lived in the apartment complex.

But Annie had a cartoon hanging on the wall. It showed several ducks walking one way and a single duck going in the opposite direction. "Do you know what I call it?" she'd tell visitors. "I call it the dissenter."

Her other walls were hidden behind filing cabinets and book shelves bearing a complete library of Marxist thought. At the climax of any political discussion, she could reach for a volume and clinch the argument.

"Look," Annie would tell Eleanor, "I lived through the 1930s when the capitalist system was on the ropes. Labor unions were strong and men were out of work, on breadlines." Pausing for effect, she would light a cigarette, sip her scotch and soda, and go to the bookshelf for her copy of Lenin's *What Is to Be Done?* "It was obvious in 1917," she would say, waving the book in her daughter's face. "The workers were in the streets. Who is going to run the means of production in your revolution? The hippies? You've got to be kidding."

Eleanor turned the key to her mother's apartment and made certain that it was empty. She was not in the mood to hear any of Annie's homilies today.

Her purchases were laid out like she was the Avon lady when Cathlyn Wilkerson arrived. Cathy's house had been demolished, and she remained dazed and deafened by the explosion. An organized network that she had only faintly known about had taken over her movements, and friends all over town were working to spirit her from the city. She had little interest in any of that. Her comrades were dead, and no one seemed to want to talk about it.

Eleanor worked quickly. She dyed Cathy's hair and globbed on the makeup. When she was done, the hippie had become a secretary from the boroughs, one of a million others whom no one noticed. Eleanor gave her the wigs so she could change her look, and the job was complete. Cathy was passed off to the next conductor on the underground railroad and disappeared.

•••

> Name: Jeffrey Carl Jones
> Age: 23, born February 23, 1947
> Height: 5'11"
> Hair: Blond, worn long
> Eyes: Blue
> Build: Slender
> Caution: Jones reportedly may resist arrest, has been associated with persons who advocate the use of explosives and may have acquired firearms. Consider dangerous.

The solar eclipse barely registered on the West Coast. In northern California, only 27 percent of the sun was blocked. It looked like a chipped china saucer. My father hated to miss it. In a world without Vietnam Wars and Richard Nixons, he would have taken the day to drive up the Pacific coast. He'd find a deserted spot on a rugged Marin County beach and remove the fragrant leather pouch from his jacket pocket. Pinching some green sinsemilla buds and laying them in a cigarette paper, he'd take the extra time to roll a perfect joint and then light up.

He had been raised in the San Fernando Valley before it was entirely paved over by the Los Angeles suburbs. Some of the best hours of his life had been spent wandering through the Mojave desert with his YMCA camp friends and, since childhood, he had liked nothing better than to get lost in the wild and then find his way back home again. He had gone east for school and, after two years at Antioch College in Ohio, dropped out to work full time for Students for a Democratic Society.

For four years he had been at nearly every milestone of the anti-war movement: he had charged the Pentagon in 1967 and stood face-to-face with National Guardsmen during the 1968 Democratic National Convention in Chicago. The parades had turned into marches and then riots. As the years dragged on, desperation grew. In the summer of 1969 Jeff was elected—along with Mark Rudd and Bill Ayers—to the national office of SDS. He had brought the politics of rage to the largest student organization in American history and, within months, it was finished, splintered and destroyed. All that remained was the true fringe: Weatherman.

Jeff had never stopped wandering. There were few neighborhoods he didn't know, and in each new city he took the time to map out the fastest escape routes. In October 1969, he had led a few hundred Weathermen against the Chicago cops in a full-blown street fight that would come to be known as the Days of Rage. After that, there had been no way to avoid the law. Police officers trailed him constantly. He had no time for walks or meditation. Only at night, when the day's organizing was complete, did he allow himself the respite of a joint.

On March 7, instead of watching the eclipse, Jeff filled his pockets with rolls of quarters and went to work. He had come to San Francisco when Chicago became too dark and threatening. Going from pay phone to pay phone, he used his quarters on long-distance calls: making connections and scheduling meetings. He was lying low, still using his real name but also forging false IDs and learning to live under an alias. At supporters' homes around the city, he had left escape bags filled with clothes, money, and driver's licenses.

At the end of the month, Jeff was due to appear in a Chicago courtroom to face charges of rioting and punching a police officer that he had incurred during the Days of Rage. Lawyers around the country were preparing his defense, and the press was gearing up for another sensational political trial. But it wasn't going to happen. Jeff was going to disappear. With the IDs and secret phone calls, he was building the network to support an underground. He planned to skip his day in court and become a wanted man.

Jeff checked his watch on the evening of March 7. It was time for another in the endless series of phone calls. When he picked up the receiver, a frightened voice asked him one question: "Have you heard?"

"No," said Jeff. The voice hesitated. Obviously, he didn't want to say too much over the phone.

Finally he spoke in code. "Mister SDS is dead," he told Jeff, who knew the name could only refer to Teddy Gold, a leader of the Columbia chapter who had personified the passions of the cause.

"How did it happen?" Jeff asked.

"Go buy a newspaper."

Reading about the townhouse explosion in the *Chronicle*, Jeff was upset but not surprised. In the previous months, bombings had spread like an infection. From a localized outbreak in Vietnam, they had been borne by frustration to Laos and Cambodia, India and Algeria, Paris and Germany, Chile, Argentina and now America. Less than a month earlier, Jeff had been shocked when a bomb killed a police officer in San Francisco. With the accident in New York, it seemed as if the violence was still escalating and, sure enough, four days later, a different group detonated explosives inside three corporate offices in midtown Manhattan.

It was not a contagion that the government could ignore. The Federal Bureau of Investigation would use all its resources to find Jeff and the others. Its agents would track down every friend, every college professor, every employer, every neighbor. They would watch his parents at all times.

The court date approached, and the rescue workers sifting through the rubble in Greenwich Village uncovered enough additional sticks of dynamite to level the entire block. Miraculously, they had not gone off. Rescuers also discovered two more bodies. The woman was decapitated, and her arms and feet had been blown off. By tracing prints on a pinky finger found among the bricks, specialists had identified her as Diana Oughton. Jeff knew that the final body, belonging to a young man, was Terry Robbins, but to people outside the organization, he remained a John Doe. Nervous parents with wayward sons around the country worried that he was theirs.

Jeff knew he was about to become a fugitive. Once he had

skipped his day in court, there would be no way to go home and see his family. It might be years before he and his father could meet again, and Jeff did not want him to spend that time wondering whether his son was alive or dead. To reassure him, he would have to see his dad face-to-face, and if that was going to occur, it had to happen now.

A stranger meeting Al Jones for the first time could take a hundred guesses and still not figure him right. He was fifty years old in the early spring of 1970 and stood six feet two inches tall. He was broad across the middle. In full regalia—cowboy boots and hat—he was a truly giant man. He refused to drive any car that wasn't built in America and was less than seventeen feet long. Yet despite his resemblance to an extra on the set of a Hollywood western, he was a man of peace who would never lift his finger against a living thing.

Al was a Quaker. During World War II, he had been among the tiny minority of Americans who refused to wholeheartedly support the good fight. Instead, he had been shipped to a work camp in the mountains. Jeff's father couldn't abide cussing and didn't approve of his son's new friends. He hated the Vietnam War too, of course, but the Weathermen weren't opposing the war in the Quaker way. Before the Days of Rage, Albert had given Jeff a warning. In his sternest voice he had said, "Son, I believe very strongly in your goals. But if you set out to hurt somebody, I would hope and pray that you are hurt first."

Al worried that Jeff had taken him at his word. It had been months since he had heard from him. Then at the end of March, Jeff called from San Francisco. He wanted to come down for a short visit. The tone in his voice, clipped and flat, left Albert with little doubt that serious things were happening in his son's life. Jeff flew down, carrying only a rucksack as luggage. The family home was in Sylmar, at the northern edge of the San Fernando Valley. It was part of a recent development providing, according to the realtors, a combination of "away-from-it-all privacy and . . . nearby shopping areas." Al lived there with his daughter, Julie. Jeff's mother, Millie, had left Albert in 1966.

The small bedroom where Jeff had lived as a preppy high school senior was as he had left it. That had been only five years earlier. Now the hard-charging boy, the kid who had been class president and won the Disney scholarship, was coming home.

Albert preferred not to know what his son was up to, and Jeff was in no hurry to fill him in. Still, the comforts of the family nest—sitting on the sofa drinking a beer and watching TV—were a welcome change from the rigors of organizing. In the evening, Jeff walked out of the house and wandered through the foothills of the San Gabriel Mountains, listening to the coyotes as the sun swept west across the valley.

Back at home, Jeff locked himself in the bedroom and removed a brown paper bag from his rucksack. Moving quietly and carefully, he hid the bundle on the closet shelf.

The next morning, Albert drove him out to Burbank Airport. They waited together in silence until his flight was called. After a quick hug, Jeff left the gate and walked across the tarmac toward his waiting 727. Albert watched through the terminal window. He saw Jeff climb the steps of the movable ladder that led to the hatchway of the jet. It was getting late for work, but he waited. Jeff was at the top of the gangway, facing the plane. He stood there, hanging fire between staying and leaving, for several seconds. Then he seemed to reach a decision and, without looking back, vanished inside the plane.

Albert walked to his car and steered toward the office. He turned on the radio as it flashed to news: the notorious Weathermen had skipped a court date in Chicago scheduled for the day before. Jeff Jones was one of them. The judge had issued bench warrants. They had officially become fugitives. Albert pulled past the guard and into the parking lot at the Disney Studios on the morning of April 1, 1970. It would be a decade before he saw his son again.

•••

In New York City, the Federal Bureau of Investigation was working its way down a sheet of names listing every soul who had ever been associated with the Weathermen. Annie Stein was home when two men in dark suits rang her bell. She opened the door but kept it tethered on its chain. The agents told her that her daughter was dead and asked to be allowed inside. Annie refused to let them into the apartment. She had spent most of her life not talking to the FBI.

Many parents were informed that it was their child who was lying in the rubble on West Eleventh Street. Some might have believed it and told what they knew. Others, opposed to the politics of their children, may not have needed much prompting. Annie knew her daughter was safe: she had already received a bill in the mail from Lord & Taylor's department store. When she saw that wigs had been purchased on her account on the day after the explosion, she had known that Eleanor was fine.

Weeks after his son had left, Albert was rummaging through his closet when he discovered the bundle wrapped in old clothes that Jeff had stuck there. He pulled it out and laid it on the bed. Unwrapping the package, he found two handguns—a 9mm and a revolver—and some shells.

It was late afternoon. Albert tossed the guns on the bench seat in his car and steered down California State Road 14. There was a place he often drove by, a deserted lot overgrown with sage and chaparral. Pulling to the side of the road, he climbed out and waited a few moments to make sure no one was around. The brush sloped down a steep incline for several hundred feet. The desert night was falling, and he felt a creeping chill. Cactuses on the far hilltops stood out in silhouette.

Taking a final look around him, Albert stepped back and heaved the guns into the arroyo.

CHAPTER 1

Cobblestones

Two young women climbed the stairs to an elevated rail platform in Brooklyn during the summer of 1929. One of them walked with a cane, and the other's legs were hampered by a long black coat that was anything but stylish. Their school day had just ended, and they stood a few paces apart waiting for the train to Coney Island. On the street below, nothing stirred unless it had to. Glass, steel, stone, concrete: everything in the borough absorbed the sun and was too hot to touch. Carefully shaded groceries were rank and rotten by midmorning, while fat flies swarmed around the steaming trash piled on the sidewalk.

Evelyn Wiener, known to her Yiddish-speaking friends as Chavy, was taking summer classes because she had flunked geometry. Only fifteen years old, a childhood case of polio forced her to walk with the aid of a wooden cane. Her father had been a charter member of the American Communist Party, and Chavy remembered well the night when the czar had been overthrown. She had been only three in 1917 and had toddled out in wonder to watch her parents and all their friends drinking vodka in celebration. She had grown up in the Party. As a girl she had been a Young Pioneer and recently, though she was not yet sixteen and had lied about her age, she had joined the Young Communist League.

Chavy and her radical friends had their own language and style. The men wore leather jackets, and the women went without makeup. Looking at the second girl on the train platform, Chavy thought she spotted a fellow traveler. Only a Red would wear that loose-fitting coat that whipped around the stranger's legs every time a train tornadoed by.

The girl in the distinctive outfit was Annie Steckler, my grand-mother. She was a year older than Chavy and also in summer school. Until recently she had been a fine student, but her father, Philip Steckler, had died a few years earlier, and her mother had sent her to stay with relatives and gone looking for a new husband. Annie, not surprisingly, had developed a willful stubbornness, a temper, and a sharp tongue.

But as Chavy discovered after a brief conversation, she was no radical. Jumping at the chance to make a convert, Chavy started bragging about the fearsome strength of the Young Communist League. Finally, carried away with enthusiasm, she warned, "We are becoming a menace!"

"What," Annie asked, "a little two-by-nothing like you, a menace?"

The conversation might have ended there. Instead both girls boarded the same train, and Annie listened to stories about the Party. By the time they reached Coney Island, the girls were friends.

A year later, when Chavy turned sixteen, Annie gave her a copy of Marx's *Das Kapital*. "If you must be a Communist," she said a bit scathingly, "at least you should know what you're talking about."

•••

Annie's father had a widow's peak like a ship's prow. He could comb it forward, backward, or to the side, and still it would point down unmercifully to the bridge of his nose. Philip Steckler was born in 1875 in the village of Romny in the Ukraine, which had served for centuries as a farmers' market and a Cossack stronghold against the czars. Narrow and uneven stone streets separated short and moldy stone buildings. It was a place one hardly needed an excuse to leave, but for an ambitious Jewish man, there were excuses aplenty. Violence against the Jewish communities in Russia could break out at any moment, and when Steckler was twenty-eight, it did.

Kishinev, near the Ukraine's southwestern border, was the kind of city that a young bumpkin from Romny might someday aspire to visit. It was a commercial hub where Jews and Moldavians, Russians, Bulgarians, and Albanians tolerated each other with varying degrees of loathing. In April 1903, during the Easter festival when religious zeal was at its annual zenith, the Christians of the city sacked the houses of the Jewish quarter. After two days of rapine and slaughter, the Jews of Kishinev had forty-three new graves to dig. In the telegraph age, the details of the Easter pogrom were printed in the world's newspapers without delay. International committees denounced the czar, and benevolent societies from every Western capital gathered alms for the victims. Jews living in the town of Romny, one province over, didn't think of Kishinev as a far-off place. For them, the violence was a present threat. Within a year of the pogrom, Annie's father had left the Ukraine and stood on a quay in Hamburg, Germany.

It was a late December day when he clutched his ticket and climbed uncertainly up a narrow gangplank of the steamer *Patricia*. The ship's great black stack burped out a breath of coal smoke, and her twin screws started churning the greasy waters of the River Elbe. Philip leaned over the rail or, unused to the motion, lay in his berth as the vessel gathered way toward two European stops—at Boulogne and Plymouth—and then the open ocean.

Patricia was one of the Hamburg–American Line's newest steamers, built a few years earlier with room for nearly 2,500 passengers. She offered a luxurious crossing for the lucky few who could spend at least fifty dollars for a private cabin. The remaining four-fifths, almost certainly including Steckler, settled for third-class berths on the lower decks, where they slept in bunks and ate in a common mess. At an average speed of thirteen knots, the passage, even during the rough winter months, was scheduled to take twenty days. Steckler's trip was marred by head winds and heavy seas, including a tidal wave that staggered the ship just as she was entering the Atlantic. Even Captain Reessing, a mariner with more than twenty years of salt in his blood, was rattled by the storm. "I have not known such weather for many years," he said. "The winter of 1882 was very similar to this, but none since then has been nearly so bad."

On January 11, 1904, the ship, only two days late, navigated between the ice drifts of New York harbor. Steckler's traveling days were nearly done. He had just a few miles more to cross, from Ellis Island east to Brooklyn. Once settled, he married Bessie Volozhinsky, who also came from the Ukraine, and moved into a tenement on Siegel Street in Williamsburg. He and his wife had three daughters: Frieda, Sylvia, and, on March 3, 1913, Annie.

Siegel Street ran just a few blocks from Manhattan Avenue to Bogart Street, through the center of the busy neighborhood. Shop signs advertised in English and Hebrew. The streets were paved with bumpy stones and carried a stream of trucks to the local centers of industry—Max Blumberg's Lumber Yard and the six-story factory of the New York American Bed Company—which were the Stecklers' near neighbors. Annie was raised amid the ruction and grew as accustomed to it as her cat, Beryle, who liked to sleep in the gap left by a missing cobblestone and whose slumber went undisturbed even when the trolley car passed inches above her whiskers.

The Steckler family was poor, but Annie didn't realize it because everyone she knew lived in poverty as well. She shared a bedroom with her sisters, and the only heat in the apartment came from the kitchen stove. On Siegel Street, it was common for several families to use the same bathroom but uncommon for the faucets in that bathroom to run hot water. There were almost no parks or playgrounds in the neighborhood, so Annie would beg her mother for six cents so she could go to Coney Island. The subway ride cost a nickel, and the penny purchased a piece of gum. Then she had to find herself some boy and get him to pay the train fare home.

Annie's father was a pushcart peddler. He sold sweaters on street corners, barking his spiel and haggling with customers from sunrise to evening. During holidays, savvy vendors staked out a desirable location at night and then slept beneath their carts. But on most days, Philip Steckler left for work near dawn and took Annie with him. She watched him unchock the wooden wagon wheels, lean his shoulder-weight against the bars, and creak his rolling shop down the block. It was a delight to go along with her papa, who accented his Old World upbringing with the charming habit of stopping the cart whenever a lady passed so he could bow and doff his cap.

Arriving at his accustomed spot, Philip folded and arranged the sweaters to their best advantage; the merchandise would soon be subject to very close inspection. He could afford to carry only a few sweaters at a time. If a customer tried one on—say, a size 36—and found it was too small, Philip would tell her, "Oh, don't worry, I have it in all sizes." Then he would hand the sweater to Annie, who crept down beneath the cart and found not sweaters but boxes—each labeled with a different size. She took the same sweater the customer had just declared too small, placed it neatly in a box labeled "Size 38," and handed it to her father. He returned it to the lady, who never failed to proclaim it a perfect fit. Then Annie took the money to a nearby wholesaler and bought a new sweater.

On a summer's night when Annie was ten years old, the thousands of stacked softwood boards in the nearby lumber yard caught fire. Apartment walls along the street were stained black, and windows shattered from the heat while families fled with all their movable possessions. Soon, thousands were watching—from rooftops and sidewalks—as every single fireman, fire truck, and fire hose in Brooklyn pitched in to stop the blaze from spreading. "The borough enjoyed a spectacle of destruction that grew more beautiful as darkness furnished a background for an acre or so of billowing flame," a reporter for the *New York Times* wrote, with the placid objectivity of one whose house was far away. The fire leapt from the lumber yard to the adjacent factory. "After that there was only a seething mass of flame-scoured ruins."

•••

It was a gloomy horde of revolutionaries that descended on Union Square around midday on May 1, 1932. Bucketfuls of rain collapsed their hat brims, warped their placards, and threatened to turn their May Day into a depressed and drippy mess. Still, 35,000 braved the weather and gamely tried to sing the "Internationale," though the words, instead of rising up to frighten the capitalists in their sky-scrapers, got trapped beneath all the umbrellas.

May Day had begun in America fifty years earlier. Originally held in honor of the anarchists executed in Chicago after the Haymarket riots of 1886, the date was adopted and embraced by the world labor movement. By 1900, the world's assembled Marxists, anarchists, Proudhonistes, Mensheviks, and Bakuninites urged workers in all nations to put down their tools each spring and march in a massive demonstration of unity. While it grew in Europe, the tradition wasted away in America. The previous parade, in 1931, though held in perfect weather, had drawn fewer than ten thousand workers. Only now, with the Crisis—as the Communists called the Great Depression—lengthening and worsening, were the crowds begin-ning to demonstrate again in force.

The gray and dismal day dampened their enthusiasm, but still they looked formidable trudging past William Z. Foster, the leader of the Communist Party, who watched from a reviewing stand. The coun-try's capitalists had taken only token steps to ease the economic crisis and by their unconcern had given the Communists the means to make a movement. They had, in effect, written these signs—these sodden placards heavy with damp—that named the demands that workers were suddenly willing to march for: free rent, free coal, free food, unemployment insurance, pensions, work.

The crowd showed its first spark when it passed by the rival gath-ering of Pinks in Rutgers Square. The only thing a Communist could tolerate less than a capitalist was a Socialist, and as they passed by the headquarters of the *Jewish Daily Forward,* the Socialist news-paper, they whistled and jeered. "Down with the yellow press," they shouted. "Down with Socialism!"

Otherwise, the procession's only outward vigor came from the students who marched under banners from Columbia, New York University, and City College. The women wore red dresses and ker-chiefs; the men had blue shirts and caps. They were happy and fervent despite the slick streets and heavy downpour. Every so often they shouted, "We Confess Communism" and then burst into self-conscious laughter or looked around to see who was yelling loudest.

For Annie, a sophomore at Hunter College, and Chavy, who had never completed high school, May Day was the highlight of the year. Entering from any of the narrow streets into the open space of Union Square, they could see crowds of people packed in, craning and peering at the speakers. The square had been the site of protest rallies for Emma Goldman in the 1890s, and though it was actually named for the intersection of the Bowery and Broadway, the name Union Square had an irresistible attraction for the labor movement. Walled in by fading stone and brick office buildings, the square had movie theaters and discount department stores that were popular with working-class crowds. Standing side-by-side-by-side on Fourteenth Street were the offices of the city's three progressive newspapers: the *Forward,* the *Daily Worker,* and the Yiddish-language *Freiheit.*

After a few hours of marching, Annie and the other students arrived at the rally point. There they learned that the adults had thrown in the towel and cancelled the speeches. Still in a holiday mood and with the sudden gift of a free afternoon, they dispersed noisily into the subways. May Day was over; leaflets and signs littered the sidewalks. The city's capitalists were safe for another year.

The Depression was an exhilarating time to be young and radical. Annie had rarely been outside Brooklyn—a trip to Coney Island had been a holiday—but in long discussions about international affairs or abstract economic questions, she widened her world far beyond the boundary of Kings County. There was a range of political opinion available: one could be a Socialist or a Communist. The Democratic Party was for the Irish. As for becoming a Republican, neither Annie nor any of her wide acquaintance could ever recall meeting one.

New York was the center of it all. There, young workers and young students could read dozens of newspapers or listen to soapbox street speakers. Unlike other cities, New York also had two free institutions for higher learning. City College, in Harlem, was overrun with Jewish radicals who scorned their tired old professors and skipped class to hold rambunctious debates in odd corners of the cafeteria. Hunter College, with campuses on the East Side and in the Bronx, provided the best, and usually the only, chance for New York's poor but promising girls to attain their degrees. The students came from workers' families that could spare the extra paycheck that a girl could bring home from the typing pool or shirtwaist factory. Hunter women were acutely aware of the opportunity they had being given and remained impeccably respectable in their marcelled hair and V-neck sweaters. But by the time Annie arrived in 1931, even they were dabbling in politics.

In a questionnaire given to Annie's class of 750 incoming freshmen, only one girl reported that she intended to marry. Most of the others planned careers in medicine, journalism, teaching, and the law. Between cigarette advertisements for Lucky Strikes and Chesterfields, the *Hunter Bulletin* was crowded with their intellectual activity: from debates on the "Present Economic Status of Woman" or the "Prospects of British Empire" to reviews of the college production of *The Mikado*. These refined attainments masked the fact that the Hunter girls were drifting to the Left. In the 1932 election, when Democrat Franklin Delano Roosevelt knocked Hoover into a cocked hat, beating him by 7 million votes, he failed to carry Hunter College. Instead, the students handed Norman Thomas, the Socialist candidate, an easy victory.

The time seemed right to start a militant campus organization, so Annie joined with the boys at City College and founded one: the National Student League. They rented an office in Union Square and put out a magazine, the *Student Review*. Most of the league's objectives would be familiar to student protesters of a later era. It was antiwar and opposed the presence of the Reserve Officer Training Corps on campus. Its members were horrified by the brutal conditions faced by striking coal miners in Harlan County, Kentucky, so they sent two busloads of freedom riders to investigate the conditions in the South. When the bus, "with which most of the Hunter group were," attempted to cross the state line, officials were waiting with a lynching party. "Several members of the delegation were beaten," reported an eye-witness in the *Hunter Bulletin*. "One, a teacher in a New York public school, was hit on the head with a revolver."

Annie's first organizing lesson came as she was gliding down an escalator into a train station. In her arms she carried antiwar propaganda to hand out to army recruits setting off for basic training. "The American bosses are preparing and arming themselves for the coming world war," a typical Party leaflet ran, "Fight for the overthrow of the bosses' government and for a workers' and farmers' government. Join the Communist Party of the United States of America, 26-28 Union Square." Annie came to the bottom of the escalator, and as she stepped off, she tripped over her own feet and sent the pages flying all over the room. The army recruits, chivalrous young men, bent down and picked up all the leaflets, gathered them together, and politely handed them back to her.

From that beginning, she spent more of her spare hours at the league headquarters. She was elected to the position of secretary, a post she would hold in many future organizations. Membership expanded monthly, and the increasing subscriptions for the *Student Review*, at seventy-five cents a year, nearly covered the cost of publication.

Millions seemed to share Annie's vision of the future, and the fiery red center was the Soviet Union. In November 1932, members of the league issued a warm greeting to their Bolshevik counterparts: "You are now celebrating the 15th Anniversary of the October Revolution. You are now glorying in the fulfillment of the Five Year Plan in four years. You are now reviewing the new life you have created upon the ruins of the old. We, the revolutionary students of America, are proud to call you brother."

Annie and the others understood that the Soviet Union was still a new experiment, but it had existed their entire conscious lives. So far, they had no hint that this nation was other than a paradise. Joseph Stalin was just beginning to eradicate his rivals and it would be years before most American radicals heard about the Moscow trials and learned to dread the word *purge*.

Two of the three leaders of the National Student League were members of the Young Communist League. Annie, the third, had so far avoided joining the Party. The others urged her to get her card and in the meantime held fraction meetings without her. They made the important decisions behind closed doors and admitted Annie only once most questions had been reconciled with the Party line.

The league had a membership of a few thousand students, but its influence spread far beyond its numbers. Some of the greatest writers of the day—Theodore Dreiser, John Dos Passos, and Malcolm Cowley—put their names on an appeal in the *Student Review*, saying, "The new student movement has crystallized around the alert organization known as the National Student League. The League has affiliations now on more than one hundred campuses. It has shown infectious vitality. . . . So far the students have done all we older men and women off campus could have expected . . . and more. Let us now do our part."

The adult Communist Party had been unable to capitalize on the Depression, even though the Crisis was in its fourth year. Membership remained below 20,000 in 1933, and most of these were unemployed. Far from building a revolutionary proletarian movement, they couldn't even find jobs in the factories themselves. There were so many Jews in the party that a few years before Annie got involved, the Young Communist League had gloatingly reported on a membership drive: "The results are also good in national composition, the majority of the new recruits being young Americans and not Jewish."

The main thing holding back Communist Party membership was the unwillingness to cooperate with other leftist groups. Socialists were not seen as allies but as "social fascists." When the *New Masses,* a literary magazine published by the Party, editorialized about the movement, it praised "the militant sections of the working class, the living core of which is the Communist Party." For the remaining "enemies of the working class, the upholders of capitalism: bankers, militarists, imperialists, Fascists, labor fakers, Social Fascists, and all other open or hidden defenders and apologists of the capitalist order," the Communists had nothing but contempt.

•

The organizers of the 1933 May Day parade were determined that it would be a true display of strength. The *Daily Worker* relentlessly called on its subscribers to attend, promising an enormous turnout. Whether or not the readers believed it, the police certainly did. In the days leading up to the first of May, groups of sergeants were quietly trained in special street-fighting drills. On the night before May 1, the department cancelled all leave and ordered every one of its 19,000 men to remain on duty. The officers' deployments seemed more appropriate to an invasion than a parade:

> More than 1,000 policemen will be on duty in the immediate vicinity of Union Square. With about 600 of these in the square itself, another 400 will be stationed in nearby office buildings and on roofs. Another 1,000 men will scatter along the line of the Communists' march. Assisting the patrolmen will be emergency squads armed with tear-gas bombs, machine guns and rifles. Several district squad cars, their occupants armed with rifles, will cruise through the streets to be traversed by marchers.

By 11:00 A.M., tens of thousands of Communists were mobilizing into two divisions. The first, which met at the Battery and was to march north into Union Square, was led by masses of the unemployed, followed by the Marine and Transport Workers Union, the Ex-Servicemen's League, and fifteen antifascist organizations.

Annie and Chavy were in the second division, which met in Bryant Park on Forty-Second Street and was to proceed south to the reviewing stand at Union Square. There, the first column was made of women in "the needle trades." Column Two consisted of tradesmen: builders, shoe and leather makers, metal, office, furniture, and laundry workers. Column Three was set apart for "Fraternal Organizations." Column Four, the important one in Annie's mind, belonged to "Youth and Cultural Organizations."

At noon, the masses started moving. The route was carefully chosen so as to sweep through Manhattan's major business areas. Annie and Chavy swung south on Seventh Avenue, through the garment district, where many onlookers raised their fists in support. But the southern unit, invading Wall Street and passing city hall, was met with a nervous silence. Stockbrokers and bankers leaned out from their office windows and slowly shook their heads at the street beneath them. The workers were an unbroken crowd, punctuated every few yards by angry banners. They kept mostly to the sidewalks, but for as long as their parade passed by, all business was forced to cease.

Instead of marching all together in a unified demonstration, the Socialists staged their own parade, gathering at Union Square earlier in the afternoon and dispersing—while policemen kept the two factions apart—before the Reds arrived. This division lessened the effect of the demonstration, but, for the first time, it truly seemed as if Chavy's prediction had been correct: the Communists were becoming a menace.

As if to prove this beyond all doubt, Stalin was celebrating the International Day of Labor with a military review in Moscow. At exactly 10:00 A.M., the spectators in Red Square were startled by the sharp report of 101 hidden guns firing a salute from behind the Kremlin walls. Foreign attachés watched in glum silence as the Soviet Army marched the Russian version of the goose step, for two unbroken hours, past their leader. The infantrymen were joined by more than 500 tanks and, overhead, 350 planes executed low-altitude maneuvers above the onion-topped turrets of St. Basil's Cathedral.

Following the military spectacle came almost a million workers and peasants, all straining their eyes toward the reviewing stand near Lenin's Tomb, to catch a glimpse of Stalin, who took his pipe from his mouth and waved.

Back in New York City, the two divisions had converged in Union Square by the middle of the afternoon. The speakers and the crowd worked each other into an ecstasy of passion. Shortly before the meeting broke up at 6:00 P.M., the entire assembly joined together in this solemn promise:

We pledge ourselves to do everything in our power in the shops, unions and organizations to forge the united front of all workers for: Unemployment and social insurance; immediate adequate cash relief; for increased relief and higher wages to meet the rising cost of living . . . for the immediate safe release of Tom Mooney, the Scottsboro Boys, the Centralia and Kentucky I.W.W., and all class war prisoners; for Negro rights; against the Hitler fascist terror and pogroms; down with the assassin of the Italian masses, the butcher Mussolini; against imperialist war; smash the provocations against the Soviet Union.

It was an overwhelming moment, as if just to speak these goals meant that they were as good as accomplished. Annie looked around at the faces and recognized the power and discipline of the masses. Uplifted and exuberant, she found a recruiter and joined the Communist Party.

•••

When she wasn't quaking the knees of capitalism, Annie lived with her sister, Sylvia, in an apartment on Jerome Avenue in the Bronx. The two had always been a team, adventurous and independent, allied against their mother and their dour eldest sister. Sylvia was older, taller, blonder, and more beautiful. She attracted a solar system of orbiting admirers while Annie sat by unattended. Once a friend had tried to comfort her. "Sylvia," he said, "is a fine French pastry but you are a loaf of brown bread." Somehow this didn't have the intended effect. All photographs of Annie—taken without exception in dim light and out of focus—suggested a crisis in self-confidence.

Before he died, Philip Steckler had graduated from pushcart peddling to owning a small store on Myrtle Avenue. When he died from a heart attack in 1925, he left enough money to provide all three of his daughters with funds for a college education. Frieda, the eldest, married a Zionist and left for Palestine. Sylvia was still playing the field. On Friday nights, she and Annie hosted parties at their apartment, and Sylvia's various boyfriends would come to visit. Chavy went home and mentioned Sylvia's affairs to her mother and was instantly banned from ever going back to the Steckler sisters' bohemian love nest.

One of Sylvia's men had a friend, Arthur Stein, and he took notice of the younger sister. He was five years older than she, athletic and handsome, though his red hair was already receding. To strangers he seemed brusque and brooding. In company, he could disappear from conversation until everyone forgot he was there, only to surprise them twenty minutes later with a wicked rejoinder. Chavy refused to be in the same room with him lest he turn that wit on her. Before the Depression, his family had been wealthy by Annie's standards. The Steins had had a chauffeur and could afford to send their son to Columbia University.

But by 1933, when Arthur was taking mathematics courses in graduate school, his father's business had been ruined. Arthur got a job as an accountant and considered himself lucky. From the Columbia campus, he could see the makeshift houses of a Hooverville in Riverside Park.

Arthur's father, Charles, had come to America from Mazritch, a shtetl in Poland. The tiny village—which the family referred to in Yiddish as a *fevorvineh vinkel,* or a little nothing—had, centuries earlier, been home to a Hasidic holy man called the Maggid of Mazritch. The pious would come to worship in the town, and somehow the spectacle was enough to create in Charles Stein a disgust with religion that he would keep faithfully his entire life. Charles married Sadie Gordon, a trash collector's daughter from Minsk, and went into business in the Bronx at first as an umbrella manufacturer and later as a speculator in real estate.

Arthur attended Evander Childs high school in the Bronx, where his IQ was tested and rated at 150. His professor of statistical inference at Columbia remembered that he "possessed ability well above average and a character beyond reproach." He was a powerful swimmer and had fenced when he was younger, but Columbia's school physician examined Arthur and diagnosed him with an "arrested pulmonary tuberculosis condition." Medical wisdom of the day recommended that an underdeveloped heart be protected from exercise, which in effect made a weak muscle even weaker.

Arthur skated through four years at Columbia without straining himself. He never joined a club or made a single appearance in the school newspaper. A mathematician coming into Butler Library to interview Arthur for an important job found him fast asleep with his head down on a table. He didn't even show up for senior picture day, preferring to leave a blank space beside his name in the 1929 college yearbook.

Annie Steckler became Annie Stein on August 12, 1933. She was twenty years old. New York State law allowed underage couples to be married only in religious ceremonies, so they found a rabbi willing to perform the service in his own basement apartment. Arthur's parents didn't come. Though he was the family's pride and joy, they refused to set foot inside a rabbi's house. The wedding was so poorly attended that they fell short of the *minyan* of ten men that was required by Jewish law for important ceremonies. Luckily, in the Depression this was not such a problem. The rabbi went into the street and rounded up some vagrants to fill the void and make everything kosher.

The young couple moved into a modest apartment on Maple Street in Brooklyn, one of the few properties that Charles Stein had managed to retain. Annie was frustrated with her husband's lack of politics. Then she got some advice from a columnist in the *Daily Worker* who suggested leaving copies of the *Worker* around the house so that the benighted husband would be forced to read it. Inevitably he would be overcome and converted. So Annie left newspapers in every room, on each table and chair. Artie found them and at first threw them in the garbage. But it wasn't long before he started reading them himself.

•••

Three different student organizations had plans to hold their national conventions in Washington during the Christmas vacation of 1933. The first was the National Student Federation, from 250 "leading American colleges." The organization had met annually for

a decade and each year resolved agreeably to do nothing about anything. The *Washington Post* greeted their arrival with a paternalistic
chuckle. "The boys and girls," the paper reported, "are taking time
off from holiday festivity to settle a few world problems before
classes recommence in January." Franklin Roosevelt was glad to have
these students in the capital and sent an encouraging statement to be
read at their convention.

The members settled comfortably into a fancy hotel where a
room ranged in price from $4 to $15 per day. In the glittering lobby,
baize-covered registration tables had been provided by the
Washington Board of Trade. "A half dozen young ladies sat there
ready to sign up students and hand out programs," reported one
observer. The students themselves were "slick-haired fraternity men
and authentic sorority girls, strolling among the great potted plants
and marble and bronze statuary." Their usually placid affairs were
interrupted by the two other groups present in the capital, whose
passionate meetings were making the federation's convention look
like a tea party.

No Board of Trade was rolling out a red carpet for the Student
League for Industrial Democracy. Yet few viewed this moribund
socialist group as much of a threat. In previous decades, it had
claimed John Reed, Jack London, and Upton Sinclair as members,
but for the 1933 convention, fewer than fifty delegates bothered to
make the trip to Washington. It would be thirty years before the
League for Industrial Democracy would spring to life again under a
new name—Students for a Democratic Society. In the meantime, its
former leaders had been driven even further to the Left, into the
waiting arms of the third group.

Annie and the other delegates of the National Student League
had come to Washington by bus. Arriving at 3:00 A.M. and finding
that their hotel refused to rent rooms to blacks, they marched right
out of the lobby and back onto the bus to spend the night. Their
convention was bent on action, and the *Washington Post* had warned
of their coming: "Radical Group Is On Its Way Here . . . and There
May Be War."

Representatives of the league, which at the time claimed 5,000 members nationwide, met in a spired red-brick chapel on the campus of Howard University. Racial issues had never been the league's priorities. "The section of our program on the problems of the Negro students had reposed rather peacefully since the day of its writing," Annie confessed in an article in the *Student Review*. But at this convention, the three hundred delegates turned toward integration. The league hosted interracial dances, and Annie wrote that "Howard students attended the sessions and participated in the discussions. . . . For three days Negro and white students shared the same dormitories, ate at the same tables and worked out a line of attack on common problems."

After a long day of discussions, Annie and a group of students walked down Connecticut Avenue in downtown Washington. None of the city's restaurants would willingly serve a black customer, but the students, still feeling powerful and inspired from the day's speeches, marched in and demanded service. And they "were not thrown out. There were too many of us," Annie reported. "It struck some of us that a sizable N.S.L. group could make jim-crow restaurants tremble." It was an idea that she wouldn't forget.

On December 29, the three conventions wrapped up. "Early in the afternoon," reported the *Washington Post:*

> The League for Industrial Democracy and the National Student League, numbering several hundred students, paraded before the White House with placards demanding an end to war and R.O.T.C. At the same time the National Student Federation, which considers the former groups "too radical," was having tea with the First Lady inside the Executive Mansion. L.I.D. officials previously had termed the N.S.F. group "stuffed shirts."

Annie rode the bus back home to her husband in New York City. Her twenty-first birthday was a few months away, and after that it was only a few more months before her graduation from Hunter College with a degree in math. Already, she had made one of her strongest public impressions. In front of hundreds of spectators, she had risen to defend the league against charges of being a front for the Party. "The National Student League is not a Communist organization nor one affiliated with any political party," she said, although by joining the Young Communist League on May Day, she had in fact made it just that.

"Let's not spend our energies proving that we are not Reds," she said. "If fighting for lower tuition fees, for the rights of the Negro, for higher wages for student workers, for lower prices for the lunch room—if that be a Red then let's be Reds."

One of the listeners in the audience, someone with a pen and pad, probably wearing nondescript clothing and trying not to attract attention, wrote down her speech, noting especially the remark, "If that be a Red then let's be Reds." From that day forth, for the rest of her life, the Federal Bureau of Investigation would carefully watch Annie and all her activities.

CHAPTER 2

L'Enfant Jones

MALCOLM Barton Jones, my great-grandfather, steeled his will and left his wife's bedside. His first child would soon arrive, and Yosemite Hospital was not known for its maternity care; only a few years earlier, its doctors had specialized in treating cavalrymen wounded during the Indian Wars. Malcolm's heavy boots made it impossible for him to leave silently, so he stomped his way down the row of beds and stepped outside as the sun cleared the crest of Half Dome. The light slid down the mountain's granite edge until the treetops returned from silhouette to evergreen, and morning—the morning of October 15, 1919—arrived on the valley floor.

Malcolm started the ignition of the large touring car with seats for seven. He engaged the throttle and set out on the twelve-mile ride from Yosemite Village, in the heart of the national park, to the train station of El Portal. With the sun on his back, the breeze in his face, and the tires crunching gravel, his anxiety about the birth began to fade. He was the official driver for Yosemite Park and was not missing his son's birth for nothing. On this morning, he was going to chauffeur the most famous visitor in the valley's history.

Malcolm arrived at El Portal before 9:30 A.M. Like everything man-made here, the rail station was dwarfed by the trees and rising mountain walls. Soon the expected funnel of smoke appeared, followed by a clatter from the special train, lavishly appointed and pulled by two galloping locomotives. Malcolm watched the train snort and buck against the wooden quay. A final anxious moment and then Albert I, king of the Belgians, stepped onto the platform and gazed with the delight of a true nature lover at the wonders of the valley.

The king was finishing a tour that had brought him a hero's welcome from New York to San Francisco and at dozens of rural junctions in between. He had earned this acclaim in 1914 when tiny, neutral Belgium was overrun by the gray German army during the first weeks of the Great War. American sympathy had taken the form of millions of dollars in relief. As soon as the peace conference at Versailles was finished, Albert had steamed across the Atlantic to celebrate the victory, thank the American people for their contributions, and secure some loans on generous terms.

Albert was a keen outdoorsman, but he had spent most of his North American tour trapped inside convention halls suffering through long, albeit praiseful, speeches. He had been looking forward to seeing the park for weeks.

Malcolm busied himself with bags, loading up the car and making sure his passengers were comfortable. He wore the clothes of a workingman, pleated and washed this day to appear at their most presentable. His old fedora, floppy as a mutt's ears, probably was on its usual perch, sitting uneasily atop his head and ready to fly off at any opportunity. At thirty-nine and about to become a father, Malcolm was no longer young. He still had a boyish face, though, and an expression that suggested he was looking for a prank to pull. If Malcolm didn't look kingly, neither especially did his passenger. Albert was only five years older than his driver, yet the trials of the war had marked him. He wore an officer's cap and an olive uniform buttoned tightly to the neck.

Malcolm released the brake for the second time that morning and the car put-putted up among the souvenir postcard sights: El Capitan, Bridal Veil Falls, and the Three Brothers. Arriving at

Yosemite Village around midmorning, Malcolm stopped the car in front of a two-story building at the center of town. Flags with forty-eight stars hung from a balcony, and ladies watched from the veranda as the king and his entourage appeared.

Albert was eager to explore the wilds, but before he could escape he was faced with yet another bevy of local functionaries. Finally the last speaker, a doctor, took the stage and offered his own words to the crowd. "Your Majesty," Doctor Frederick L. Stein told the king's party, "There has been another arrival in the Valley today. A male child was born here this morning and his parents have decided to name him in your royal honor: Albert Leopold Jones."

Malcolm had missed his son's birth because of his duty to the king. Now, before he had even seen the child, he was learning he'd missed out on the opportunity to name him. The king told Dr. Stein that he wished to meet the father. Malcolm stepped up and was formally introduced to the man whom he'd been driving with for hours.

At 9:00 A.M., half an hour before the king's arrival at El Portal, my grandfather had been born, delivered within earshot of the rushing plummet of Yosemite's waterfall. Albert's parents always claimed that he was the first white baby to be born within the valley of the Yosemite. His name, Albert Leopold Jones, given in honor of a military hero, would turn out to be almost perfectly unsuitable.

The Belgian party's two days in Yosemite provided the press with a series of minor insights into the habits of royalty. The queen had a fright when a caged mountain lion nibbled her coat sleeve, and King Albert terrified his company by venturing out onto a spit of rock that dangled precariously above a fatal fall. The monarch reportedly was disgusted by the nervousness elicited by his derring-do, though in retrospect—he would fall to his death in a mountaineering accident in 1934—there was some cause for concern. The king and queen spent the night at the brand-new Glacier Point Hotel, and Leopold, the royal heir, camped in a tent nearby, where he learned the subtle secrets of flapjack flipping.

When the season ended a few weeks later, Malcolm and Christine took their baby back to their winter home in Los Angeles. A few days after they arrived, the *Evening Express* ran the headline, "King Hails 'L'Enfant' Jones," over a story about the baby born with a royal name. A flurry of ambassadorial memoranda shot back and forth between the Joneses of 279 Henrietta Court, Pasadena, and the royals of the Palais de Bruxelles. The king, sensing an opportunity for good publicity, instructed the Belgian vice consul in Los Angeles to "go to the best store in Los Angeles" and purchase, as a present for the baby, a "silver knife, fork and spoon and a silver loving cup." He also instructed his agent to "extend the best wishes of the king for the health of the mother and child." The fancy gift arrived a few weeks later: $200 worth of silver plating over dishes decorated with figures from Mother Goose.

Malcolm and his wife sent a picture of the baby Albert to the queen, and a final letter arrived a few weeks later, saying, "Her majesty desires to let you know how happy she is to possess the picture of the beautiful baby born when the Royal party arrived in 'Yosemite Valley.' "

•••

By the time of his son's birth, Malcolm's career path was well established: his destiny was to work hard and fail. A laborer most of his life, the wrong decision would always come easy to him when an opportunity for investment presented itself. His greatest business asset was a patient and perspicacious wife whose advice he would repeatedly ignore.

Malcolm had been born in 1880 on the eastern bank of the Republican River in Kansas. The town, Clay Center, was named after Henry Clay, the drafter of the Missouri Compromise. The land was a pioneer's dream, and an early booster described its "low, rounded, bordering hills, with others beautifully rolling and rising behind them . . . and the serpentine course of the broad river, traced by its trimming of forest trees and the silver sheen appearing here and there."

When Malcolm was born, raids by the Pawnee and Delaware Indians were a fresh and terrifying memory. Settlers had been on the land for more than a decade, yet they were still outnumbered two to one by their horses. Malcolm was born in a boom time, and though Clay Center was still a decade removed from electricity, the wooden architecture of transience had begun to be replaced with permanent stone, dominated by the community's pride and hope, a newly built $25,000 redbrick schoolhouse.

Despite its gaudy price tag, the schoolhouse held little attraction for Malcolm, who lit out of the classroom at the end of the sixth grade, never to return. Staying within four walls seemed perverse when just outside lay rowed fields of winter wheat, rye, barley, and Irish potatoes. It was an Eden, with apples, plums, peaches, pears, cherries on the vine, as well as vast open fields of blue grass and prairie meadow. But Malcolm was a rover, and soon he would leave all this behind in the manner of young men before and since: bearing arms.

In 1898 a Cuban rebellion against Spain provided America a perfect opportunity for "a splendid little war." Everyone wanted a fight: the government wanted colonies, newspapers wanted readers. The only thing they lacked was a *casus belli,* and when, on February 15, "with a bursting, rending, and crashing sound," the *Maine* exploded in Havana harbor, killing 266 crewmen, a fight was ensured. President McKinley sent out a call for 125,000 patriotic volunteers to join the army and travel to Cuba to vanquish the enemy. Men all across the country joined up.

On May 7, Malcolm traveled ten miles northwest to the town of Clifton, where he stood in line with other Clay County men and signed his name. Then the new recruits were transported by train one hundred miles to Topeka, given physicals, and mustered into the service of the United States as the Twenty-Second Kansas Regiment. The unit was composed, according to the official state history of the war, "largely of farmers' sons." Malcolm was now a private in I Company. His muster-in card says he stood 5 feet 10½ inches. His complexion was fair, eyes brown, and hair light. In fine copperplate script, his occupation was listed as painter. A week after induction, the nearly one thousand men of the regiment boarded trains of the Missouri Pacific railroad and decamped for the East. The troop of prairie men hooted and waved their caps as the train vanished down the lines toward a training base at Camp Alger in Virginia and eventually, it was supposed, an appointment with the Spaniards.

While the volunteer army was drilling stateside, the regulars had landed in Cuba and were cheerfully campaigning. A week after arriving, the Americans won the major battle of the war at San Juan Hill. It was July 1, and the fighting would be over in a little more than a month. Virginia was as close to Cuba as the Twenty-Second Kansas would ever come.

Camp Alger was a far more dangerous place than the front for an American soldier. Malcolm suffered from dysentery, but typhoid fever was the most common malady. More than 40,000 men were stationed there during the summer of 1898; there were no bathing facilities, and the nearest water source was a stream four miles away. By early August, 39 men had died of typhoid, and another 375 were ill. Fourteen men in Malcolm's regiment died, at least 8 from the fever. The conditions at Alger became a national scandal, and finally even the general in charge of the camp succumbed to disease and dropped dead.

In early August, Malcolm's regiment, its uniforms dulled by dust, marched out of camp to the railroad, pausing just long enough to desecrate some Confederate graves. After two months of drill, 5:25 A.M. reveille, and almost no women to be seen, it was a relief to be moving, even if the chance to go to Cuba was gone. On August 12, Spain agreed to a preliminary peace agreement. The fighting continued in little outbreaks, but the need for McKinley's huge volunteer army, if there had ever been a need, was over. Two weeks later, the regiment boarded trains to Fort Leavenworth, Kansas, and was mustered out of existence. Malcolm was honorably discharged, still owed $29.17 of his pay.

Fort Leavenworth was 150 miles from home, and the government had issued traveling money to all returning veterans. With cash in his pocket and a wider experience, Malcolm returned to Clay Center. His ability as a soldier remained untested and largely conjectural, as did his regiment's, but the state's official history was confident that "had the exigencies of the service called the regiment to the field,"

Malcolm's Twenty-Second Kansas's record "would not have discredited the fair name of the state it represented."

A war veteran and not yet twenty, Malcolm needed to find a career. His job as a house painter now seemed dull and Clay Center impossibly small. Camp Alger had boasted no high-rises, but with tens of thousands of inhabitants, it had been a city. Malcolm signed on as a brakeman for the Rock Island Railroad. With track running from St. Louis in the West to Chicago in the East, the Rock Island line was the road to ride in the Midwest at the turn of the century. One of its stops was Clay Center. One of the brakeman's jobs was to insert a pin into the coupling that secured two cars together. A skilled brakeman could perform this task so quietly that you could hear the pin drop. It was far more dangerous than being a soldier, and a man applying for a brakeman's job with all ten fingers was instantly recognized as a greenhorn. Having lost the tip of his thumb in a coupling accident, Malcolm was no greenhorn.

When the automobile appeared after the turn of the century, Malcolm jumped the tracks and became a mechanic, as all drivers were then called, since every long trip included a few breakdowns. He worked as a truck driver and a chauffeur. During one trip from California to the Midwest, he spent an evening at a boarding house in Minneapolis where he met a plump young widow.

Mina Christine Tande was a woman who looked hardy enough to raise a family in the frontier, which she was. Her parents, immigrants from Norway, died when she was a teenager, leaving her to live with an austere Lutheran aunt and an uncle who worked as a Bible salesman. Her first husband was a man named Frank Lee who had invested in a steam tractor. It was an era when men believed that a good idea could make their fortunes, and Frank's idea was to take his tractor to South Dakota and till his neighbors' fields. Christine followed him to the Badlands, where they lived in a sod hut in a field of flat mud. Around 1910, before he could strike it rich, Lee was betrayed by his tractor, which snapped a valve and boiled him to death in the escaping steam. The tragedy for the Lees was a boon to the Joneses. When Malcolm arrived in Minneapolis a few years later, Christine was a free woman.

They were married in July 1918. After the ceremony, Malcolm, in a black suit fine enough to be buried in, posed side by side with his new wife for a photograph. They didn't touch each other as the shutter snapped, but kept a tiny space between them. She wore a white dress with a frilly collar and flowers, her arms stiffly at her sides. For a honeymoon, Malcolm carted his bride across the country's dirt roads. During the ride, they wore through nearly a dozen tires. But somewhere between Minneapolis and southern California, they overcame the physical tentativeness evident in their wedding photo and conceived Albert.

Following their brush with royalty, the Joneses put a $7,000 down payment on a home in the San Fernando Valley, north of Los Angeles. Until the turn of the century, the valley had been cattle land. At the time Malcolm and Christine arrived in the town of Girard, the entire area was still dominated by farms. The settlement boom that would transform the valley into a notorious suburb was beginning, and, of all the wild builders' schemes, Girard was the least baked. It had streets, sidewalks, and building lots but no tenants. At the center of town, where Topanga Canyon and Ventura boulevards intersected, there was a block of false fronts with slanting wooden beams supporting them from behind. The buildings could have easily come from the set of Valentino's *The Sheikh:* towering minarets, onion-domed mosques, and an arabesque fountain. Girard was a Californian Xanadu, part film set and part Potemkin Village.

Most of the lots stayed vacant throughout the 1920s. On weekends, tour buses filled with prospective buyers left Los Angeles at 9:30 A.M. and rumbled past the Jones house. Brochures promised a free lunch, horses to ride, dancing, a golf course and swimming pool, most of which had not been—and never would be—built. For years, the Jones family was the only one on the block. The unclaimed lands were used by farmers, who planted barley where the sidewalks ended.

For young Albert, it was an ideal place for exploration. Whenever he could wriggle out of his mother's clutches, it was out into the arroyo, barefoot and muddy-legged. He spent his days hurtling through the chaparral or in the wondrous inspection of a family of squirrels. The entire valley was his playground: orange and walnut groves, irrigated pastures cross-hatched in growing swaths across the desert. Here and there were roads and village centers, though in the whole valley there was hardly a score of traffic lights.

Malcolm had somehow come into a little money—probably from the sale of Christine's Minneapolis home—and as the man of the house he had to figure out how best to use it. His wife wanted to invest in real estate. He ignored her and started a business. Since autos were what Malcolm knew, he started a trucking company and soon owned three rickety rigs, each with a tall cab open to the elements and a big wood-enclosed flatbed behind. Maintaining them himself, Malcolm hauled produce from many of the valley's farmers to market. He wanted to be his own boss, and there was a need for trucking in the valley, but his business sense would fail him, and by decade's end he'd be out of work.

Malcolm's political creed was to vote Republican and mind your own business. Nothing bothered him so much as vote canvassers, bleeding hearts, and busybodies. Bend your back to the load and work was his philosophy, and even when his money-making ventures inevitably failed, he never looked to cast blame on anything so abstract as a system or a society. Socialist promises—Malcolm, Christine, and most of their neighbors believed—were just so much hokum.

And if they started to doubt it, there were newspapers and radio dramas to remind them. California had its labor problems, and the business owners took every opportunity to drum up a little Red Scare. There existed few better symbols of authority and stability than a beloved monarch. So when King Albert had come to California in the fall of 1919, the governor had pressed his point. "As King Albert stood against the invading Hun," he reminded businessmen in a San Francisco ballroom, "so must you and I stand against other Huns that would invade this country. No man who advocates anarchy or Bolshevism must be allowed to enter America. We must also see to it that any man now in America who raises his voice against the flag or against America must be punished—and punished properly."

In Girard, the fear of bolshevism was remote. On most evenings, the Joneses sat around the house and sang. Malcolm couldn't hold a tune in a wheelbarrow, but he could chord the piano, so as long as he remained sotto voce, the family sounded good together. On other nights, the neighbors would sit on lawns to listen to the radio. Different houses played different programs, and switching lawns was like changing channels.

The 1920s were boom times in the San Fernando, and there seemed no reason why they should ever end.

•••

On October 21, 1929, a distinguished group of Los Angeles's leading capitalists gathered downtown, and they were sweating. Rivulets of perspiration slipped along their beefy jowls and slopped down into their shirt collars. It was the hottest day of the year. By early afternoon, the heat reached 100 degrees. Dressed in suits, roasting slowly on a dais, bankers, brokers, and leading men suffered through a ceremonial groundbreaking for what was to be the new Los Angeles Stock Exchange. It was to have a modern granite facade with etched bas relief depictions of Research and Discovery, Finance, and Production. The trading floor, when it was finished, would be second in size only to New York's. It would be the great exchange that the city fathers felt it was LA's manifest destiny to possess.

At a signal from the mayor, an elephantine steam shovel drove its tusks into the dirt. A bottle of water was smashed into that first shovelful of soil, and the ground was officially broken. The crowd cheered and melted away in general relief to find some cool dark space and wait for dusk.

Three days later, the stock market crashed in New York.

•••

The late-night sounds of the San Fernando were no longer a source of midnight fear for ten-year-old Albert. The creak of yawning floor boards, the scuttle and thrash of wildlife outside, even the coyotes' yawps that echoed across the valley had grown familiar to him. He slept on a sun porch that was paned on three sides by windows.

From his room, he could hear the noisy passage of automobiles as they hiccupped and belched along Canoga Avenue.

Once night fell, the windows turned opaque as stone, and the outside world vanished behind the reflecting glass. The valley became as dark as a desert: no street lights, no headlights, no billboards or signs. The world shrunk to the size of his bedroom, and in his private space, the ten year old's mind savored exciting dreams. He'd be a fireman or work on the railway like his father had done. Cowboy novels and the boy hero stories of Tom Swift provided other fantasies, and once the light was off and he was snuggled under in his flannel pajamas, the possibilities seemed endless, delicious, and unknowable.

As the summer days of 1930 shuffled by, anxiety began to steal into these nighttime visions. His parents had worries that he could only guess at, and Malcolm had warned him to expect few birthday or Christmas presents. Then, deep into a summer night, the curtain was thrown aside, and he saw just how bad things were with them.

Albert slowly woke. He had to pee. He padded toward the bathroom in his one-piece pajamas. Suddenly a terrifying noise, one he'd never heard before on the sun porch, left him wide awake. What he listened to now was the sound of crying. Peering through an open door, he saw his father slumped on a straight-backed bench in the kitchen, weeping. His head was cupped in his hands and tears sluiced through his fingers. Christine stood over him, rubbing his back and cooing. "Don't cry, daddy," she said. "Don't cry, daddy."

Albert, protected by the dark, crouched to watch his parents. A bare bulb in the kitchen lit the worry lines on his mother's face. His father's was hidden in shadow. The boy could hardly imagine a calamity awful enough to reduce Malcolm to such a state. Soon Albert himself was crying and then he hurried back to bed. His worst fears were hardly as bad as reality. The Depression had ruined far better businessmen than Malcolm. Bad investments, poorly negotiated contracts, and unwise speculations had already crashed his trucking business. Now the bank had initiated foreclosure proceedings. He was losing the house as well.

Malcolm had looked like a young man far into middle age. Almost overnight, it now seemed, he had lost his impish vigor. His face was suddenly wrinkled and squashed like a crushed beer can.

A count of the unemployed in Los Angeles, conducted as part of the 1930 census, showed that more than 50,000 men were either "out of a job, able to work, and looking for a job" or had jobs but were "on layoff without pay, excluding those sick or voluntary idle." The next year, 100,000 had fallen into these categories.

In Girard, one man who suddenly found himself out of a job, able to work, and looking for a job was Malcolm Jones. Finally, in desperation, his wife's business acumen was allowed to flourish. Christine, cheerful and efficient, rolled up her sleeves. She earned a few extra pennies and nickels by cooking for unmarried men who worked at a nearby ranch and took boarders into the little house on Canoga Avenue.

When there wasn't enough money to buy food, the family provided its own. Malcolm built a rabbit hutch in the backyard, and Christine could fry the creatures up. Stews filled with home-grown vegetables and carefully rationed meat simmered for hours in the huge soup kettle to stretch the flavor to its fullest. Want had never tasted so good.

Girard town, which had been growing unsteadily since the family moved there, suddenly shriveled to almost nothing. Eventually only seventy-five families were left. There were so few residents that the Joneses, in exchange for upkeep on the property, were allowed to stay in their house rent free even after the bank foreclosed.

Albert entered Canoga Park High School in 1933. He had curly blond hair, stood over six feet tall, and weighed 125 pounds. When he tried out for football, the coach ordered his burliest linebacker to stand still and then told Albert to go tackle him. He considered the prospect, turned, and walked off the field for good. On weekdays he was up at 5:30 for the three-mile walk to school. Later, for fifty dollars, far more than the family could afford, Malcolm bought him a mustang from the Nevada desert. From then on, Albert rode to school and tied his horse up outside during class.

Albert still remembered the image of his teary-eyed father. Privately, he began to question a society where such a thing could happen to hard-working people. But he didn't have many places to turn for politics. Malcolm remained a Republican, even though Roosevelt's Works Progress Administration had found him a job doing street construction. The only progressive force in the community was the church.

Every Sunday in the Jones family, life had followed the same pattern. Christine, whose chilly Minnesota Lutheranism had hardly thawed through all the years in California, gathered and washed the kids. Malcolm put on his suit and trudged along behind. The family became Methodists since that was the only Protestant congregation within walking distance. Malcolm sang in the choir and often, to the family's chagrin, fell asleep on stage during the sermon. The church was central to the community, but only to part of it. No Mexicans or Japanese were allowed.

Teenagers were encouraged to join the youth program called the Epworth League. Albert went to sing-alongs and met other upstanding Methodist boys and girls. They were asked to "take an out-and-out stand for Christ" and spend fifteen minutes a day in religious meditation. Members were expected to forbear from drinking and gambling, and "attend movies only after consulting unprejudiced reviews such as those found in the *Parent Teacher's Magazine, Christian Century* or *The Epworth Herald.*" The Epworth Leaguers were not wild-eyed Bolsheviks, but they believed that a better society would come when people followed the simple doctrines set forth in their own radical manifesto: the Bible.

The Epworth League, which had formerly marched in parade-step with rifles, made pacifism its main cause during the Depression. In 1931, a poll of almost 20,000 Protestant ministers taken by a religious magazine showed that more than 12,000 thought the church should stand against all future wars. By 1939, when the mainstream Protestant peace movement was at its height, the *Christian Century* printed an editorial that could have come from the speeches of any of the Socialist orators back in Union Square: "War has lost its glory and stands forth as the naked iniquity which it always was. For the Church to bless war, now appears to the Christian conscience as the absolute contradiction of the Christian faith."

Albert was naturally predisposed to agree, having suffered through his father's war stories for years. Though Malcolm had never made it farther than a camp in Virginia, he often claimed to have been present at Teddy Roosevelt's charge at the battle of San Juan Hill. The story had not filled Albert with a thirst for glory. Rather, he had been repelled by it. Now, as a teenager, he became convinced that a socialist society was the only kind that could prevent war and live up to the spiritual principles of Jesus Christ. With that idea as a starting point, it was clear that many things would need to change before southern California could become a decent place.

He traveled hundreds of miles to hear speeches by John Steinbeck, who would soon publish *The Grapes of Wrath*. He marched in Armistice Day parades and had the anti-war signs yanked from his hands by angry veterans. The logic of pacifism seemed so clear to him—so integral to Christian thought—that when he had an opportunity to make his commitment official, he did not hesitate.

In July 1936, Albert hitchhiked to Arroyo Grande, a popular campground, and paid six dollars to participate in one of the Epworth League summer programs. For a few days, he woke up early and ate the camp fare in the dining hall. As the retreat ended and campers were winding up their sleeping rolls and packing suitcases, he remained in a serious mood. He was young, yet it was only the youth, he figured, who had the will and desire to make changes in the world. The words had mingled with the campfire smoke, had dropped with the embers in front of him, and had started to work a change in his mind. There were enough problems on earth already and enough well-wishers whose talk came to nothing. Albert's life was going to stand for something.

At the end of the session, the director erected a table. At a chair behind it, a Methodist operative was present to take down young idealists' declarations to avoid participating in wars through the legal means of conscientious objection. Few signed. Albert did. The paper traveled to the headquarters of the Methodist Episcopal church in

Chicago. By return mail, they sent him a blue wallet card with a picture of a cross indicating that he was a principled objector who
could not be made to fight. Issued on stationery of the Methodist
Peace Commission, the card carried about as much weight with a
draft board as a mother's permission slip. But it was a pocket-sized
reminder and spine stiffener. In the hands of a seventeen year old, it
felt pretty weighty.

Albert started speaking out in the churches of the San Fernando
Valley. He hitchhiked to the different congregations scattered
through the regions of the valley: North Hollywood, Ventura, Santa
Maria, Robertson Boulevard, and even the First Methodist Church
in downtown Los Angeles. Dressed in his best church-going rig, he
claimed a seat on one of the front benches and waited for the collection plates to jangle around the congregation. During the period
reserved for announcements, he took several deep breaths, and
offered a quiet prayer for eloquence. Then he was standing in the
aisle, or sometimes even at the pulpit, and hundreds of eyes were on
him.

His message was forceful and had a logic that could not but affect
his audience: nonviolence was stressed repeatedly in the Ten
Commandments. Avoiding combat was the primary teaching of Jesus
Christ. Even the Golden Rule, that cornerstone of decorum, was in
effect a call for pacifism. His doctrine, the social gospel, was not
exactly revolutionary, and his elders usually viewed this skinny
young idealist with amused interest. When he was done, he'd sit back
on the bench, filled with relief, and listen to the pastor's sermon.

After the service was over, a small group would always form
around Albert. They were polite and thanked him for coming to
speak to them, but he wondered if he had actually reached anybody.
Albert was living his faith, that's how he saw it. He knew what was
right and was going to stick to that path and spread word of it to
others. He began to feel that maybe the only way to inspire people
would be to become a minister himself.

In 1938, Albert enrolled at Los Angeles Community College.
During his first year, he conducted the college orchestra and caught
the eye of a young violinist. Mildred Meyer was seventeen and, like

Albert, a freshman. He noticed her noticing him, and he approved. Millie had a big smile and wore her hair shoulder length as the styles from Hollywood dictated. They would sometimes skip class to sit in Albert's car and flirt. The main thing that impressed Millie about Albert was his politics. She had never heard of a pacifist or imagined that anybody could be anything but unhesitatingly patriotic. As she sat in his car listening to him describe his beliefs, she felt like a rebel and a radical.

Like Albert, Millie had grown up in the San Fernando Valley. Her home life had not been happy. Her parents had kept a low-grade conflict active for decades until eventually her father fled the field of combat. They had met at a church social in Pasadena and were married on November 10, 1918, a day before the armistice ended World War I. Carl Meyer's family had come from Prussia to work their way across the continent.

Millie's mother, Helen Wentworth Brown, was born in Chicago in 1890 and could trace her family back to Cromwell's England. The Wentworths had come to Boston in the 1600s, when the continent still had that New World smell. The Browns came from Maine, and everywhere they traveled they founded a church. Some time in the middle nineteenth century, a great-great-grandfather in Maine won roughly ten square miles of San Fernando Valley real estate in a bet. The deed was passed down through the generations until, finally, Millie's grandfather and his family went and claimed it. There was no irrigation, and the soil was rough and thin. They built a house for themselves and founded the Pacoima Community Congregational Church with a white steeple like the ones in New England.

Millie grew up on the family land in a house that her parents had built themselves. It had a slouching roof and, until she was eight years old, neither electricity nor indoor plumbing. In high school she was too embarrassed to invite friends over, and for years her only acquaintances were the children of the Japanese farmers who grew alfalfa on the land nearby. In the spring, Millie's father borrowed seed money from the bank and tried to pay off the loan at harvesttime. Then he did the same the following year. In the Depression, this system failed. Millie lived on bread and milk for weeks on end, and sometimes it was hard to unearth even a nickel for the loaf. She and her mother both began to dread the sound of a car in the driveway, followed by the rap on the door that announced the arrival of a bill collector.

It was hard living, but everyone around them seemed to be struggling as well. The great advantages Millie had were kin and music. Her mother played the flute, and as a toddler, Millie had joined her at rehearsal and sat beneath her chair. Every cousin played an instrument. Millie picked up a violin when she was seven and started lessons at eight. She learned quickly and one day rode to Burbank, stood in front of a microphone, and played "Etta's Waltz" over the radio. Soon her teacher arranged for her to play at banquets and box socials all across the valley. She formed an eight-piece orchestra with her family, and they performed at church on Sundays. She studied hard, spent every night doing homework, and was her high school valedictorian. Instead of making a speech at graduation, she played a solo.

By the time she was in college, her parents had separated. It was an open secret that her father had a mistress. With Albert, Millie saw an opportunity to build a relationship that would work better than the example she had seen in her own home. They decided that he would quit school and find a job so that she could continue working toward a teaching certificate. Then their roles would switch: Millie would teach and Albert would return to school.

On May 10, 1940, Nazi divisions blitzed into Western Europe, invading France, Belgium, Holland, and Luxembourg. In Belgium, King Leopold III, the teenage heir who had learned to flip flapjacks in Yosemite, was placed in the same position as his father twenty-six years before. Albert had held, but Leopold surrendered to the German army; his subjects never forgave him. In Los Angeles, Albert Leopold Jones watched the advancing war. He hoped that America could remain neutral. He hoped that his belief in pacifism would never be tested in a time of war. But he knew in his dark thoughts that the moment was coming when he would have to decide just what kind of a man he really was.

CHAPTER 3

Konspiratsia

THE devout were up before dawn on Easter Sunday 1939. They cherished the warmth of their coffee mugs and adjusted the radio dials past the static to find the broadcast of Pope Pius XII's high mass at the Vatican. The Latin ceremony was unchanged, as soothing and inscrutable as it had been in the time of Pius the First. Yet Rome was fascist territory now, and all the prayers from all the faithful hearts in the listening audience could not forestall the war that would darken the next six Easters.

It was an overcast morning in Washington, D.C., and still the inhabitants felt blessed. They were thankful for the appearance of the first green sprigs of the season and grateful for the ocean that lay between themselves and the sins of Europe. "In other world capitals there are trouble and apprehension," reported the *New York Times,* "but in Washington the cherry trees around the tidal basin are in bloom. . . . In Prague and Warsaw, in Berlin and Rome, in Paris and London spring must come with a more somber touch. Here no troops parade in field equipment, no spies hang on innocent words, no iron hand shuts off the truth."

President Roosevelt spent his Easter taking the cure in Warm Springs, Georgia, and his First Lady remained at the family home in

Hyde Park, New York. But 200,000 tourists were in the capital. They came for a solemn moment at Arlington Cemetery. They came to worship at Washington Cathedral or the Foundry Methodist Church. And they came for the concert.

Parks Department workers had hauled a grand piano up the steps of the Lincoln Memorial. They had unrolled green carpeting before the columns and lined two hundred wooden chairs neatly into rows. A platform had been constructed for newsreel cameras, and six microphones belonging to NBC's Blue Network were connected to the largest amplification system the nation had heard since Roosevelt's Inaugural Address. Lincoln's temple made a stunning backdrop for a performance. Looking out through the eyes of the thirty-foot-tall statue, the view stretched across the long reflecting pool to the distant Washington Monument. The scene's only blemish was a muddy construction site, which eventually would be the Jefferson Memorial.

At midday, an anxious black woman, huddling in her mink coat against the chill, walked out onto the stage. With the parade a few blocks away, not many were around to see her. While her accompanist banged out scales on the piano, she leafed through her sheet music and sang some notes into the microphones, testing the acoustics. Marian Anderson, suddenly the world's most famous singer, had not asked to become a political symbol, and the pressure had kept her awake all night.

In a few hours she would be back, so nervous that she would almost forget the lyrics to songs she had performed dozens of times. In front of her, the empty Mall would be thronged with an audience of tens of thousands.

Annie and Arthur Stein left their apartment on Euclid Street in northwest Washington. They joined the holiday masses in the journey downtown. The trolleys were jammed. Cars dodged around the rails; the older models still were tall and black and looked like carriages, but the new designs came in red and silver and were sleek and curvy. The passengers all looked their best. "Costumes were a Roman holiday for new shades," commented the *Washington Post,* "cyclamen, lime, jonquil-yellow, japonica, every variety of purple from lilies to royal." For men, fedora hats and three-piece suits were the fashion, but Arthur, with his brim down around his eyes and a cigarette dangling from his lip, made it seem almost rakish.

Not just the finery set this crowd apart. Washington was a southern city, and the races rarely mingled. Annie and Arthur had learned this already; every time they invited black people to their apartment, they were rewarded with dirty looks and cutting silence from the neighbors. Nothing less than the promise of hearing Marian Anderson, and for free, could bring black and white together for an evening.

The singer had returned from a European tour to sell out Carnegie Hall, and Washington had thrilled to learn that she planned to appear in the city. The only auditorium equal to her stature was the 4,000-seat Constitution Hall, which was owned by the Daughters of the American Revolution. The Daughters considered themselves the guardians of the spirit of 1776, and their attitude toward race was indeed centuries behind the times. If black people wanted to hear a show in Constitution Hall, they were forced to sit in the last rows of the balcony. As for performers, the Daughters permitted white artists only.

"They stand almost in the shadow of the Lincoln Memorial," the *Washington Times-Herald* complained, "but the Great Emancipator's sentiments about 'race, creed, or previous condition of servitude,' are not shared by the Daughters." Marian Anderson, hearing the news during a tour of California, was "shocked beyond words to be barred from the capital of my own country after having appeared in almost every other capital in the world."

Eleanor Roosevelt announced her resignation from the Daughters in her nationally syndicated column, and the concert was transformed from a scandal to a cause. Annie and Arthur joined the hastily formed Marian Anderson Citizens' Committee. They picketed and petitioned, and still the Daughters refused to change their policy. Only a few weeks before Easter, Harold Ickes, secretary of the interior, came up with a plan to stage an outdoor concert, free to the world. It had taken on its own momentum, and as five o'clock neared, it was finally time.

First-comers arrived hours early to claim spaces directly before the stairs of the memorial. Since then, the crowd had fanned out, trampling the newborn grass of the Mall, surrounding the reflecting pool entirely, and stretching all the way back to the base of the Washington Monument. Constitution Hall could have held a few thousand of the well-to-do; best guesses put this outdoor gathering at 75,000. Those who were too far away to see Anderson could still hear her through the amplifiers. NBC would carry the sound of her voice live, from 5:00 to 5:30 P.M., to audiences around the country.

Just as she stepped to the microphones, the sun came out from behind the clouds. It was in the western sky behind the memorial, which cast a shadow hundreds of feet long across the spectators. The Colorado marble, muted by clouds, came to life, shimmering like the silver waters in the pool. Marian Anderson shut her eyes; she could hardly bear to look out at the huge crowd. Annie and Arthur were out there, silent and waiting. As the deep operatic voice reached them, they knew they were witnessing the birth of an important new movement. At the same time, they were still in mourning for the death of another: just one week before the concert, the Spanish republic had surrendered to the fascist armies of Generalissimo Francisco Franco.

Free Spain had slowly bled to death during three years of civil war. While Franco had received unlimited help from Mussolini and Hitler, only the Soviet Union agreed to sell armaments to the democratically elected government in Madrid. American policy, as spoken by the secretary of state, opposed arming "irresponsible members of left-wing political organizations."

Never had so large a proportion of the country's people been so ashamed by the policy of their leaders. Morally, it was as if those were American planes bombing Guernica and the other villages of Spain. If Roosevelt wouldn't help, then it was up to his citizens. Tens of thousands—Communists, Socialists, and many who were neither—had gathered in Union Square and Madison Square Garden. Volunteers solicited change on subways, and trucks drove through the cities collecting old clothes for the orphans of Madrid. More than three thousand Americans had volunteered to fight. Men whom Annie had known, citified college boys who had no business taking up arms, had gone to Spain. Only a little more than half made it back.

With the surrender of Madrid on March 29, the fight was over. The pope wired his congratulations to General Franco, who was a Spanish Catholic in the tradition of Torquemada. Germany, Italy and, a day later, America, hurried to recognize the new government. On April 1, callously—almost, the Steins thought, shamelessly—Roosevelt lifted the embargo on arms to Spain. American companies could do business again—with the fascists.

A few days later, Marian Anderson gave Washington one of its finest memories. Here, immobile, was the statue of Lincoln who, seventy-five years earlier, was supposed to have made all Americans equal. And here was Anderson, tiny but animate, who was still being barred from the city's halls of culture. "I had a feeling," the singer remembered, "that a great wave of good will poured out from these people, almost engulfing me. And when I stood up to sing our National Anthem I felt for a moment as though I were choking. For a desperate second I thought that the words, well as I know them, would not come. I sang, I don't know how."

The administration could never wipe the Spanish blood from its hands. Yet here was the same government providing a world stage—and sending a global message of equality—to a black opera singer.

Marian Anderson sang six songs, and the concert lasted only thirty minutes. Her crowd was spellbound throughout the performance. For her encore, she did a slow and mournful rendition of "Nobody Knows the Troubles I've Seen." Then she thanked the audience in a few breathless words and stepped back from the microphone. "When she had finished," the *Washington Post* proclaimed, "a thunderous burst of applause broke around her and continued to roll up from the far reaches of the crowd for several minutes." Overcome with emotion, hundreds surged toward the stage. They wanted to get close to the singer, to meet her, to thank her. "In attempting to congratulate Miss Anderson," said the *Post,* they "threatened to mob her and police had to rush her back inside the memorial where the heroic statue of Lincoln towers."

In the crowd, Annie was moved along with the others. But Arthur felt strange. He had known chest pains before but nothing like this. During the concert, the sensation had grown more intense. He was nauseated and dizzy. The crowds pressed in on him. He collapsed, or nearly did, while his wife frantically tried to find out what was wrong. It was a heart attack—his first—at the age of thirty.

•••

It had been a sad day for Chavy when Annie left New York City in the autumn of 1934. Comradely hugs were exchanged all around, and the Steins departed for their waiting apartment in Washington. Arthur had found a New Deal job as a statistician with the National Recovery Administration. His salary of $3,200 a year was almost twice what he had made working for his uncle's struggling real estate company in Brooklyn.

If you were an unemployed laborer during the Depression, you went along to a Federal Emergency Relief or Public Works Administration site and applied for a job digging ditches or building dams. If you had a degree from Hunter, City College, or Columbia, you went to Washington and found a desk in the bureaucracies that kept these emergency agencies operating. Thousands of young couples, a regular migration, had passed down U.S. Highway One, the same road that Arthur and Annie were driving.

Washington offered good, socially relevant work, and unlike in the rest of the country, there was plenty of it. In Roosevelt's first five years in office, he expanded the federal payroll by a quarter of a million employees. Many were the same young fire-eaters who a couple of years earlier had been with Annie in the National Student League. Now they had families and responsibilities. Later it would be said that Communists had infiltrated the government. It wasn't true— they inundated it.

The National Recovery Administration, where Arthur worked, was just one of the dizzying collection of new agencies trying, with unequal success, to pull the country from the crisis. The New Deal consisted of more than sixty of these bureaus. They shot up overnight; were applauded, criticized, or sued; operated frantically for a few months or years and then disappeared. Less than a year after Arthur arrived, his agency was declared unconstitutional by the Supreme Court, and its offices were allotted to another department.

Arthur's next job was with the Works Progress Administration, where his salary rose again, this time to $3,600 a year. There he joined a radical new union, the United Federal Workers of America, and soon he became the president of its WPA chapter. In 1938, Arthur traveled to Pittsburgh for the first constitutional convention of a new giant in labor politics, the Congress of Industrial Organizations. The delegates in the flag-draped hall represented more than 4 million union members, and, united together, they instantly became one of the most powerful forces in the American economy.

This was the best work Arthur would ever do. He looked at organizing as a puzzle to be solved, and he wheeled and dealed and devised strategies in smoky rooms. He drove coworkers mad by making wisecracks and refusing to take things seriously. He and Al Bernstein, lawyer for the union, would disappear at crucial moments, only to be discovered playing at a pinball machine, completely engrossed. Once Paul Robeson spoke at a labor convention, and his words had reduced Arthur and his buddies to tears. Hearing this, one of Annie's friends wondered what the singer possibly could have said that could "make those characters cry."

Though Arthur was still a wise guy, his heart attack at the Marian Anderson concert had changed him. He seemed to lose the sharpest edge of cynicism and sarcasm that had made him such a terror. In New York, Chavy had refused to be near him, but now when she visited, she found him friendly and mild, a new man. Annie controlled his regimen. She limited his tennis and swimming and kept him strictly to the healthy habits of the day, which seemed to include cigarettes, whiskey, and plenty of red meat.

If Arthur's new outlook allowed him to take hardship and defeat with some perspective, it was definitely a timely adjustment. A Communist was always torn between his personal affairs and the fortunes of the world movement. Within a few months of the concert, both would suffer severe reversals.

In the early 1930s, Communists had enjoyed the luxury of friend-lessness. They took more pleasure denouncing their Socialist rivals as "social fascists" than in doing anything to topple capitalism. Each May Day, the Reds and Pinks divided their strength, marching sepa-rately while New York City police kept them apart to prevent fist-fights. But Hitler's rise in Germany had put an end to that frivolity. All progressives were suddenly needed to join together in the United Front. Everyone was welcome: Socialists and Stalinists, liberals and Leninists, Trotskyites . . . well, maybe not Trotskyites.

Even the National Student League and the Student League for Industrial Democracy, formerly bitter rivals, joined forces to create a briefly flourishing mass student movement.

It was the age of the front organization. More numerous even than Roosevelt's agencies, they had innocuous names such as the American League for Peace and Democracy, or the National Federation for Constitutional Liberties, and they allowed the Communist influence to spread among those who never would have joined the Party itself. The fronts gathered aid for Spanish orphans and organized hundreds of thousands of people into the battle against fascism.

Then in August 1939, Hitler and Stalin promised that neither of their armies would attack the other. In America, the calls for war on Hitler ceased. New front organizations, such as the American Peace Mobilization, of which Arthur was a member, pushed isolation-ism and neutrality. When Nazis invaded Poland in September, Communist leaders no longer denounced fascist aggression as they had in Spain. Rather, they lumped together Hitler and the democra-cies, weakly calling the fight "an imperialist war in which the rulers of both sides are equally guilty."

Mass support for the popular front vanished, and American Communists were once again relegated to a tiny fringe group with-out allies or influence.

Franklin D. Roosevelt may have had closer ties to organized labor than any president who had come before him, but that didn't mean he wanted a union stirring up dissatisfaction among his own employees. Since 1937, the United Federal Workers, with roughly 15,000 members divided among the government agencies, had heckled both the president and his labor secretary, Frances Perkins.

When Congress passed the Hatch Act, in the same month that the Soviets and Nazis signed their agreement, Perkins finally had a tool to use against Arthur and the union. Section 9(a) barred federal employees from belonging to "any political party or organization which advocates the overthrow of our constitutional form of government in the United States." The Communist Party, though legally recognized and constitutionally protected, was one of nine groups that no loyal person could belong to. If the government could prove that the leaders of the United Federal Workers belonged to the Party, it could use the Hatch Act to get them thrown out of their jobs and crush the union.

In early 1941, the labor secretary mentioned this annoyance to the attorney general, who dictated this note to J. Edgar Hoover: "Miss Perkins told me at a Cabinet meeting that the four persons on the attached list were in their employ and that their conduct has excited suspicions on her part that they may be engaged in subversive activities. She asks us to make an investigation, which you are authorized to do." The appended suspects were all leaders of the United Federal Workers, including Arthur Stein. The director of the Federal Bureau of Investigation then lit a fire under the special agent in charge of the Washington field office. "In view of the fact that the request for this investigation originally came from the Attorney General," Hoover wrote to his subordinate, "you are instructed to continue investigation concerning Arthur Stein, affording this matter expeditious attention until it is brought to a logical conclusion."

For the next eight months, Hoover's men magnified, dusted, and analyzed Arthur's past to prove he was the subversive their boss believed him to be. They talked to residents in the Bronx neighborhood where he grew up. They secured his records from high school and interviewed old college professors. They ordered the mailman to report any suspicious magazines or newspapers the Steins received.

They found Arthur's criminal record and unearthed the following record of law breaking:

November 1, 1935	Parked at hack stand	Fine $3
February 7, 1938	Improper lights	Fine $2
September 8, 1941	Passed stop sign	Fine $5

The FBI agents soon discovered they were not the first to be suspicious of Annie and Arthur. The couple's landlord said neighbors "were annoyed by persons calling at the apartment building and knocking on the wrong door, thinking they were at Stein's apartment . . . these included Negroes and whites." The people who lived next door were so eager to get rid of the Steins that they offered to let the agents use their house as a post from which to spy through the window. And one woman had done some spying on her own. On a night when the Steins had guests, she and another housewife had "attempted to overhear the text of the conversation at one of these meetings by listening at the airshaft in the bathroom of her apartment. However, she stated that she was unable to overhear anything with any degree of satisfaction, although normally any conversation could be easily overheard."

On February 10, 1942, the day before the agents were set to turn in their comprehensive and, they believed, damning report, Arthur was invited to confess his sins in person. By this time, he had left the WPA and was applying for a more sensitive job at the War Production Board. Since the invasion of the Soviet Union, all American Communists had shifted again. The isolationist American Peace Mobilization, which followed the slogan "The Yanks Are Not Coming," had become the interventionist American People's Mobilization, which rallied behind the slightly different motto, "The Yanks are Not Coming Too Late." Since the surprise attack on Pearl Harbor, the aims of the Communist Party and the American government were one and the same: defeat Hitler.

Arthur entered a small room and was greeted by an FBI agent and a stenographer. "The purpose of this interview," the agent said, "is to allow you an opportunity to answer questions concerning information which has been received by the Federal Bureau of Investigation about alleged activities on your part." When the interview was finished, Arthur asked to put something else on the record:

> Since I have been questioned by the Federal Bureau of Investigation in connection with its investigation of subversive activities, I wish to make the following statement at this time: I am not, nor have I ever been a member of the Nazi Bund or any of its affiliates. I am not, nor have I ever been a member of the Communist Party or any of its affiliates. I am not, nor have I ever been a member of any subversive organization or of any organization whose purpose is to overthrow the government of the United States. I do not advocate or believe in the overthrow of the Government of the United States. I am a loyal citizen of this country and will do my utmost to defend it and its government from any attack, whether from without or within. I am willing, at any time, to refute any specific charges that may be made against my loyalty to the government or against my willingness to support it in any way.

Then Arthur left the interrogation room. He may or may not have believed that what he had just said was the truth. He may have hoped that the agents had taken him at his word. But one thing was certain: the twenty-six-page FBI report didn't contain any definitive proof that Arthur was subversive. For all their legwork, the agents had interviewed people who would be the least likely to possess secret information. The FBI felt that Arthur posed a security risk, but to Hoover's chagrin, the heads of the War Production Board refused to be swayed by this collection of hearsay and conjecture. In the opinion of the board the evidence submitted "exonerates Mr. Stein," to whom they offered the job.

In the Roosevelt years, it took more than a few snooping neighbors to ruin a man's career. But that wouldn't always be the case.

•••

The first duty of every Communist—and though Hoover couldn't prove it, Arthur was a Communist—was to read the *Daily Worker* from cover to cover each day. In Washington, this task was even less pleasant than it sounded.

A secret Party operative, who could lose his job if his true allegiance was discovered, could hardly walk up to his neighborhood newsstand each morning to get his copy. "Members," recalled one veteran, "were told which news dealers carried the paper, and were instructed that they were not to go to a stand two days in a row. . . . It took considerable time to get the paper each day, and yet it was considered imperative that comrades buy and read the paper regularly."

The *Worker* was the conduit, running from Union Square in New York to Union Station in Washington, that kept comrades up to date on the latest zigzags in the Party line. But once the paper was acquired and perused, the reader was left with the most difficult task: getting rid of it. Many editions vanished into fireplaces, but some apartment dwellers "tore papers into small pieces and spent hours flushing them down the toilet. Some concealed them within the regular 'capitalist' newspapers and disposed of them. Others saved them for trips to New York and took home suitcases filled with old papers."

When you joined the Party in Washington, you were warned that it had gone "deep underground." Comrades were not issued the membership cards that would later inspire the phrase "card-carrying Communist." Even before the Hatch Act made it illegal, a government worker who had a reputation as a Red was not likely to be in line for the next big promotion. The underground included roughly one hundred members scattered through the various bureaus and departments. They were organized into isolated units consisting of about eight people each who, in theory, knew only one another and no one else in the network. "We would try to limit our knowledge of other members," a former participant wrote, "in case of interrogation, possible torture. Such an idea . . . might seem rather remote in the radical Washington climate, but climates could change fast."

Each unit was commanded by a captain who collected dues—10

percent of a member's salary—and delivered directives from the semimystical leaders "upstairs." Arthur became a captain in the WPA unit in the mid-1930s and each week hosted a meeting of his group. Annie would leave on that particular night, and the guests would carefully park their cars down the block from the apartment. These precautions certainly gave the impression of conspiracy, but while FBI agents copied down license plate numbers, peered through windows, and strained their ears at airshafts, the Communists inside were doing nothing more sinister than talking politics. "Procedures at meetings varied little from group to group," one jaded former participant told federal agents years later. "Part of the evening would be devoted to political discussion. . . . Part of the evening was devoted to a discussion of trade union questions. Each person present was expected to list all the meetings he had attended during the week, all the responsibilities he had undertaken in the union and how he had fulfilled them."

The Communist underground must have been the most boring clandestine organization in history. Unlike most other secret cadres that existed to carry out some illegal revolutionary campaign, the Communists in Washington stayed underground simply in order to stay underground. Keeping Party membership secret was the only goal. So week after week, the menacing Reds subjected one another to endless conversation, which in a room full of theoretical Marxists, could get oppressive fast. They bickered and pursued each other's wives. Once the initial thrill wore off, members were left with the competition and claustrophobia of the units. Not surprisingly, few stayed for long.

It may have been pointless, but it wasn't easy. The Party demanded commitment and total discipline. Arthur proved his mettle during a surgical procedure when he insisted that Annie stay in the operating room to make sure he didn't blab any Party secrets while under anesthesia. He had little patience with others who couldn't use the same kind of self-control. When Louise Gerrard, a rising unit captain, wanted to complain about the way things were being run, she was told to talk to Art Stein.

"I hadn't known Stein was important 'upstairs,' (though I probably should have known)," Gerrard later confessed, "and even then I didn't know how important he really was. . . . I talked to Stein in the office one afternoon when we were alone, but instead of discussing the situation with me, he 'laid down the law.' I was to mind my own business, do what he told me and stop worrying . . . in short, he told me to 'forget my gripes' and get back to work."

It was this type of interaction that ensured that twenty years later, when details about these secret meetings became the most sought-after commodity in Washington, there would be plenty of people, like Louise Gerrard, who were eager to turn informer for the FBI or give their testimony to a congressional committee.

•••

Chavy had risen to prominence during the war years. With the men in Europe and the Pacific, she had taken the post of Communist organizer for all of Manhattan, by far the most important district in the Party. She was doing nothing illegal since she didn't work for the government, but Chavy's activities were closely watched. It seemed as though every time she finished a speech at a Party meeting, a young woman would approach her and say, "That was an excellent presentation. Could you say it to me again, so that I get it just right." Chavy figured she was the stenographer, though, of course she was an informer and Chavy was dictating the incriminating speeches directly into her rapidly expanding FBI files.

That kind of laxity was not tolerated in Washington. When Chavy came to visit, she found a whispering city filled with secrets. The units that had once sat around driving themselves crazy had finally been given a mission. Word had come down from "upstairs" that the underground should begin intelligence gathering. "I was instructed," one former Communist later explained to the feds, "to find out from each member in my group precisely what data he had access to. What kind of papers, what did they include, to whom were they routed, how important did they seem, what was the security classification?" Few Communists had access to anything top secret, but the Soviets were interested in the political climate. For instance, they were pushing Roosevelt to open up a second front in Europe and wanted to learn where different politicians in Washington stood on the question. The unit members themselves were told that the information was for domestic use only; that it was being sent to Earl Browder, the Party leader, who would then "get it to the 'right people' at the White House." In actuality, Browder was going straight to the Soviets.

Some did have direct contact with the NKVD—Stalin's spy group. Like Arthur, Victor Perlo was a progressive who had landed a job in the New Deal. In fact, when Arthur joined the WPA in 1935, he had taken over Perlo's underground unit. After World War II, Perlo would be named as an agent by Elizabeth Bentley and Whittaker Chambers, the two most voluble sources of Communist names. Perlo had been a terrible spy. His Soviet handlers were constantly distressed by the poor output and sloppy *konspiratsia,* the Russian word for tradecraft. "They gathered at meetings in each other's homes, and their wives typed the reports," Perlo's contact complained in a secret message to his superiors. "Taking into account the state of *konspiratsia,* one can not do much. I am persuading [Perlo] to stop holding the meetings so regularly and to work individually as much as possible."

Arthur had known Perlo since they were both children in the Bronx. For Hoover, this acquaintanceship was tantamount to guilt and proved that Arthur himself was a spy. Perhaps he was. He briefly held a sensitive position in the War Production Board, where he could obtain "very confidential information regarding the water supply and power lines in defense areas." If he was a spy, he didn't confide it to Chavy. During one of her visits to Washington, Annie and Arthur invited her on a long drive through the countryside. When they were well out of the city, the Steins told their friend that a Party operative had asked Arthur to pass along any sensitive information he could gather. The three old comrades discussed the question at length and finally, as Chavy recalled, they decided not to do espionage work.

That's not to say that Arthur wasn't up to something. Once a week, he went off to play chess at the Marshall Chess Club. It wasn't until thirty years later that Annie learned the truth about this routine. Sol Adler was a high-ranking New Dealer who had been driven out of America during the McCarthy period and sought refuge under Maoist rule in China. "I guess it's safe to tell you now," he confessed to Annie in the 1970s, "I was your husband's Party contact. We used to meet once a week to play chess."

•••

Arthur had his second heart attack in 1946. He and Annie were moving a few houses down Conduit Road, newly renamed MacArthur Boulevard, and Arthur was hauling the furniture himself. He collapsed on the sidewalk while pushing a wheelbarrow filled with books. From then on, Annie lived on the edges of panic. Whenever he was ten minutes late, she began to fear the worst. Under no circumstances was he allowed to exercise. Instead, he stuck to pursuits of the mind. In the mornings, he sat with his coffee in front of a chessboard, patiently puzzling out the day's game problem in the newspaper. He knew the game like a master, and whenever accomplished players came to Washington looking for a competitive match, they were directed to meet Arthur at the local chess club.

Soon after their first son, Philip Steckler Stein, was born in August 1942, Annie had been forced to decide what to tell him about his father's health. It was not surprising, considering the importance the new parents placed on secrecy and discipline, that Philip was never told about Arthur's weak heart. When he was old enough, he would beg his father to come play catch. Annie would cajole and plead, and then yell. Her son was left with the feeling that his mother was completely unpredictable. Without provocation, she would suddenly become hysterical.

In 1943, Arthur took a full-time job with the union, which had joined forces with state and local employees to become the United Public Workers of America. At the founding convention in Atlantic City, he had stood amid the crowd of delegates and presented the resolution to "pledge ourselves to organize the unorganized, to win full citizenship, both economic and political, for government and public workers, and the service of the American people." Truman sent his support to the convention, and Hoover sent his spies. The

Bureau planted its informants within the union and were soon receiving reports on all of Arthur's activities. On March 16, 1946, Eleanor, my mother, was born. Within a few days, an FBI informant reported overhearing Arthur "talking about the birth of his little daughter at the Homeopathic Hospital."

The Steins and their friends knew they were being watched. They discussed it and speculated to the point of paranoia, and still they underestimated the resources that the government was using to record their every action. From December 1946 until September 1947, Annie and Arthur's telephones were tapped, and the FBI was making transcriptions of their calls.

Few people, even in government, knew that the Federal Bureau of Investigation was preparing, despite the disapproval of Congress, a special vacation retreat for people like the Steins. "There is enclosed herewith information on the above Subject," an agent had written to J. Edgar Hoover regarding Arthur, "in order that he might be considered for custodial detention in time of national emergency." Both Annie and Arthur were placed on the FBI's Security Index, a list of thousands of progressives who were to be rounded up—as Japanese-Americans had been during the war—and taken into internment camps in the event of a serious crisis.

•••

The Eightieth Congress, elected in the autumn of 1946, was among the most reactionary in history. Democrats had controlled the White House and both chambers of the legislature ever since the New Deal landslide of 1934. In the interval, it had seemed that the Republicans might never regain power, that they would be relegated to the permanent role of minority party. But the world war was over, and Roosevelt had died the previous year. It had never felt natural to call those Godless Soviets our allies, and when Winston Churchill came to Missouri in March and told a room of nervous housewives that an "iron curtain has descended across the Continent," well, that sounded more like it. Fear of Communists won the Republicans both houses of Congress in 1946, and it seemed inevitable that in the presidential election two years later, their candidate, Thomas Dewey, would defeat Truman.

Truman himself knew that "the Communist bugaboo," as he called it, presented no real threat. America, the president believed, "was perfectly safe so far as Communism is concerned—we have far too many sane people." In his mind, the real menace was J. Edgar Hoover running amok and building a "citizen spy system." But the Red Scare was on, in the newspapers and on the radio. Within three weeks of the Republican victory in the election, Truman abandoned his fine sentiments for political expediency, created a temporary Commission on Loyalty, and ceded to Hoover more power than ever before.

Truman's Executive Order 9835—the Loyalty Order—was as damaging to civil liberties as any law issued to protect national security in a time of emergency, except there was no emergency. For a federal worker to lose his job, the loyalty boards only had to show that "reasonable grounds exist for the belief that the person involved is disloyal to the Government of the United States." The accused were not allowed to hear the specific charge brought against them, nor were they likely to learn the name of their accuser. The word *disloyal* was not defined. The law was perfectly written so that it could be abused, and the people responsible for enforcing it—the FBI and the House Committee on Un-American Activities, which had been hunting Communists since 1938—were precisely those most likely to abuse it. "A liberal is only a hop, skip, and a jump from a Communist," a military investigator said, expressing the mind-set of the loyalty boards. "A Communist starts as a liberal."

The Loyalty Order gave Hoover a chance to settle some old grudges, and it wasn't long before he recalled a certain government worker who had kept his job despite the FBI's recommendation that he be fired. Hoover dropped a line to the assistant attorney general requesting "that a loyalty investigation be conducted relative to Arthur Stein in the event he was still employed by the Federal Government." But Arthur had quit the government a few years earlier to work as secretary-treasurer for the union. Before the Loyalty

Order, it had not been a very important union; now it was at the very center of the struggle for civil liberties. Hoover was looking for liberals and progressives to hound out of government work, and Arthur's union consisted of liberal and progressive government workers. His members would represent a hugely disproportionate number of those investigated, and he and Al Bernstein, the union's lawyer, would do their best to defend every single one of them.

Arthur wrote letters of protest to Truman, Eleanor Roosevelt, and New York City mayor Fiorello La Guardia. He commissioned a radio show, making sure it presented a middle-of-the-road message that could not easily be characterized as Communist. He drafted a print ad, which was refused by the New York Times but appeared in the New Republic. Annie became her husband's researcher. She dug up a statement Truman had written when he was still a senator calling loyalty investigations a waste of time.

But now he was president, and his agents were checking up on millions of government employees. Little attempt was made to keep track of who was being dismissed or why. "I don't think the people are concerned with any breakdown," one investigator explained. "They don't care if they are drunks, perverts or Communists—they just want to get rid of them." More than one thousand workers were dismissed as subversives before Dwight Eisenhower took office as president in 1953. Five times that number resigned rather than have their personal foibles and scandals aired in public. After all this effort, not a single charge of espionage was ever made.

By that time, Arthur would be out of work and out of Washington. The union would be broken, and nothing would remain of the promise that the New Deal seemed to hold out for a young couple out of college. They had done little to curb the abuses of the loyalty cases, but Annie had found one memorable quote during her research: "A little more patience," Thomas Jefferson had said in the days of the Alien Sedition Act, "and we shall see the reign of the witches pass over and the people recovering their true right, restoring the government to its true right."

It would take a lot more patience.

CHAPTER 4

The Other Cheek

THE entire Jones family came out to the depot to see Albert off. His father, mother, and sister were there. His new wife, Millie, still a little shy around her in-laws, hadn't cried yet, but the tears would come soon. Twenty-three-year-old Albert carried his duffel bag over his shoulder. Inside were the recommended items for his destination: three pairs of blue jeans, six pairs of work socks, one suit of clothes "suitable for Sunday wear," and a Bible.

The driver climbed up the stairs into the silver bus. A moment later, the engine shook itself awake and the Greyhound vibrated eagerly in anticipation of some exercise. The Joneses shared one last round of hugs, tighter and more desperate than before. Albert's mother and sister were crying, and Millie's eyes were growing red. Albert gave his father a firm handshake and thought of the words he had spoken a few nights earlier. "I don't believe in one thing you're doing," Malcolm had told him, "but I'll whip the man who calls you a coward."

It was late April 1943. In North Africa, the Allies had finally chased the German army into a trap on the Tunisian peninsula and were throttling it slowly day by day. There were soldiers on Albert's bus, probably returning to base after a home leave, and he couldn't help notice the deference they were shown and the disapproval that fell on him, a healthy young man in civvies. Imagine how they would look if they knew where he was going.

Through Los Angeles, Millie followed behind the bus. When it stopped in the San Fernando Valley, she pulled ahead and was at the station to see her husband off again. This time she was crying for real. She waved him out of sight and then her hand fell back down to her side. He was off to an adventure, and she was a war wife, one of millions whose husbands had gone away.

The Greyhound pawed its way up the steep grades of Highway 395. It was late in the afternoon, and Albert's ride into the Sierras would last all night. He was too excited to sleep; instead, he put his face to the cold glass of the window and watched the road signs and the black trees file by. In the morning, the bus stopped at yet another tiny rural post office. Albert climbed down the stairs into the mountain air; it was boot-stomping, hand-rubbing weather. A man was waiting for him with a station wagon, and together they drove three miles, climbing up to 6,000 feet into the high mountains, to Civilian Public Service Camp #37, in Coleville, California.

The first conscientious objectors had arrived in Coleville the previous year. "They were transported on luxurious Greyhound busses," the local *Minden Times* reported. "Young fellows, soft collared with soft hands—principally office men. Very few were of the hardy rough and ready outside class. . . . We were informed that these brave (?) gents will be under the supervision of the Forest Reserve and will be worked on improvement projects in that area."

The objectors, seeing the snow-topped Sweetwater Mountains that surrounded the Antelope Valley, had immediately started taking snapshots. The district attorney and sheriff, on hand to see them arrive, confiscated all the cameras and stowed them under lock and key. It was bad enough the conchies were here. The least they could do was not act like tourists on vacation.

At first, the inhabitants of Camp #37 proved their detractors right. They had little experience in country living, and even basic bunkhouse improvements posed a major challenge. "Crews Build Shelves" was a lead headline in one of their early newsletters. "After two weeks of discussion," the story read, "and no less than four 'final' plans, a three-man crew started work on the sets of shelves for the dormitories."

But Albert was not this type of man. He had been working in railroad sheds and shipyards, and his hands were coarsened. He took a look around the camp, which was made of several narrow pine cabins built in a scattered pattern like wooden matches dropped and left as they had fallen. He set down his bag on an iron-framed single bed, walked past the sage and piñon pine trees in the center of the compound, and reported to the camp director. Albert handed him his orders, a single sheet of paper headed "Assignment to Work of National Importance," and signed at the bottom by General Lewis B. Hershey, the director of Selective Service.

Ever since the war began, Albert had waited to arrive here. In that time, he'd had support from his wife and at least a pact of nonaggression from his parents, but his church had deserted him, and he could look for no sympathy from neighbors or coworkers. In Camp #37, he was surrounded by pacifists. Each Sunday they held a silent Quaker meeting, and that was the only time in the week that the men were not in heated discussions about their faith. Coming here, Albert finally felt welcome.

•••

Two years earlier, in early December 1941, Albert was putting in six-day weeks at the Southern Pacific railroad's Los Angeles maintenance shop. He earned fifty-four cents an hour and put every penny aside for the day when he and Millie would be married. Sometimes he worked sixteen consecutive hours for two or three nights a week, arriving at the shop in midafternoon and leaving near daybreak. On Sundays, he was pooped.

After twelve years of almost universal underemployment, the factory machines were spinning again. It was not just tanks and bomber planes either, but wheat and beef, wool blankets and boots, paper and rubber. Sunday was the day of rest, and on that day Americans were busier doing the things that made them feel American than they had ever been before. It was the day for driving the new car, for ball-games, beach trips, home repairs, and window shopping. All leisure activities were penciled in for that one day each week and were accomplished with the giddy excitement that comes in the shadow of disaster.

December 7, 1941, was supposed to be such a Sunday. Albert's parents had gone off to church early in the morning, and the house was empty. He stayed home, stealing some extra moments of sleep. The sounds of the Mormon Tabernacle Choir floated in from the kitchen radio. He finally dragged his weary bones from bed and stumbled into the bathroom. And so he was sitting on the toilet when, shortly after 11:30 A.M., the radio announcer interrupted the choir's singing to announce the news. "President Roosevelt says that the Japanese have attacked Pearl Harbor in Hawaii from the air." The attack had already been in progress for more than an hour.

Alone in the house, Albert started picturing his future. It had just changed for the worse, he knew. His first concern was for Millie's parents. Could they accept a conscientious objector as a son-in-law? All afternoon, he stayed within earshot of the radio as details of the disaster drifted in like the smoke that was wiping out the sky in Honolulu.

Conversation between Albert and his father was limited to essential topics only, and pacifism was not among them. Malcolm had never understood his son: Why would a strong, healthy American, a rough-housing Jones, have such an abhorrence for fighting? Albert was a congenial, hard-working young man who just happened to hold a serious and highly unpopular belief, but someone could know him for months and never hear him talk about it. After Pearl Harbor, it became a topic to discuss. That night, Malcolm turned his eyes on his son and asked him what he would do. "I'll wait and see," Albert said. "When the time comes, I'll see how sincere I really am."

The time was coming, and Albert had already taken the first step more than a year earlier. On October 16, 1940, the day after his twenty-first birthday, every man in the United States between the ages of twenty-one and thirty-six was told to report to his local draft board. It was R-Day, the day for registration. Before dawn, men were lined up on sidewalks outside draft sites in every town and city. When it was over, 17 million of them had been tagged, cataloged, and issued draft cards. In one day, the army learned most of what it needed to know about the men who would soon provide its human fodder.

Four years earlier, Albert had signed a pledge saying he would never fight. That pledge, and the blue card that confirmed it, were fragile shields against the pitiless questioning of the army and the draft registrar. He knew that members of certain religions were allowed to seek alternative service. They could become medics or noncombatants in the army, or perform "work of national importance" in isolated camps scattered around the country. Or a pacifist could refuse to register and face up to five years in prison and a $10,000 fine.

Albert's church, which had guided his path toward peace, now betrayed him. An older minister, hearing that he was going to be a conscientious objector, grabbed him by the shoulders and said, "Think about what you are doing young man." After Pearl Harbor, the Methodists abandoned twenty years of peace work. Once the fighting started, one leader bragged, "We are sending over a million young men from Methodist homes to participate in the conflict. . . . God himself has a stake in the struggle and he will uphold them as they fight forces destructive of the moral life of man."

Many young men around the country who had grown up in the same pacifist movement were left to face a grave dilemma alone. The most famous were eight students at Union Theological Seminary in New York. David Dellinger, who would still be leading the antiwar efforts two decades later, refused to register and was sentenced to a year and a half in prison. During the trial, Dellinger and the other defendants made clear their position that "in order to live in harmony with the will of God," it was necessary to "obey our conscience before we obey the State." Albert felt the same way.

He registered in the late morning, before an afternoon swing shift at the railroad yards. The registrar asked him eleven questions, none of which gave Albert the opportunity to discuss his deep objections to violence. He filled in a card, which read: Race, white. Height, six foot two inches and a half. Weight, one hundred thirty-five pounds.

For Eyes, he checked blue. Hair, blonde. Complexion, ruddy. Then Albert stepped outside of the procedure. Next to his signature he wrote the words "Conscientious Objector."

···

A quick look at the map showed many amateur tacticians that California could be the next target of the Japanese lightning attack. A skittish Los Angeles was transformed into an armed camp. Antiaircraft cannons, surrounded by sandbags, were placed around airplane factories and oil depots. The army mounted a gun battery near the Hollywood sign, and searchlights, formerly used to celebrate film premieres, were conscripted into the war effort and stood ready to crisscross the skies at any sign of enemy bandits.

Albert waited for his draft number to be called. In the meantime, he and Millie had a wedding to plan. She had always wanted a traditional ceremony, had dreamed of a long, trailing dress and her handsome groom waiting at the altar. They scoured the local venues until she found a Methodist church in Magnolia Park that had a wide aisle, perfect for walking down. Then they cobbled together the rest. They were married on Easter Sunday, 1942. They took a tiny house and set about being married. It was a perfect interlude. Each morning Millie caught a bus to school, and Albert drove to Hollywood, where he was now working as a film technician at Consolidated Studios for the fabulous sum of $1.27 an hour.

But the war was closing in. Millie's earliest friends had been the children of Japanese farmers working on her family's lands. These same people were being taken from their homes and sent to Manzanar, one of the barbed-wire encampments where many were to spend the duration of the war. For forty dollars, Albert and Millie bought a beautiful Plymouth coupe from a Japanese man who was forced to leave everything behind on his way to internment.

So many wartime marriages were broken up that the full year they spent together seemed generous. In April 1943, Albert's draft number was finally called, and an army doctor classified him as 1A: ready and able to fight. He wasn't willing. Through the year and a half that his decision had been postponed, Albert had watched the fate of his fellow objectors. News from the camps was bad. The men there were paid no salary by the government and just $2.50 a week from church donations. Worse, the work they had been given, far from being nationally important, was just keep-busy stuff. Men with unsympathetic draft boards never even made it to the camps. They either buckled under and joined the army or were sent to jail.

As Albert's interview with the draft board neared, he prepared himself for all outcomes. If they denied his status as a conscientious objector, he decided he would go to jail rather than fight. Before his meeting, Albert filled out Form 47, the special questionnaire given to those claiming CO status. Suddenly, the army was concerned about individual feelings:

1. Describe the nature of your belief which is the basis of your claim . . .

2. Explain, how, when, and from whom or from what source you received the training and acquired the belief . . .

. . . .

4. Under what circumstances, if any, do you believe in the use of force?

5. Describe the actions and behavior in your life which in your opinion most conspicuously demonstrate the consistency and depth of your religious convictions.

It was a long drive from Girard, where Albert and Millie were now living, to the draft board in Tarzana. At the time, the board in the San Fernando Valley presided over a population of roughly 100,000 people. When Albert arrived for his hearing in April 1943, a year and a half into the war, it had yet to offer a single draftee conscientious objector status. Albert could not be optimistic, but he did have some reason to hope. Most of the seven men on the board were familiar to him. Some were fathers of his classmates. All were aware that he was a dedicated pacifist. For years they had listened in church as he rose to speak, naively they might have thought, against war. Still, they were not about to go easy on him.

Albert dressed in the soberest clothes he possessed. He was a tall man, too skinny to be physically imposing but still a large presence. Yet sitting on the hot seat, he could not help but feel like a child being scolded for some wrongheaded idea. They asked him, "How can you not join the military and fight when my boy is overseas right now risking his life?"

One said, "You say you're a pacifist but what would you do if somebody attacked your mother?"

Then they asked, "If everybody felt the way you did, what would happen then?" That was an easy one to answer.

"If everyone felt like me," Albert said, "there would never be any wars at all."

Something he said must have been convincing because the board granted his request to enter Civilian Public Service. The army stamped him with a new draft rating, IV-E: wrongheaded, incorrigible, hopeless. The bearer of such a classification was not allowed to remain long among his neighbors. He was separated from society as soon as possible and shipped off to a remote work camp in the mountains.

•••

Camp #37's military drill consisted of a bullhorn that sounded reveille at 8:00 A.M. each morning and an American flag that was hoisted to the top of its pole. After that, no soldier could have recognized the routine. There were usually between 150 and 200 men in camp who gathered for a quick breakfast and then scattered into the mountains to their work assignments. Albert's first camp job was as a dishwasher in the kitchen. It was clear from the start that he did not belong to the soft-collared classes; he was handy about the camp, and such men were valuable. Soon he was hauling hewn logs in the camp's enormous Walters Snowfighter, which rolled on ten tires and handled like a Sherman tank.

From June through mid-October, all the men were on call to combat forest fires. They watched the weather conditions and prayed for rain. "The summer work program," Albert wrote in a spring newsletter, "is planned around an expected bad fire season. Moisture content of last winter's snowfall is far below normal, giving rise to our worst fears, a long dry spell."

Even this dangerous work failed to impress the locals, who never warmed up to the conchies in their midst. When a flooded stream destroyed a store and motel in nearby Lee Vining, Albert and some others offered to help clear out the debris. The store was waist-high in mud and rocks. For two days they worked on the site, digging out cars on the street that were almost completely covered. Most of the merchandise was ruined, and some things had been washed a few hundred feet down the highway. After Albert and the crew were done, the store owner didn't offer a single word of thanks. Later, they heard that the town was speculating on how much the conscientious objectors had stolen.

In the late afternoons, Albert filtered in with the others from the work groups. Chores were done, and the social life of the camp began. First was the clamor of dinner, followed by the long evenings and dark nights. Almost all of the talk concerned the war. Everyone had friends or relatives at the front. One man got a letter from his brother in North Africa. "You in the states," he wrote, "are likely forgetting the campaign here already but the bloody details of it will lurk in our minds as long as we live, though we may try hard to forget them. It's not a pleasant sight to see one's own countrymen being killed. It's not a pleasant sight to see groups of little white crosses, not even if they are German."

Of course, the men in Coleville could not forget the campaigns that they were missing. At lights out at 10:00 P.M., each was left with his own thoughts. Luckily, they had aching backs and screaming joints to ponder too. The blessed physical exhaustion of the day's work usually meant that sleep came fast.

If possible, Millie was in an even worse position than her husband. He at least was a government-sanctioned conscientious objector who was doing something he felt was honorable. It was also simple: he worked all day, talked with like-minded young men in the evenings, and went to sleep exhausted. Moreover, he was isolated from those who disagreed with him. She had no such protection.

Millie moved back in with her mother when Albert left for the camp. She had earned her teaching credential from UCLA and found a job working in an elementary school in Burbank. She hated it, except for music lessons. Even the classrooms had been mobilized for the war effort. Millie was expected to sell war bonds to her students. Their parents would be informed of the day when they'd be sold, and every little boy and girl would come in to class with a $5 bill to buy a bond. Millie refused to sell them, and on sale days another teacher came into her classroom and handled the actual transactions. It was little more than a gesture. On other days she'd lead her students in singing the navy anthem, "Anchors Aweigh."

Millie visited Albert sometimes on weekends. Her mother would drive her to the San Fernando depot, and she would settle into a well-traveled seat for the long bus ride north on 395. From the highway she could see the sentry towers from Manzanar, the Japanese relocation center where some of her best girlhood friends were incarcerated. Albert would meet her and take her to camp. It was a pleasure to eat Cheerios in the mess hall and not have to cook her own meals. There was a piano, and she could play some music. The men had done little to decorate the camp, and Millie did her best to add some color.

•••

Night was the only time that the outside world, via an uncertain radio reception, entered Camp #37. There was too much static to hear in the daytime, and power went out at 10:00 P.M., so there were a few hours of radio broadcast each evening. It was then, sitting around the set thousands of feet up into the High Sierras, that Albert followed the progress of the war: Guadalcanal, Stalingrad, the Kasserine Pass. In June 1943, the momentum of the conflict was changing. The Allies, not yet advancing, were no longer collapsing on all fronts. The battles for the Atlantic and North Africa were won; the invasion of Sicily would begin in a few weeks. Albert felt an ever-increasing alienation from world events. The action out there was so fierce and his setting was so remote.

Everyone had doubts about the conscientious objectors' courage. And in the long nights, sometimes they doubted themselves. It had taken a principled stand to enter the camps, an unpopular choice in the face of public opinion, but that didn't count for much when they heard of a high school friend who had died in battle. Fighting fires and building roads might be important, but it was not the stuff— storming beaches in open boats, hand-to-hand combat—you could tell your grandkids about. Albert and all the other men in the camps around the country longed for that opportunity that would prove to everyone, especially themselves, that they possessed physical bravery too.

It was stormy on the night of June 21, 1943. Albert was in a spike camp near June Lake, a few miles from Coleville. Millie was there too, visiting for the weekend. The rain exploded on the corrugated iron roof. The wind outside threatened to lift the entire ceiling off the shoddy barrack walls. They held their blankets up to their chins, gripping tight at each thunderclap. Around 9:30 P.M., Albert heard the faint buzzing of airplane engines amid the general symphony of the storm. He wondered for a moment what the conditions up there must be like on such a night.

Second Lieutenant William E. Hunt and his crew had already had a long day. At 1:45 P.M., Hunt had steered a fourteen-ton B-24 Liberator down the strip in Salinas, California. He and his crew, eleven other members of the Second Air Force's Thirty-Fourth Bomber Group, Seventh Bomber Squadron, had been flying training missions like this one for months. Hunt himself had already logged over three hundred flight hours, including eighty hours in the B-24. The plane had been inspected thoroughly the day before. It was a routine 350-mile flight, and they touched down safely and on schedule in Tonopah, Nevada, at 6:36 P.M.

The only difficulty of these flights was clearing the High Sierras. Since the mountains topped out around 13,000 feet and the Liberator had a service ceiling above 31,000 feet, even these were only a minor obstacle. The army trained its pilots on this route to prepare them for the far more dangerous flight over the Himalayas, known as the Hump, which was being used to supply China from Allied bases in Burma.

There was not a lot to do at Tonopah. Hunt could have gotten a cup of coffee and a bite to eat in the canteen. He probably received a mission briefing for his return flight to Salinas. If so, he would have heard that the weather conditions on his route were deteriorating. Nevertheless, at 8:19 P.M., Hunt and a crew of six were back in the bomber, facing down another runway. He reported that three of his generators were not functioning, but since the Liberator was equipped with an auxiliary power plant, he was ordered to proceed. He throttled up the four Pratt & Whitney engines. The plane roared down the tarmac and lifted hesitantly into the air.

An hour into its flight, the bomber was in trouble. Scattered cloudbanks limited visibility. The tail winds were veering wildly between forty compass points, blowing as hard as fifty miles an hour. Among the mountains the turbulence was intense. The bomber was flying dangerously low. At 9:25 P.M., the plane was at 12,800 feet, dancing amid jagged peaks that rose hundreds of feet higher.

In his final seconds, with wind rattling the bomber like a tin can full of nails, Hunt could have seen the mountainside appear from out of the tumult. Only a hundred or so feet shy of the top, the B-24E crashed into the side of Kuna Peak. On impact, the bomber left a long black score in the snow. One engine came loose from the wing and burned a hole six feet deep. At 9:30 P.M., the Mono Lake weather station alerted the army air force that a large plane had slammed into the granite mountain. Flames could be seen for miles. Then flares started soaring up from the crash site. There could be survivors.

Around 4:00 A.M., a forest ranger burst into the cabin where Albert slept. He asked for volunteers to climb up and help the crew. Albert quickly dressed. He wore heavy work boots and a hooded parka and threw a coil of rope and a blanket into his knapsack. As he was leaving the cabin, somebody pressed a whiskey bottle into his hand. He hopped in the back of the ranger's truck with about a dozen other men and drove to John Toms's house.

Toms was a Paiute Indian who lived in a small cabin surrounded by falling-down sheds. He had seen the flames from the crash and, as the fire started to die down, had driven a pickax into the earth with its handle pointing directly at the crash site. Now that the flames had stopped completely, the ax handle was the only marker of the plane's location. The men gathered in a circle around the pickax. Each took a turn to kneel down and sight along its length as if it were a rifle barrel. Albert took his bearings. It was aimed so close to the peak; just a few more seconds, and the plane would have flown clear.

They drove up an old fisherman's trail to Parker Lake. It was dawn as the men jumped down from the truck, their shoes crunching the dirt. Albert thanked God for his heavy boots; some of the others were in sneakers. The ranger addressed them, telling each to set out on the route he thought was best. Albert tried to remember the plane's position, picturing the long ax handle in his mind's eye. Then he chose what he took to be the most direct path, straight up the mountainside.

Sierra granite erodes into jagged shards called talus. As Albert started his ascent, he noticed these pieces all around him. The slope turned into a cliff. He had never climbed anything so steep but didn't hesitate. There seemed to be good footholds, but time and again the rock gave way beneath him, crumbling in little avalanches to join the razor-like talus below. Sometimes whole handfuls of rock vanished just as he grasped at them. He pictured what the shards beneath would do to his body if he fell. He composed a silent prayer and pushed himself upward. About 10,000 feet up, he came to a frozen lake. Overhead, a spotter plane circled the crash site, dropping sand to mark the position of the wreckage.

Albert rushed across the lake and began the last climb, 3,000 feet more through the deep snow. He was the first to reach the plane at 3:00 P.M. Hunt and his crew were dead; there were no survivors. The flares that had given hope to witnesses in the valley had been touched off by the burning fuel. The other volunteers arrived a few minutes later. They found some deflated yellow life rafts and decided to wrap the corpses and slide them down the slope. Even in the high altitude and with his stuffed-up nose, Albert could smell the burned skin of the pilots, a sickly sweet, never-to-be-forgotten stench. They dragged the bodies, sometimes pulling them through brambles, at other times racing to catch up as the rubber rafts sledded down ahead.

At the frozen lake, they were met by members of the army engineering corps who had plowed a blocked mining road to get there with their vehicles. Immediately, the army demanded to take command of the bodies, eager to get them out of the hands of the conchies. The ranger drove Albert and the others back to camp.

"There's nothing more you could have done," he told them.

Millie had dinner waiting, and Albert wolfed down his first meal of the day. He returned the whisky, untouched, to his friend. The next morning, he could not open his eyes. To look at a light bulb was agony. He was snow-blind. Other men had suffered too; the ones who had attempted the climb in just their sneakers had only narrowly avoided frostbite.

The word got around that the conscientious objectors had gone up the mountain when the bomber crashed. They had found the bodies, the locals said, and robbed them. It was rumored that by the time the army personnel had taken charge of the corpses, all of their wallets were gone. It was partly true. So desperate had been one of the men in sneakers for warm shoes that he had peeled the boots from off a corpse and worn them down the mountainside. Back in camp, the boots stood at the doorway for a few days, giving off a faint, nauseating smell. Finally, somebody took them into the woods and quietly buried them.

•••

Albert was hauling seventy-five-foot logs toward Carson City in Nevada in early August 1945 when a news report on the radio announced that the United States had just dropped the world's first atomic bomb on Hiroshima. It didn't take a belief in pacifism to be staggered by the damage done by the explosion. Literally in a flash, tens of thousands of lives had winked out of existence. Japan surrendered less than two weeks later, and men in the armed services began clamoring for release.

Meanwhile, the Civilian Public Service men—12,000 in an army of millions—were only a few hundred miles from their families. The war was over, their job—such as it had been—was done. And they wanted to go home. The heads of Selective Service knew they'd be the least popular men in uniform if they let the conchies go home at once while soldiers were still stuck on distant continents. They decided that the conscientious objectors would be the last men discharged. Disaffection was the mood in Coleville. Albert had risen to assistant director, and Millie was living in camp with him, yet he was as eager as any other to get back into the world.

The peace churches, which had spent millions of dollars bankrolling the entire CPS program, informed Selective Service that they would no longer pay, not if the boys were just kept in limbo. As an alternative, it was suggested that some of the men could continue their service by enrolling in the United Nations relief efforts that had been launched to rush food to a starving Europe. Albert applied to the United Nations Relief and Rehabilitation Administration, and as Camp #37 in the High Sierras prepared to shut down, he packed for a trip to Europe.

Albert and Millie were the last to leave Coleville. She had lived there for more than a year. For Albert, the simple wooden barracks had been home since 1943. Now the camp was empty. They made dinner for two in the huge kitchen that had once served hundreds. The sense that they were ending a phase in their lives was inescapable. Leaving early in April 1946, they locked the offices, pulled on the door to make sure the bolt held, and took a car to the post office to catch a bus.

The war years had changed Albert and Millie. They had both become Quakers in everything but name, having lived for so long under the auspices of the American Friends Service Committee. In some ways, being in camp was like being in jail, Albert had lost touch with changes in the world, and rarely had so much changed so fast. The war mania that had repelled him in 1943 had been replaced with disgust for death and fighting. Since the war had ended, full disclosure of Nazi atrocities had been released to American civilians. The American economy that was just revving up when Albert left had become the most powerful industrial force that anyone had ever seen, far more productive than any capitalist's wildest prewar fantasy. Albert and Millie had the long bus ride to Los Angeles to get used to the changes. Then, after a visit, they boarded a train for New

Windsor, Maryland. During the long, monotonous days of the trip, they began for the first time to think about the future.

Only in America did the future look comfortable. In Europe, millions were starving. Conscientious objectors were volunteering to crew on UNRRA cattle boats. The livestock was badly needed in Europe and, for Albert, it would be a chance to earn points toward his discharge while at the same time living up to his conception of a pacifist's ultimate duty. He had always felt that after the war, he would be able to make a contribution to the peace—that a pacifist's greatest power came when the fighting was over and the combatants were sick of blood. Then his testimony about the benefits of peace would receive its most receptive audience. By shipping out with UNRRA, Albert was getting a chance, in a small but personally important way, to help the worldwide recovery effort.

They arrived in Maryland and took a train to Media, Pennsylvania, where Millie was to stay at the home of a Quaker family. Albert kissed her goodbye and left for Baltimore. It was April 16, 1946. After a week of beautiful spring days, the city was suffering under a bed of clouds. A fresh northwesterly wind whipped up whitecaps on the Patapsco River. He arrived at the docks to report for duty.

Never in its history, not even during the peak of the war, had Baltimore's port been busier than it was in the spring of 1946. About a dozen relief ships, floating high, arrived each day, and another dozen, loaded to the gunwales and riding low, steamed out of the harbor into Chesapeake Bay. The ships ferried back and forth across the Atlantic, but unlike most trade routes, the goods were going one way only. After six years of war, Europe had little worth exporting.

Albert picked his way across the crowded dock. His previous maritime experience consisted of a three-hour ride with his parents to Catalina Island, where he had watched the barnstorming Chicago Cubs play against the local San Fernando Valley nine.

He smelled his ship before he saw her; barnyard odors, incongruous at a dockyard, wafted onto the shore. But with one glance at his appointed vessel, the *Edward W. Burton,* he saw his fears had been unfounded. She was huge, hundreds of feet long, with a fresh coat of gray paint and a rail that loomed high above his head. The deck was crowded with cattle stalls holding placid beasts. In its two-week stay in harbor, the ship had been loaded with 866 head of cattle, all cows. Each animal was with calf, so that a gift of a cow to a Polish farmer would soon multiply. There was trouble with the ventilation system, and for almost a week, the manure had been allowed to pile up below, accounting for the smell. Albert and his shipmates threw down their bags and suitcases on the slightly swaying cots, then went back on deck to escape the stench and watch the port vanish in their wake.

The sun set behind the continent, casting the city of Baltimore in silhouette. A few minutes later, it was high tide and the *Burton,* with Albert and almost 900 cows, hauled up the four-ton bower anchors and steamed down the harbor into the bay. Albert's thoughts were lost amid the spreading wake when the crew members caught his attention. They took pleasure in making the volunteers uneasy, and this evening they had some especially unsettling news: a storm was brewing in the Atlantic.

The swell grew enormous as they approached the entrance to the sea. In the distance, Albert saw a fleet of navy vessels, an aircraft carrier and support ships, steaming in toward the bay. Out there, the waves were so steep that at times, the towering carrier was entirely hidden from sight by intervening crests.

During four days of constant tumult, the seascape was recast into an aquatic alpine range. The *Burton* became a mountain climber, scaling one peak before dashing down its far side into the valley beyond. At times the stern was completely out of the water. The rudder flailed noisily side to side. The huge eighteen-foot propeller, churning only air, threatened to vibrate the hull to pieces. In the troughs between the waves, Albert could look up at the cliffs of water fore and aft, ready to crash down and scuttle them. The cattle men spent most of their waking hours among the animals, trying to keep them on their feet. If one fell, the other cows would kick and stomp it to death. For four days it was too rough to light the galley fires, and they lived on cereal and sandwiches.

When the storm finally broke, the volunteers returned to their regular chores. Soon the calves began to arrive, and then the whole crew enjoyed fresh milk. There were quiet hours each day to sit and read, pausing between sentences to look up and scan across 360 degrees of ocean. The *Burton's* wake now stretched for hundreds of steady miles behind them. Ahead, all was not so peaceful.

In Poland, where Albert was headed, there were more than 2.5 million starving children. Battles had swept over the country three times during the fighting, and Warsaw was 90 percent destroyed. The country's Jewish population, comprising a large percentage of the professionals who were most needed to rebuild the nation, had been almost completely destroyed behind the gates of Chelmno, Treblinka, Sobibór, Majdanek, Belzec, and Auschwitz-Birkenau.

Land's End, the western tail of southern Britain, was the first dry earth that Albert had seen for days. The *Burton* anchored until a pilot came aboard to steer her through the still partially mined channel. On the other side of England another pilot arrived to lead them through the most treacherous leg of the voyage—the North Sea.

From England to the Kiel Canal, the sea is shallow and cold. In the war, these waters had been among the most heavily fought over. More than a year after the fighting had stopped, uncleared mines still posed a fatal danger to wayward vessels. The safe path through the North Sea was clearly demarcated on each side by sunken ships that had struck the mines. The water was not deep, so their superstructures were still visible. Below each was a steel shoal, home to bones and herring, slowly corroding. On this leg of the voyage, they were almost never out of sight of a sunken ship, marking the channel like runway lights.

Steaming through the Kiel Canal, Albert could see the devastation of Germany. It was a Sunday, but farmers on both sides of the waterway were in their fields, turning their soil with hand shovels or whatever other tools they could find. The *Burton* crossed through the Baltic at night and dropped anchor in Danzig harbor, which had been repaired to receive vessels only a few months earlier. The job of the cattle men was almost done. They had arrived with 866 head, the same number as when they had departed from Baltimore. A few animals had died, but the same number were born, so Albert figured their success rate was 100 percent, a new United Nations record. It took two days to unload the cows. Each was marked with an UNRRA brand that did more than any other method to spread the word about the program. Sadly, the cows were not destined for dairy use, as had been intended. One Pole confided that the peasants were too hungry to do anything but eat the beasts.

It took another two days to unload the manure.

Danzig was a brickyard. All around the outskirts of the city were burial mounds covering dead Polish soldiers. The dead Germans still lay as they had fallen. Russian soldiers and Polish troops lived in mutual unease. Gunfire was constant in the city night and day, there were so many spare rifles lying around. Albert and the others had a few days to see the sights. First they were taken to a luncheon reception, hosted by the local UNRRA officials. In front of their plates were two glasses of clear liquid. One was water. For Albert the other glass was an introduction to a new kind of alcohol, vodka.

The crew was homeward bound after a few days of sightseeing. Halfway across the Atlantic, Albert saw a huge cloud of smoke coming from the direction of Europe. He was sure some unlucky ship had hit a mine. Soon, however, the enormous luxury liner, the *Queen Mary*, steamed into view, blowing torrents of black smoke out of her three red stacks. Headed to New York, loaded to the railings with more than a thousand war brides, she steamed past the dumpy *Burton* as if it were sitting still.

Albert pulled into Norfolk, Virginia, a month and a half after he had left. His discharge from the army was waiting for him. Millie was waiting for him too. Albert's war was finally over. He had not raised a finger to harm another, nor had he faced death. Instead, he had spent four years of his life without pay or any of the other benefits—pensions, money for education—that military veterans had earned. He had been unable to make any provision for his wife. He had helped in the little ways the government had seen fit to allow him, but he had been barred from making any real contributions. He had witnessed a historic upheaval, and like millions of other Americans, it was time for Albert to return to living a sensible life with everyday concerns.

He found a job in central Philadelphia in a converted medical instruments factory commandeered by the American Friends Service Committee. The machines used for manufacturing scalpels and retractors were set out of the way, and in their place, the Friends brought tons and tons of donated clothing. Women's dresses were shipped in 150-pound bales, wrapped in plastic or burlap. Freezing families in Norway, Finland, and Russia received bales containing winter coats. With a little ingenuity, a shipment of old-fashioned foot-powered sewing machines and yards of residual muslin that were donated by a window shade manufacturer could be combined to produce hundreds of pairs of underwear in Poland. There was a shipment of 10,000 army boots, all for left feet. Shoemakers in Eastern Europe were happy to receive them; they turned every other one inside out to make pairs. Good-intentioned Quaker matrons knitted colorful shawls, which an industrious German housewife undid and recast into valuable socks.

A bale of cast-off tuxedoes went to outfit a symphony orchestra in Vienna. Another orchestra was festooned (no doubt, ludicrously) in donated costumes that once had clothed the Horn and Hardart Automat company's marching parade band. In 1947, Henry Cadbury, head of the American Friends Service Committee, accepted the Nobel Peace Prize in recognition of the international work of the Quaker faith. Before he traveled to Oslo to accept the award, he stopped by the warehouse in Philadelphia to pick up one of the donated tuxedoes, which, Albert heard, he wore in the ceremony.

On February 20 the worst snowstorm of the year descended on Philadelphia. Almost a score of people in the city died, and it was two days before traffic and trains were running normally. On the evening of February 22, 1947, Albert took a very pregnant Millie to the Homeopathic Hospital in Philadelphia. He was not allowed to stay the night. The next morning, he was heading off to work when the phone rang. His son was due any minute. He hurried onto the train. It was freezing outside. At the station, the platform was slicked with ice. In his rush, he fell headlong onto the track, almost sliding under the wheels of an oncoming train.

In the maternity ward, he was directed to Millie Jones's room. When he opened the door, the bed was empty. For a dreadful second, Albert feared the worst. Then a nurse led him down the hall to a large window facing a room filled with bassinets. He felt somebody behind him, Millie. A nurse then lifted up a baby boy to show Albert and Millie what they had wrought. His name was to be Jeff; Millie had been quite firm about that. Like his own father, who had been chauffeuring a king, Albert had missed the birth of his firstborn son.

Thirty years later, Jeff would also be absent from the birth of his first child.

CHAPTER 5

The Committees

ON February 18, 1953, an FBI informant notified the Washington Field Office "that the Coordinating Committee for the Enforcement of the D.C. Anti-Discrimination Laws was planning a farewell party for secretary Annie Stein, who is leaving for New York." As far as the Washington office was concerned, good riddance.

Hundreds of friends and colleagues, almost the entire progressive population of the capital, received invitations to Annie's farewell party. "We shall miss her as a secretary—'The Greatest Secretary in the World' I have called her," said the letter, signed by world-renowned civil rights leader Mary Church Terrell, the leader of the Coordinating Committee.

In the spring of 1953, Washington was a picketed city. Inhabitants had grown used to seeing marchers on almost every corner. There were protesters on Seventh Street, in front of small five-and-dimes and huge department stores; sign-waving marchers circled in front of the board of education, demanding integration of the district's public schools. In front of the White House, from June 1952 until January 1953, a silent vigil urged clemency for Julius and Ethel Rosenberg, the convicted "atom spies," whose executions had been delayed and delayed but were now fast approaching.

It had been a perfect picketing winter, the mildest in recent memory. As March began, the cherry trees around the Tidal Basin near the Jefferson Memorial were threatening to blossom a month early and ruin the annual festival. Even the Stein family's apartment in a drab housing development, filled with packing boxes bound for Brooklyn, seemed bright and almost cheerful.

On March 2, the mild winter ended with the worst snowstorm of the season: schools were cancelled and traffic snarled. March 3, ruined by rain, rivulets of melting snow, and drops trickling down shirt collars, was Annie's fortieth birthday. She still looked like a young woman.

The next morning, the papers announced that Joseph Stalin had suffered a brain hemorrhage. It was a cloudy Friday afternoon in the capital two days later when Moscow's news bureau announced, "The heart of the comrade and inspired continuer of Lenin's will . . . has stopped beating." Stalin was seventy-three and had led the Soviet Union for almost thirty years. There, he had been a monster, but for American Communists, he had been the big brother who would come to their defense in a schoolyard fight.

For Annie and Arthur and the rest of the Party's dwindling membership, the turmoil and loss were not discussed. Reaction to his death, like most other party functions, remained a private and secret matter.

In Washington, journalist I. F. Stone noted, "Amid the burst of bad manners and foolish speculation, there was remarkably little jubilation. A sudden chill descended on the capital." While half the world mourned his death, the other waited anxiously for a successor to be named. Flags on the diplomatic headquarters of the Soviet Union, Poland, Czechoslovakia, Hungary, Finland, and Romania were lowered to half staff; other nations made no sign of mourning. The Soviet embassy, inscrutably closed for years, opened its gates for one day. Visitors were allowed to enter and sign tributes in a public guest book, a tantalizing document, no doubt, to the Federal Bureau of Investigation.

On Sunday, crowds eight abreast filed past Stalin's red casket in Moscow's House of Trade Unions. At home, it was the day of Annie's testimonial dinner. At 6:00 P.M., guests came to Alpha Phi Alpha's Howard University sorority house, the site of many earlier Coordinating Committee celebrations. They were handed a copy of a souvenir pamphlet as they filed into the room and dispersed to find their seats. Donations to the dinner had raised more than $400, a major windfall for an organization that gladly accepted donations of a quarter or fifty cents. On the program's inside page was a picture of Annie, posed in the attitude of demure housewife. Sitting at their tables, waiting for the keynote address to begin, the guests read the caption beneath the photo. "Those of us in the Coordinating Committee who have worked with Annie Stein will see at once that the picture accompanying this program, handsome as it is, is all wrong. It shows her seated, hands idle in her lap."

Few Communists allowed themselves to be publicly honored in 1953; it was an invitation for investigation and reprisal. Annie had become a well-known Washingtonian. She was quoted often in the local press. In 1951, she was named to the *Afro-American*'s honor roll and had her picture in the newspaper. In 1952, a sorority at Howard University had named her "Woman of the Year." She was facing the public at a time when most of her comrades were scrambling for cover.

Years earlier, during a violent storm, Annie had ducked into a five-and-dime lunch counter for a cup of coffee. A few minutes later, an elderly African-American man came through the door, soaking wet from the rain. He had stood at the counter near her—blacks were not allowed to sit—and asked the white soda jerk for a cup of coffee. The counterman, a teenager, ignored him, ostentatiously continuing to mop down the counter and tend to other things. The man asked again, and the boy still ignored him. Annie sat quietly, growing increasingly uncomfortable. After a few minutes, the older man, clutching the collar of his coat against his neck, retreated back out into the rain. The teenager caught Annie's eye on him and gave her a broad grin and a wink. By not intervening, she had made herself complicit. She realized then that racism didn't need everyone to be a racist; it just needed everyone to be complacent. Jim Crow was founded on the wink. From that moment on, she vowed always to speak up.

The highlight of the farewell dinner came when eighty-nine-year-old Mary Church Terrell made her careful way to the podium. She put on her reading glasses and said, "I must confess it is a great temptation for me to take the time right here and now to relate in detail just how much Annie Stein has done to make Washington a real, genuine, sure enough, honest to goodness democracy."

•••

When Annie started working for integration four years earlier, no African American could have mistaken the nation's capital for a genuine democracy. In 1949, the government monuments were surrounded by a southern city. Trolley cars tracked down the main streets, and blacks rode only in the rear seats. The city's schools, playgrounds, and swimming pools were segregated by law. In all of downtown, only a handful of federal cafeterias, and one in Union Station, would serve everyone. The government discriminated too; only clerical or menial jobs were open to blacks.

White neighborhoods were kept pristine by law. The code of ethics of the Washington Real Estate Board bluntly required that "no property in a white section should ever be sold, rented, advertised or offered to colored people." Meanwhile, to the shock and outrage of foreign visitors, ghettos metastasized within view of the Capitol. In 1947, the *Washington Evening Star* wrote, "The Confederacy, which was never able to capture Washington during the course of that war, now holds it as a helpless pawn."

The Russians recognized racism as America's weakness and kept scoring points off the situation. In 1947, the Soviet newspaper *Trud* told its readers of Jim Crow abuses and said, "Let us remember this is all taking place in the city which, according to the reference books, has the residence of the President and the Capitol building in which Congress sits." The Russian reference books had it right. "Will Washington 'democrats,' " needled the Soviets, "dare restrict the Liberian Ambassador to movies and restaurants only in the Negro ghetto?" For President Truman and, later, Eisenhower, it was a Cold War sore spot.

The Communists, who had a bad habit of speaking in propaganda, referred to the "race issue" or the "race question." It was, without doubt, their best issue and most pointed question. While civil rights was still years away from inspiring a national movement, American Communists recognized it as the most glaring discrepancy in the discourse of democracy.

This pressure was forcing the government to at least consider integration. If pushed and prodded, there was a possibility of reform. A 1948 report, titled *Segregation in Washington,* had mentioned that the District of Columbia had passed a law in 1872 forbidding restaurant owners to refuse service to any "respectable person" regardless of race. Sometime "around the turn of the century," the report said, the law had "mysteriously disappeared," yet it had never been repealed. Annie and some of her colleagues read that line and got to thinking.

The Civil War had left Washington a shambles. In 1865, after four years as an armed camp, the city had thousands of new inhabitants and was in urgent need of a sewer system. Cobblestone avenues had been shredded by the passage of artillery and army wagons. There were other problems, too, according to the *New York Tribune's* Horace Greeley. "The rents are high," he wrote, "the food is bad, the dust is disgusting, the mud is deep and the morals are deplorable."

For all these faults, the city was a haven for its black population. It was the seat of the federal government, which had proclaimed emancipation and remained a protector of civil rights. Black officials were elected to the district's council, and in 1872, council member Lewis Douglass, son of the abolitionist Frederick Douglass, proposed the law that would one day inspire a mass movement. "Keepers or owners of restaurants, eating-places, bar-rooms, or ice-cream saloons, or soda-fountains . . . barber-shops and bathing houses," the law decreed, had to serve "any respectable well-behaved, person, without regard to race, color, or previous condition of servitude."

Young Mary Church, in her first visit to Washington, danced at

President Garfield's inaugural ball as the guest of Frederick Douglass in 1881. She came from Memphis, born there in 1863, the year of emancipation. Her father became the South's first black millionaire by snatching up real estate devalued by a yellow fever epidemic. Mary was sent to Antioch College and then to Oberlin, where she earned a master's degree. She traveled to Europe, kept a personal diary in French, then moved to Washington, D.C., in the 1890s, where she married Robert Terrell, a lawyer who became the first black man to serve as a municipal court judge in the district. Her complexion was so light that upon receiving her photo for a "Scroll of Negro History," a publisher wrote to her apologetically, "In our desire to make it quite clear that you were not a white person . . . we had to touch it up."

Mrs. Terrell recalled that "in the 1890s colored people could dine anywhere in the nation's capital, but near the end of the century, these rights were taken away from us. I remember stopping at the drug store on the corner of 9th and F street for service. The white clerk told me that it was my last service, that the behavior of a loud Negro man there previously had caused them to alter their policy of serving colored people."

In 1901, when Congress approved the first official codification of district laws, the two antidiscrimination statutes were noticeably absent. And by the time Mrs. Terrell and her husband were finally able to purchase a house in the district, after being rejected several times and finally paying an exorbitant fee, the laws of 1872 and 1873 were universally ignored.

By middle age, Mrs. Terrell had accumulated a dizzying correspondence with the world's great and small. She was an internationally known and respected voice for civil rights. Yet "as a colored woman," she wrote, "I may walk from the Capitol to the White House; ravenously hungry and abundantly supplied with money with which to purchase a meal, without finding a single restaurant in which I would be permitted to take even a morsel of food."

Copies of the antidiscrimination laws of 1872 and 1873 remained in the Supreme Court library, the Library of Congress, and the District of Columbia public library, available to anyone who wished to find them. For a half-century, nobody connected with official Washington had an interest in their discovery. Segregation became law in the capital, and by the end of World War II, not a single privately owned downtown restaurant would serve blacks.

In the Berlin Agreement of 1945, where West Germany was recast as a modern democracy, Americans had inserted a rebuke to Hitler's ethnic repression: "All Nazi laws, which . . . established discrimination on grounds of race, creed or political opinion shall be abolished. No such discrimination, whether legal, administrative or otherwise, shall be tolerated." Few could read this without being reminded instantly that discrimination—legal, administrative, and otherwise—was the explicit law in Washington.

On June 25, 1949, a group of more than twenty people met at a local YWCA, home to one of the few integrated downtown cafeterias, to plan strategies for the implementation of the lost laws. Annie was named secretary. Even in its first meeting, the group realized that simply negotiating with the municipal government would lead nowhere. "It is a forgone conclusion," they declared, "that all those interests in our city that have found segregation financially profitable will want to keep these laws perennially 'under study.' " By the fall, the organization settled on its cumbersome official title—the Coordinating Committee for the Enforcement of the Anti-Discrimination Laws of 1872 and 1873—almost always shortened simply to the Coordinating Committee. There were no dues or rules, and anyone who could "exhibit unrelenting determination and willingness to work for the reinstatement of the laws" was welcome.

Annie invited Mrs. Terrell to join as honorary chairman. "We appreciate, of course, that we are asking a great deal of you," she wrote, "knowing as we do what tremendous demands there are on your time." Three days later Mrs. Terrell responded: "It will afford me pleasure to comply. . . . I shall be glad to render any service in my power and I should be very much ashamed of myself if I were unwilling to work for such a just cause." After all, this was her cause. For fifty years, she had not been allowed to eat in a restaurant in Washington. Mrs. Terrell had lived a long, fighting life. She was out of a different age. She was frail and had a romantic way of speaking. Her clothing was always fashionable, although the fashion was of fifty years earlier.

This campaign was going to be Annie's finest. She was in her preferred role of general, and the strategy called for pincer-like flank movements, multiple theaters of operation, and a steady, grinding frontal attack. Her opponents were to be hampered by discord and confounded from all their positions.

To legally test the status of the lost laws, the Coordinating Committee needed to catch a restaurant denying service to black customers. Annie suggested that "four outstanding citizens, three of whom are colored go to lunch at a first class hotel . . . after they are refused service, they sign affidavits describing what took place." It was a big request. "We are asking," she realized, "a small group of prominent citizens to submit to the indignity of being refused service."

In late January 1950, four outstanding citizens, three of them black, entered Thompson's Restaurant in downtown Washington. Thompson's was a cheap diner with cafeteria-style service. In the Depression, when ham and egg sandwiches went for a nickel, it had been a favorite among the city's down and out. By the 1950s, its patrons were mainly tourists and office workers on their lunch break.

Mrs. Terrell and the others entered and took trays from the pile and started sliding them down the counter. Almost immediately, they were stopped by Sylvester Becker, the superintendent of all area Thompson's Restaurants, who had most likely been warned by the FBI to expect special guests. "We do not serve colored people here," he said. "It is against the laws of the District of Columbia and against public policy . . . individually, I have nothing against you—but the company will not allow it."

Mrs. Terrell had not had time to choose anything more than her cutlery before the confrontation occurred. "Do you mean to tell me that you are not going to serve me?" she demanded. When he said, no, she asked if Washington was in the United States and if the U.S. Constitution applied.

"We don't vote here," Becker said.

She and the others then left the restaurant and walked over to present affidavits at the nearby office of Joseph Forer and David Rein, progressive lawyers who were spending most of their time defending witnesses before the House Committee on Un-American Activities.

"My congratulations on a splendid job!" Annie wrote to Mrs. Terrell. "According to the press the Corporation Counsel really feels that he is on a spot now and may have to do something." At first, the counsel, who was responsible for bringing lawsuits on behalf of the city, had refused to accept the affidavits, but as news of the test began to spread, the pressure grew, and by late February his office issued a ruling that the laws of 1872 and 1873 seemed to still be in effect.

The case was argued in municipal court, and more than two hundred spectators filled the courtroom to witness the first modern antidiscrimination trial in the capital. Other restaurant companies had rallied around Thompson's, raising a $100,000 defense fund. They called integration "economic suicide" and speculated that if blacks were served, the "place would be overrun with them in a month." The legal question was the same that would be argued all the way to the Supreme Court: Were the lost laws still valid?

Judge Myers took four months to decide, and when he did in early July, his answer was no. While recognizing the need for blacks to have more accommodations downtown, the judge wrote, "The solution of this particular problem does not lie in an attempted revival and enforcement of parts of the old municipal regulations."

Suddenly, Annie's meetings were no longer just the same small group of diehards. The newspapers were covering the legal proceedings, and the community was ready to work. While the case wandered through the courts, the Coordinating Committee began a campaign of direct action.

The main downtown shopping area for blacks in Washington was Seventh Street, a few blocks uphill from the Capitol. Lined by four- and five-story buildings, with trolley tracks running down the center, Seventh Street had several five-and-dime stores, each with its own segregated lunch counter. After a day of shopping, nothing beat a cup of coffee and a slice of pie, but all along the row of stores, the experience for blacks was marred: some counters barred them completely, and at others, they were forced to stand, leaving the seats to whites.

On September 23, 1950, to celebrate Mary Church Terrell's eighty-seventh birthday, the Coordinating Committee opened its attack on Kresge's 5 and 10 Cent Store, at Seventh and E streets. Kresge's had refused to change its stand-only policy and became the first target of Annie's three-point strategy for community action: negotiate, boycott, picket. When it became obvious that the Kresge's manager, "a hide-bound Southerner," would never negotiate, the boycott began. Within a month, 4,000 people had sent in their pledges. Each weekend, Annie and other volunteers distributed about 10,000 leaflets. On December 5, Annie wrote to Mrs. Terrell, "Our boycott is going very well," and by the end of the month she announced Kresge's was losing 85 percent of its usual business from black patrons.

Still, the store manager refused to budge, and the militants in the Coordinating Committee felt the time had come to picket. This was the tactic of the labor movement and carried more than a faint tinge of subversiveness. "Committee members and community leaders warned that race riots would result," Annie later wrote of the debate, " 'We could not win,' they said, 'we would break the heart of the community by a disastrous failure.' " The question was resolved by Mrs. Terrell who, despite a sense that picketing was not quite good manners, made the decision to proceed. She "pulled out her good fur coat, tied a warm scarf around her head and led the first picket line in a swirling snow storm."

On Christmas Eve, Terrell made her way to Seventh Street, and aided by her cane, began to walk. "None of the prophecies of disaster came true," Annie wrote. "There were threats and insults and vile language from about 5% of the whites passing by. The majority was either sympathetic or indifferent." Each weekend, the picketers circulated in front of the store, urging shoppers to go instead to the five-and-dimes that had already agreed to integrate. White people began avoiding the scene. On January 12, 1951, Kresge's caved, and the picketers were invited in for a cup of coffee.

At the bottom of each of the tens of thousands of leaflets passed out to strangers by the Coordinating Committee, on every one of the hundreds of letters posted to members, was the address of the organization's headquarters, 1103 Trenton Place, S.E. This also happened to be the home of its secretary and her family. They lived in a two-bedroom ground-floor apartment that was part of Trenton Terrace, a complex of twenty squat houses. There was nothing remarkable about the plain brick houses; similar structures were going up everywhere. The difference with Trenton Terrace was the politics.

Every FBI agent in the Washington office must have spent some long shifts staking out the neighborhood, which the House Committee on Un-American Activities had once referred to as a "leftist nest." The owners were radicals and had surrounded themselves with friends. Some, like the Steins, were Communists, others were liberals, and almost all were Jewish. No black families lived in Trenton Terrace.

Arthur and Annie moved in during 1949, an inconvenience to the Feds who had a perfectly good wiretap operating at their old address. "It is contemplated," an agent noted, "that a request of the Bureau will be made for authority to reinstall the technical surveillance . . . if this can be accomplished it is felt that this office will be in a better position to keep abreast of subject's activities."

Residents felt that they were being watched; that when they attended meetings in the complex, their license plate numbers were being taken down; that the phones were tapped. They were right. Obviously, one of the birdies in the leftist nest was singing: an unnamed informant reported in 1949 that "he knew also that the (deleted) have on several occasions had dinner with the Steins and in addition have played 'poker' at the Stein residence." One day Annie's garbage man told her confidentially that his superior had instructed him to separate out her trash from the rest, so that it could be sifted at FBI headquarters. Agents were making a careful collection of her memos and shopping lists.

On the outskirts of the city, Trenton Terrace was flanked on one side by a working dairy farm and on the other by the parade grounds of Army Camp Simms. In a third direction was a park and stream. Every family, it seemed, had young children, so political identity was not the only bond of the community. There was never such a thing as a locked door, and *kinder* ran everywhere. When the parents were meeting in one apartment, the kids would be herded together somewhere else—preferably in one of the few houses with a TV set.

The Coordinating Committee meant two things to Annie's four-year-old daughter, Eleanor: Mary Church Terrell and rugalach. Before every meeting, Annie let her arrange the pastries in a circle on the large Stangl serving plate. Eleanor would then lick her sticky fingers and hope against hope that there would be some left over for her at the end. The work of the Coordinating Committee was simple for a child to understand: there were places that wouldn't let black people sit down to eat, and that was wrong. The most impressive event of any meeting was the entrance of Mary Church Terrell, who usually had a little present for Eleanor. Together, Annie and this stately lady would get restaurants to allow blacks to sit. Compared to the finer points of socialism and capitalism, this was easy to grasp.

Each Saturday, as regularly as other Jewish families attended temple, Annie dressed up her children and stood with them on street corners passing literature out to strangers. In January or June, Eleanor and Philip were either on the picket lines or handing out leaflets. At first it could be fun, but it was embarrassing, and day after day, it got boring. The apartment had become movement headquarters; the dining room table was hidden under envelopes and papers. The A.B. Dick mimeograph machine was in constant motion, with Eleanor turning the crank for all she was worth. The *Washington Courier* once asked, "What white woman in this city of conventions, taboos and Jim Crow would risk her children's future to work side-by-side with Negroes in a fight against racial discrimination?" It was a story about Annie.

·

For National Brotherhood Week in February 1951, Hecht's Department Store, one of the largest retailers in the district, ran a full-page ad in the *Washington Post,* showing an interracial hand-shake. "Support World Brotherhood Week," the ad said, and then preached, "We can't blind ourselves to the disturbing and undermining racial and religious antagonisms in America. They will defeat our good intentions for a world brotherhood until we cast them out and live as brothers." It was a fine sentiment, but Hecht's department store segregated at its lunch counter. When members of the Coordinating Committee questioned the store's personnel manager, he called the ad a "purely commercial" gesture. "We no more believe in that stuff than the people who read it." Hecht's, he said, was "a soulless company, interested only in the almighty dollar."

Annie wrote a letter to Samuel Hecht, president of the company. She asked for a chance to meet in person, then warned that "the hypocrisy of publishing an advertisement extolling brotherhood and yet maintaining the practice of segregating customers by color at the lunch counter has aroused considerable indignation in all sections of the Washington population."

Unlike the comparatively low-rent Thompson's and Kresge's, Hecht's was one of the district's most prestigious stores. Its seven-story building on Seventh and F streets was, in fact, the largest store in Washington. Against Hecht's millions was the Coordinating Committee's spare change. In 1951, the group raised almost $1,600, from contributions ranging from a quarter given by Mrs. Mary E. Dixon, to $30 from the Washington Federation Civic Association. One member gave the committee the money she had planned to spend on Christmas presents.

Summer was coming, and it was to be an unforgettably hot one. The Coordinating Committee began weekly sit-downs at the basement lunch counter in Hecht's. All through June, around twenty demonstrators would take their seats and wait. They weren't served, but they were hurting business. On July 2, Josephine Baker, the world-renowned singer, took her shift at the lunch counter and was refused service.

On July 20, when Washington was melting in a heat wave, the pickets started marching. At 4:00 P.M., Annie and six others took up their Hecht's "Discriminates Only Against Negroes" signs, and began circling the store's entrance under the watchful eye of police officers and store officials. An hour later, there were eighteen picketers. Annie called the picket about "50 percent effective." Several black customers went inside; one woman said, "I sure hate to cross the picket line but there's something I just have to get in Hecht's today," and another said, "I would not have gone in—but Hecht's was having a sale. In these days of high prices what are you going to do, even when it hurts like the devil to go across that line?"

No matter what the weather, the picketers gathered on Thursdays and Saturdays in their Sunday best. Since the text of the 1873 law had specified that service must be given to "any respectable well-behaved, person," Annie's picket lines ranked among the spiffiest in history: men in coats and ties, women in dresses and stockings. They gathered in groups before the line was formed, their signs slung over their shoulders or resting on the ground. Annie fussed from bunch to bunch, paired people, passed out signs. Then the lead marcher started walking, and, behind them, the masses strung out into a line like a coil of chain links pulled tight.

To fight the picket, Hecht's held sales on the days when the marchers would be present. Before a major Christmas Eve protest, Annie addressed committee members at a meeting in the laundry workers' hall. Hecht's was losing business, she said. "They'll put up with us during December when business is good and during the Christmas rush and maybe a few weeks after that, but you'll see. When the January white sales start and we're still out there . . ." After the speech, roughly one hundred marchers, including one in a Santa Claus outfit, headed to the sidewalks where their picket signs warped and ran in the icy drip.

Annie's predictions were right. On January 14, 1952, a black Hecht's employee came out of the store to sweep the sidewalk. Casually, he mentioned to a picketer that the store had changed its policy: all were now welcome at the lunch counter. Annie and Mrs. Terrell went a few days later to see for themselves. It was true. Mrs. Terrell had a ham sandwich, coffee, and a slice of banana custard pie, which she declared "delicious."

•

Annie rarely had the luxury of basking in a win. Things were bad with Artie. The union was collapsing, and his health was an ever-present worry. In early 1949, Arthur had been offered a job with the Progressive Party in Pennsylvania. He had planned to take it; getting out of the capital must have been a strong temptation as the crackdowns on Communists were starting. At the last moment, he had had a change of heart; the position demanded too much travel.

In August, it seemed that they would have to leave anyway. "My personal problems are still a little complex," Annie wrote to Mrs. Terrell. "Arthur is recovering as the Doctor expected, but a little too slowly for his own peace of mind and hence mine. We are planning to take a longish vacation starting about the 6th of August . . . our first real vacation in several years." The family rented a house on Long Island. "I'm soaking up all the sunshine and salt breezes," Annie wrote. "Arthur feels practically whole again and the children look marvelous."

While the pickets targeted individual stores the court case progressed to the U.S. Court of Appeals, where it remained for more than a year. "STILL NO DECISION!," Annie wrote to Mrs. Terrell. "Can we really stand any more waiting?" When it came, there was still more disappointment: the judges, five-to-four, declared the laws invalid.

Annie responded immediately, calling the decision a "frank declaration of racial bias." Despite the setback, so much progress had been made that public opinion was now fully behind integration. The district's lawyers had enough of a stake in the decision that, spurred on by a Coordinating Committee petition with 16,000 signatures, they immediately pressed the appeal to the U.S. Supreme Court.

The case was heard on the last day of April and the first of May 1953. On June 8, the unanimous decision came down: "The Acts of 1872 and 1873 survived subsequent changes in the government of the District of Columbia and are presently enforceable." The *Washington Afro-American* ran the enthusiastic headline, "Eat Anywhere." On hearing the ruling, Mrs. Terrell said, she "could die happy." Sylvester Becker, the Thompson's manager who had barred the first test group from eating, said "The law says any well-dressed, well-behaved person, and that's the way it is." Years later, Annie would say the decision in the Thompson's Case "cracked the dam of Jim Crow."

The dam may have cracked, but it had not burst. That Annie won in such a setting, in the seat of government no less, was a testament to the strength of the committee she and Mrs. Terrell had built. But outside of her work, the foundations of liberalism were being swept down river.

In January 1953, Mrs. Terrell had written a letter to Harry Truman, in his last days in the White House. "Mr. President, I have had a life rich in opportunities and rewards. I have seen many injustices done in my time. I know America can outlive injustices . . . I believe the United States is too big, too generous to be unmerciful," she wrote. "I appeal to you with all the strength that my deep devotion to my America gives me . . . please save the lives of Ethel and Julius Rosenberg." Annie was in Brooklyn when she heard "over the press wires" about Mrs. Terrell's letter. "I feel like weeping for joy," she wrote. "It is a beacon-light in my life that I have the privilege of knowing and working with you. I feel much more hopeful now that this great injustice will yet be averted in time."

Meanwhile, she was house hunting. We are "negotiating for two . . . either one would be very pleasant living." By the end of March, Annie and her family had moved into their new home at 131 Westminster Road in Brooklyn. A Victorian frame house, it was part of Prospect Park South, a planned residential enclave, mostly of doctors and lawyers, within the greater neighborhood of Flatbush. "I can just see the plumbers, electricians and all the other mechanics as they ply their trade in what will be your beautiful and comfortable home," Mrs. Terrell wrote to Annie. "It made me so happy to know how well situated you are, that you will have a home arranged and furnished as you like it, that your dear children are surrounded by influences so much better in every way than those with which they came into daily contact here." Soon, Annie could report, "We are all well and moderately busy. . . . The children love school and are quite fully adjusted to Brooklyn."

In the summer, Mrs. Terrell came to New York and visited Annie's new house. She was given a fright by Eleanor's bouncing prowess on her pogo stick. Your "pretty daughter," she wrote "gave a perfect demonstration of the fact that she knows no fear as she 'cavorted' around on that 'machine.' " In a later visit, Mrs. Terrell spent the night in Brooklyn. "Eleanor is thrilled beyond words that you slept in her very own bed," Annie wrote, "and barely a soul in Brooklyn is left who doesn't know about it."

Both women had families and political responsibility, but they discovered, once they were separated, how close they had become. Mrs. Terrell addressed Annie as "my dearest" and closed, "I am that individual who loved to work with you and who misses you more than she can express in words." Annie wrote, "I miss you terribly and think about you all the time. You don't know how many times I forced myself to do something I didn't feel like doing by saying, 'Mrs. Terrell wouldn't hesitate a moment and you know it.' "

By the spring of 1954, Mrs. Terrell was fading. Annie had worked for months to have her autobiography republished, but in the end, the author was unable to write the two chapters that would bring it up to date. "At the age of ninety," Mrs. Terrell wrote, "one does not have the energy to do as many things as he or she did when the individual was many years younger." She was impossibly delicate, scribbling her letters on her lap in a convalescent-home bed. "Old age has destroyed a great deal of my courage," she wrote in April 1954. "I don't walk up 'arms akimbo' to tackle the foe as I used to do a few years ago."

In April, Mrs. Terrell ended a note with one of her romantic, Old World flourishes: "As long as I live and can hold a pen in my hand long enough to write a line, I shall write to you." It was the last letter that Annie had from her. Mary Church Terrell died on July 24, 1954.

...

Arthur Stein had special plans for Valentine's Day 1956: he was appearing before the House Committee on Un-American Activities. Taking the train from New York City to Washington, he emerged from Union Station to find a morning that was cold but sunny, and warming fast. It was false spring in the capital.

There was also a hint of thaw in the Cold War. By 1956, Senator Joseph McCarthy had gone too far, having dared to charge the U.S. Army with Communist infection. He had been broken, defeated, and officially censured by the Senate. In Moscow, the same week Arthur was testifying, Premier Khrushchev gave his "secret speech" about Stalin's crimes to the Twentieth Soviet Communist Party Congress. Both sides seemed momentarily to have vanquished their worst zealots, but no rapprochement was forthcoming. Khrushchev, who soon had his own crimes to hide, came to regret his secret speech. In Congress, there remained witch hunters eager to carry on McCarthy's fight against Communists, though not with the recklessness used by the Wisconsin senator. Arthur was going to face off with some of these this morning.

It was a short walk south across Capitol Hill to Independence Avenue, where the sun sparkled off the autos' chrome tailfins. The House Office Building stood on the corner of Independence and New Jersey avenues, across the street from the Capitol and the Library of Congress. Made of buttery marble slabs and decorated with columns and friezes, it looked like nothing so much as a wedding cake. Around 10:00 A.M., Arthur and his attorney, Victor Rabinowitz, climbed the broad staircase, passed through the echoing rotunda, and up to the second floor Caucus Room, reserved this day for the HUAC hearings. Outside, lawyers and their clients stood shoulder to shoulder in whispered huddles. Arthur recognized faces he had not seen in a decade. They could be here only for one reason, the same that had brought him. In that atmosphere, every old friend who knew your secrets could become a possible witness against you, a potential enemy.

Arthur made his way into the Caucus Room. Along one wall, a raised dais allowed the congressmen to look down on the crowd and their witnesses from a suitably elevated position. The committee members filed in, led by the chairman, the Honorable Francis E. Walter, Democrat from Pennsylvania. Walter was not the bulbous, jowly kind of legislator but the other type—gray, slender, and severe.

In 1952, the congressman had coauthored the McCarran–Walter Immigration Act, which made subversive intentions a deportable offense and ensured that 85 percent of all immigrants to the United States would come from Western and Northern Europe.

At 10:15 A.M., Walter banged his gavel, said, "The Committee will come to order," and started the proceedings. Talk in the room died out. The day's inquiry, Walter explained, was into Communist infiltration of government. Scanning the faces of the crowd, many of whom he suspected of having been seduced by communism, Walter gave an exhortation, the same he gave before every hearing.

"It is not an easy task," he said, "to appear before a congressional committee and lay bare all of your shortcomings of years gone by. Such persons will be subjected to all the vituperations that can be heaped upon them by the well-organized smear bund of the Communist Party and its henchmen. To those witnesses who decide they will give us the benefit of their knowledge, I have this to say: You will have the heartfelt thanks of your fellow Americans and you will have made a worthy contribution to the cause of a free world." Then he told his counsel, Dick Arens, to call the first witness.

James Gorham stepped forward and was duly sworn. He didn't need the chairman's encouragement to give the benefit of his knowledge. The *Washington Post* described him as "a dark softspoken man," but he certainly was not taciturn.

Gorham described life in a Communist cell. It had not been what he expected. The Party was supposed to operate, he said, on the "principle of democratic centralism, namely that the members could discuss policies up to a point of decision and then after that . . . loyally carry them out. It seemed to me that we were getting all centralism and no democracy in this particular unit." He had complained to Arthur about this treatment, and for his efforts he had been suspended from Party activity. Now it was time for his revenge.

As he started to name his fellow Communists, Arthur watched and waited.

MR. ARENS: Is there another person whom you could identify as a member of that Communist Party cell?

MR. GORHAM: . . . subsequent to my joining that unit, a Mr. Arthur Stein was brought into the unit.

MR. ARENS: Could you identify him?

MR. GORHAM: Yes; he is present here in the hearing room this morning, and he is close to my height and somewhat heavy-set.

Arthur must have expected it the moment he first saw Gorham in the Caucus Room that morning. He had been named.

MR. ARENS: Mr. Gorham, could you stand up and point out to this committee by physical appearance in this room, the person whom you have identified as Mr. Stein?

Then, as in a courtroom drama, Gorham turned from the committee to the crowd and looked at Arthur. He raised his hand and pointed.

MR. GORHAM: This is Mr. Stein here.

MR. ARENS: Is Mr. Stein the gentleman seated second from the aisle in the front row to the right of the committee?

MR. GORHAM: In the brown suit, smoking a cigarette, yes.

Gorham talked for an hour and forty-five minutes. He gave twenty-six names: Communists in the Works Progress Administration, in the Securities and Exchange Commission, the Senate Subcommittee on Monopolistic Practices, the Library of Congress. When he finished, he was rewarded with the ritualistic benediction of the committee chairman.

"Mr. Gorham," said Walter. "I want to express to you the appreciation not only of this committee but of the American people for your contribution to the security of this Republic. . . . In our judgment you are a great American."

"Thank you," said Gorham.

The committee then recessed until 1:30 in the afternoon. After the break, the spectators settled back into their seats, ready for more.

Chairman Walter called the committee to order and told counsel to bring forth his next witness, Arthur Stein.

Arthur, in his favorite brown suit—a three-piece, with pleated pants made from a particularly hairy wool that trapped the smell of cigarette smoke in its itchy fibers—stepped forward to the podium and raised his right hand.

MR. WALTER: Do you swear the testimony you are about to give shall be the truth, the whole truth, and nothing but the truth, so help you God?
MR. STEIN: I do.

•••

Arthur, like thousands of other progressives, had been caught in the anti–Communist machinery. Once your name came before one of the congressional investigators, your professional life was ruined, your social circle curtailed to others who had been named. Arthur and Annie were never freed from the curiosity of the Federal Bureau of Investigation, whose agents called the house every few months to harass and remind them that they were being watched.

The machinery of anticommunism was not designed for efficiency; it was complex and confusing. It had parts culled from the Senate and the House of Representatives, committees, special committees and subcommittees, agencies, boards, and bureaus. Every department of the federal government that could find an excuse got into the action of leaning on progressives: the House Committee on Un-American Activities, of course, as well as Senator Joseph McCarthy's Permanent Subcommittee on Investigations, which was part of the Committee on Government Operations. There was also Pat McCarran's and later Senator James Eastland's Senate Judiciary Committee, whose Subcommittee to Investigate the Administration of the Internal Security Act launched hearings in 1952 on the work of the United Public Workers union. Each federal department also had its own individual loyalty board, set up after 1947 when President Truman demanded loyalty investigations of his subordinates. Besides the federal bureaucracy were the state inquisitions, modeled after the committees in Washington.

It was an internal security combustion engine: pistoned and sparked by the committees and loyalty boards, powered by repressive laws passed in a climate of fear, maintained by the Federal Bureau of Investigation, and fueled by names. Names were petrol for the engine; without witnesses to interrogate and drill, the engine sputtered and the pistons froze. Whittaker Chambers told his story about Alger Hiss and spies in the State Department to all comers until the Un-American Activities Committee came along finally and listened. Elizabeth Bentley accused scores of people, including Arthur's friend Victor Perlo, of being spies.

There were no restrictions placed on the drilling for names. Anyone with an egalitarian bent or a few liberal associations—who thought blacks deserved better treatment or felt strongly about civil liberties—was cast as subversive. Since keeping the engine running was the primary goal of the investigations, all informers were taken seriously: reformed Communists who wanted to prove just how securely back in the fold they were, people like Gorham nurturing some twenty-year grudge, paid spies, the drunken, the delusional, the spiteful.

Cooperative witnesses were squeezed dry and then forgiven. No matter how vile their previous crimes had been, informing to the committee redeemed their condition. A man like Gorham, who had been a Communist for a decade, became a "great American" after a couple of hours on the stand. He was rewarded with the "thank you" of the chairman and then was cast aside.

The committees needed to hold more hearings and hearings needed witnesses, who could only be targeted by informers. The names made it all work, and it was an informer who in 1955 first named Arthur.

Herbert Fuchs was already a Communist when he moved to Washington in 1936 to work as a lawyer on the staff of a Senate committee. The Party leaders told him to meet with Arthur, who would find a place for him in the underground. Arthur at the time was the head of a clandestine unit in the Works Progress Administration. He met with Fuchs and became his contact man, gathering dues and passing on Party directives.

Fuchs and his wife became close friends with Arthur and Annie, and their children played together. Then, in 1943, Fuchs moved to Denver. In the late 1940s, after the war had ended, he quit the Communist Party with a feeling of "complete disillusionment." He left government work in 1949 and became a law professor at American University, a venerable and progressive Methodist institution in Washington. Then somebody fed the machine his name, and on June 13, 1955, Fuchs came before the Un-American Activities committee in closed session. He refused to cooperate. His employers at American University applauded his resolve, calling him "an intelligent, loyal and devoted teacher."

But Fuchs, who had moved between many underground cells, was a rich well of names. He was pressured to recant; most likely he was threatened with prison for contempt of Congress. Fuchs changed his mind. He appeared again behind closed doors and talked. He spared nobody he had known throughout a Communist career that had lasted more than a decade. The day he decided to give names, the president of American University called Fuchs into his office and suspended him. Hundreds of people had lost their jobs for refusing to cooperate with the committee. Now that one man had lost his job because he had chosen to cooperate, the press was outraged. "There are several hundred thousand former members of the Communist Party," wailed the *Saturday Evening Post*. "Naturally the Communist Party is pleased by any action that discourages repentant ex-Communists from helping the United States."

In December, Herbert Fuchs came before the committee and repeated in public the charges he had made in private session during the summer. The meeting was held in the federal courthouse in Chicago. Walter gave his same preamble about the "well-organized smear bund of the Communist Party." At 10:00 A.M., Fuchs was sworn in. His testimony lasted until 4:45 P.M. In that time, he presented the committee with forty-five names. When asked, he spelled them out slowly, letter by letter, and repeated them, like a spelling bee contestant. One name he gave was James Gorham. Another was Arthur Stein, S–T–E–I–N.

•••

The Caucus Room was high-ceilinged, muffling conversation. Arthur began to testify and was accompanied by the patter of the stenographer's typing. His hearing began cordially enough. For a few minutes, the questions pertained to his education and work background. He answered these. It was a ritual they had all witnessed dozens of times. No one expected cooperation from this witness, but the strategy was to put him at ease. Then Arens asked him if he remembered James Gorham from their days together at the National Recovery Administration.

MR. STEIN: I won't answer that question, Mr. Chairman.

MR. ARENS: Mr. Chairman, I respectfully request the witness be directed to answer.

THE CHAIRMAN: I direct you to answer the question.

(The witness conferred with his counsel.)

MR. STEIN: Mr. Chairman, I am not willing to answer the question, and I am relying on the fifth amendment to the Constitution.

THE CHAIRMAN: You say you are not willing. By that do you mean, "I refuse to answer the question"?

MR. STEIN: I refuse to answer the question.

MR. ARENS: Mr. Stein, do you feel if you told this committee a truthful answer with reference to any alleged acquaintanceship with James E. Gorham that you would be supplying information which could be used against you in a criminal proceeding?

MR. STEIN: I am relying on the fifth amendment which, as I recall it, states that no person may be compelled to testify against himself in any criminal proceeding.

THE CHAIRMAN: This is not a criminal proceeding.

MR. STEIN: It may lead to a criminal proceeding.

MR. ARENS: Mr. Chairman, the courts have repeatedly said that the status of a man's mind is as much a fact as the status of his indigestion. Therefore, I propose to request again that this witness announce to the committee whether or not it is his honest judgment that if he gave a truthful answer to the question pertaining to any alleged acquaintanceship which he may have had with James E. Gorham, he feels that answer would supply information which could be used against him in a criminal proceeding.

(The witness conferred with his counsel.)

THE CHAIRMAN: I direct you to answer.

MR. STEIN: If I answered the question, I feel it might be used against me in a criminal proceeding.

THE CHAIRMAN: Therefore you refuse to answer?

MR. STEIN: Yes, sir.

MR. ARENS: Mr. Stein, this morning Mr. Gorham stood up here after he had been sworn to tell the truth before a congressional committee, and identified you as a person who, to his certain knowledge, had been a member of the Communist Party. Was he lying or telling the truth?

MR. STEIN: I refuse to answer that question on the grounds previously given.

MR. ARENS: Mr. Stein, have you ever known a man by the name of Herbert Fuchs?

MR. STEIN: I refuse to answer that question on the same grounds.

MR. ARENS: Do you feel if you told this committee whether or not you knew Mr. Fuchs you would be supplying information which could be used against you in a criminal proceeding?

MR. STEIN: The same answer as I gave before.

At this point, some line had been crossed: it was clear that Arthur would take the Fifth, and Arens changed his tone. Now the questions volleyed fast, the famous questions that in later years would instantly evoke this period and tribunal.

MR. ARENS: Are you now a member of the Communist Party?

MR. STEIN: I refuse to answer that question on the same grounds.

MR. ARENS: Have you ever been a member of the Communist Party?

MR. STEIN: I refuse to answer that question on the same grounds.

MR. ARENS: Are you now a member of an organization dedicated to the overthrow of the Government of the United States by force and violence?

MR. STEIN: The same answer, Mr. Chairman.

THE CHAIRMAN: For the same reason?

MR. STEIN: The same reason.

MR. ARENS: Have you ever committed espionage against the United States government?

MR. STEIN: No.

•••

In the spring of 1945, the United States and the Soviet Union had been allies in a global fight against fascism. Roosevelt and an administration broadly sympathetic toward labor had controlled the White House for more than a decade. There was no such thing as an atom bomb. The Federal Workers Union represented office workers in an expanded wartime U.S. government.

By February 1956, the iron curtain had fallen between East and West. Roosevelt had been dead for more than ten years. A Republican president had been elected for the first time since 1928. Both the United States and the Soviet Union had exploded atomic bombs, and scientists had cracked hydrogen too. Arthur's union had changed its name and briefly flourished, representing 100,000 members, including the prison guards at Alcatraz and 20,000 workers in the Panama Canal Zone. As the representative union for federal employees, it had been at the front of the battle over President Truman's loyalty investigations into government workers. The proceedings retained the jargon of the law, but there were no specific charges, and most evidence came from the testimony of informers, who remained anonymous. No Communist spies were found in the proceedings, but thousands of workers either quit or were fired.

At first the CIO had supported its government union, but the once-radical labor movement quickly scurried to the right. The

United Public Workers of America were accused of having policies "consistently directed toward the achievement of the program of the Communist Party rather than the objectives set forth in the constitution of the CIO." Since the spectacle of show trials was in vogue, the CIO held one for Arthur's union, refusing to hear more than three witnesses for the defense.

At its founding convention in 1946, the new union's first decree demanded that the United States commit to good relations with the Soviet Union. This foreign policy resolution was cited as evidence that the UPWA was dominated by Communist leadership. The fact that in 1946, when the resolution passed, friendship with the Soviet Union was not only CIO policy but the policy of the U.S. government, was ruled irrelevant. The UPWA was expelled in January 1950. The leaders of the union were dragged before the Senate Judiciary Committee to swear they were not Communists, and its president was sent to jail for contempt of Congress for refusing.

By 1956, card-carrying Communists were outnumbered three to one by badge-toting FBI agents. The Party was hunted and ruined. It had never been the threat that the witch hunters had claimed. Now it functioned nowhere. J. Edgar Hoover claimed that the few thousand left were building "the most devastating fifth column the world has ever known." Actually, the remaining Communists had been driven to despair, to hiding, to political inactivity.

In the space of a decade, every political organization that Arthur had belonged to had been destroyed. Whatever professional ambitions he had cherished—as a graduate of Columbia in 1929, as a young worker in government in the 1930s—by 1956, he must have known they had become unattainable. Maybe he hoped for a time when this climate of repression would eventually turn again toward liberalism. It would turn, but he would not live long enough to see it.

•••

Arthur's lawyer, Victor Rabinowitz, estimated that he had represented close to one hundred witnesses before the House Committee on Un-American Activities. Usually he and his client would ride down together to Union Station and spend the time on the train preparing. Rabinowitz had done this so often he could predict the day's questions almost exactly. He charged $100 if his client could afford it but never turned down a case.

All witnesses were frightened, and Rabinowitz urged them just to go through with the proceedings without bluster. The trick was to get the client in and out of the hearing room as quickly as possible. Nothing could be gained by lingering, arguing, bantering with the committee members. The congressmen could throw a man in jail, cost him his job, or drown his good name in hostile newspaper ink. If everything went smoothly, the whole ordeal was usually finished in twenty minutes.

Only a few witnesses had been able to have their way with the congressmen. When Paul Robeson appeared to testify, his invincible baritone had been powerful enough to drown out the questions and turn the committee room into a stage. "You want to shut up every Negro who stands up for his rights," Robeson shouted as Chairman Walter helplessly beat his gavel to matchsticks. "You ought to be ashamed of yourselves." Finally, after an hour, Walter gave in: "I've stood about as much of this as I can—the session is adjourned."

"You should adjourn this forever," Robeson told him.

Pete Seeger brought his banjo to the hearing and offered to give his answers in song.

Arthur was not a performer, but neither was he cowed by the inquisitors. There was little the committee could do to him—little that had not already been taken away. He had not been a government employee since 1942. His meaningful work had ended when the public worker's union was destroyed. He was already being harassed by federal surveillance and forced out of his jobs on a regular basis. Arthur wanted to complete his appearance and move on, and maybe to get in one good joke at the committee's expense in the process.

The prosecutor offered fifteen names and asked Arthur to confirm that they were Communists; he refused each time. Otherwise, the questions attempted to discredit the progressive organizations Arthur had belonged to by proving a connection, through Arthur, with the Communist Party. So to condemn Arthur's union, Arens asked, "Was the United Public Workers of America interlocked in any respect with any other organization, entity, or group?"

MR. STEIN: The CIO. It was a member of the CIO.

MR. ARENS: Was the United Public Workers of America affiliated with any other group besides the CIO?

MR. STEIN: Not to my recollection . . .

MR. ARENS: I put it to you as a fact and ask you to affirm or deny the fact that the United Public Workers of America was controlled lock, stock, and barrel by the Communist Party.

MR. STEIN: I refuse to answer.

Finally, Arthur was asked if he was a member of the World Peace Appeal, an organization that in 1950 distributed a worldwide petition against nuclear proliferation that eventually garnered 200 million signatures.

"Have you been identified with that?" Arens asked. Arthur refused to answer.

THE CHAIRMAN: Am I to gather from that that this World Peace Appeal organization is an organization of such nature that if you belonged to it you might be prosecuted criminally for being a member?

MR. STEIN: Well, I have some reason to believe that this organization was on the attorney general's list of front organizations.

THE CHAIRMAN: Front organizations?

MR. STEIN: Whatever his list is. It's a bad list as far as I am concerned.

THE CHAIRMAN: It is a bad list? It is a good list of bad organizations.

MR. STEIN: Whichever way you want to put it. It is a bad list of good organizations according to some.

MR. ARENS: You are not suggesting that the World Peace Appeal is a good organization; are you?

MR. STEIN: Fifth amendment, Mr. Chairman.

That evening, Arthur got into Pennsylvania Station and rode the subway home. When he walked into the house, Annie and Philip were sitting in the kitchen. Annie went over to him and asked if anything funny had happened. One thing, Arthur said, and savoring it like the sharp aftertaste of a swig of bourbon, he recounted his verbal sparring with Chairman Walter over the good or bad nature of the attorney general's list. He'd got in his joke.

Chapter 6

Breakaway

THE reason Jeff Jones, my father, came to New York in 1966 was to get started on a career in politics. Ever since high school, when his peers elected him class president, both he and his proud father had imagined him as a lawyer and perhaps someday a congressman. A year at Antioch College had introduced him to the student movement and cemented his opposition to the escalating war in Vietnam, but it had not soured him completely on liberal politics and the Democratic Party. For his sophomore year, he came to live in Manhattan. Antioch had a work-study requirement, and Jeff was interning at a well-known New York City labor law firm. This was supposed to be the beginning of a successful, steady life of respectable opposition, but one month in the city had done away with years of planning.

Jeff spent his lunch breaks pounding the pavement thinking about the government. Wandering through Battery Park, chewing a hot dog from a vendor, he had decided to become a socialist. With all the troubles in the world, that was the only justifiable thing one could be. Of course, just declaring the fact didn't make it so. He had to live it, and what was the best way of doing that? For now the answer could wait.

When he left work on the afternoon of October 27, 1966, he was becoming a twenty-year-old radical. Walking to the subway station from the law office on Broad Street, he kept himself aloof from the bodies sprinting by him. Earlier he might have seen himself in these ambitious young Wall Street workers, but now he had nothing but disdain for the shallow purpose they had chosen. He stood out from the crowd and not just because he was a blond Californian. He was a subversive element in their midst, a hungry wolf.

At the station, he walked past a newsstand displaying the papers: the *New York Times,* the *New York Post,* the *Daily News* and the *New York World-Journal-Tribune.* Lyndon Johnson was on the tabloid covers. Two years earlier, Jeff and Albert had gone door to door supporting his campaign. Now he looked at the president's cartoonish face and saw a criminal, a murderer. "LBJ Pledge to GIs in Viet: 'WE'LL NEVER LET YOU DOWN,' " read the *Daily News.* Johnson had landed in Vietnam for a surprise visit and photo opportunity. He was in country for only three hours, touching down at Cam Ranh Bay to pin medals on every uniform within arm's reach. General William Westmoreland, commanding officer in Vietnam, received his Distinguished Service award and promised that the war was nearly won. *Another public relations ploy,* thought Jeff as he hurried past, down the stairs and onto the platform.

In the autumn of 1966, there were more than 300,000 U.S. servicemen in Vietnam; 5,500 had already died in combat. During the past week in late October, a time of quiet fighting, 74 Americans had been killed and almost 500 wounded.

The crowded train emptied steadily as it moved uptown. Jeff got off at West Eighty-Sixth Street, passed through the turnstile, and headed toward his building a block away. He climbed five decaying flights of stairs and opened the door to the one-bedroom apartment he shared with two other Antioch students. There were mattresses on the floor and a stack of dirty dishes in the sink. In the alcove kitchen, hardly large enough to flip a pancake, the AM radio was set, as always, to WABC 770, the nation's premier rock and roll channel. "Walk Away Renee" by the Left Banke, "Cherish" by The Association, and The Rolling Stones's "19th Nervous Breakdown," spun hourly, were the tunes that radio audiences in New York were trying to get out of their heads that fall.

Preparing dinner—almost certainly another in a series of spaghetti nights—Jeff looked forward to going over to his Antioch friend Jonny Lerner's huge apartment on Seventy-Third Street. There they'd listen to jazz on the hi-fi and share a joint. Jeff had first smoked grass in college. There, smokers were careful and usually lit up in dorm rooms or deep in the woods out of sight. In New York City, getting stoned was just a matter of knowing the right people and having a handy package of Bambú cigarette papers. Crumbly brown pot made the trip from Mexico, and Jeff's friend Jonny knew someone who knew someone. A nickel bag held a quarter-ounce, and a lid, enough to stoutly fill a small plastic bag, was twenty bucks. Jeff also had recently taken his first acid trip, sucking the chemicals from a paper tab and frolicking through Riverside Park.

He was in love with the city and its inhabitants who, with their studied cynicism, seemed to hold the monopoly on sophistication. Jeff made a point of reading the Sunday *New York Times* cover to cover. He ate bagels. He grew his hair a little shaggier than it had been in his senior year at Sylmar High School. But his friends might have saved him the trouble: he was so blond and sunny himself that no matter how affected he became, he would always be their Californian.

Now that he was a socialist, in theory at least, the gap between him and the family back home was wider than ever. His father, Albert, had wrestled with similar issues during World War II. Already politicized by his experiences during the Great Depression when the bank had foreclosed on his parents' house, Albert had flirted with socialist doctrines himself. Jeff had exchanged a few letters with his father, but it had been months since they had been together.

As Jeff went to sleep on Thursday night, the West Coast and his family were on his mind. His mother was traveling the country with the Roger Wagner Chorale, a distinguished classical vocal ensemble. On Sunday, in the climax of the tour, and Millie hoped, of her musical career, the chorale was scheduled to play a concert at Carnegie Hall.

The next morning, Jeff was getting dressed for work when a deliveryman rang the doorbell and handed him a Western Union telegram. Worried, he opened the envelope and read: "Meet me Park Sheraton Hotel. Love Dad." Jeff took the day off from work, and, with mounting concern, he walked toward the Park Sheraton at Fifty-Sixth Street and Seventh Avenue. Up in Albert's room, father and son hugged. Jeff stepped back and looked. It was the same dad, but he had rarely looked so upset.

Albert came right out and explained. "Your mother has been having an affair with one of her violin students," he said. The man, whom Jeff had never met, was named Roger O'Donnell and was several years older than Millie. Albert told Jeff that Roger's wife had called him to say that Roger had quit his job to follow the chartered Greyhound Bus that carried Millie and the chorale as they toured the country. Albert had come to New York for a final confrontation. He and Jeff sat in his hotel room and breakfasted together. Albert had packed a bottle of whiskey too, but that was for later. Jeff looked out the window, hoping to catch a view of Central Park but saw only buildings. Albert had an adult favor to ask: he wanted Jeff to tell Millie that he was in town. Albert must have formed this plan while watching *Rio Bravo* or *High Noon*. He would march down Main Street, Broadway in this case, confront his wife, and offer her an ultimatum: Me or the Other Man.

•••

The Joneses had moved back from Pennsylvania to the San Fernando Valley in 1950 when Jeff was four years old and his brother, Eric, was two. During their stay in the East, the family had joined a Quaker congregation. But rather than finding spiritual peace, Albert had experienced a nagging void through his entire stay in the East. It wasn't until he steered the 1938 Buick club coupe within view of the Rocky Mountains that the sight made him realize what a westerner he was.

Albert had worked as a film technician in 1943 before being drafted. Returning, he found a similar job at Technicolor. In 1954, he transferred to the Walt Disney Company, where he worked as a neg-

ative cutter. Over the years his specialty was Disney television. *Ol'
Yeller,* the *Adventures of Davy Crockett,* and ground breaking nature
shows such as the *Living Desert* and *Vanishing Prairie* all came across
his desk while traveling from the studio camera to the TV set. Many
parents in Los Angeles worked in the movies, but having a Disney
dad carried extra weight around the schoolyard. Albert took the
family to Disneyland's opening day. He made Jeff's birthday parties a
sought-after invitation by lugging in his film projector and beaming
the latest Mickey Mouse cartoon from a 16mm print.

For Albert, Walt was a familiar presence. He walked through his
studio lost in thought, and the workers knew he was dreaming up
another innovation. Albert, who would talk to anybody, once had
the temerity to break in on the process. "Mr. Disney," he said. The
imagineer looked at him and said kindly, "Call me Walt." Albert
knew that Disney had named names to the House Committee on
Un-American Activities and had heard outsiders calling him a racist
or an anti-Semite. But for each of these claims he could produce a
dozen evidences of the man's generosity toward his employees.

After school, Jeff hurried home for a glass of milk and a few slices of
Wonder Bread. He sat Indian-style in front of the TV and watched
the *Mickey Mouse Club,* gazing adoringly at Annette Funicello, the
cute and sassy Mouseketeer. Once he waited in line to have her sign
a picture and promised he would keep it faithfully beneath his pil-
low. On other days he joined the neighborhood boys for cowboy
and Indian battles amid the sagebrush of an empty lot. Jeff made his
hands into guns and blasted away, but he understood that in his family, weapons and war were not glorified. The Korean War had just
ended, and World War II was only a decade past; nearly every kid he
knew boasted a father who had fought in one of these conflicts.
Jeff's father boasted about his refusal to fight. His son was forbidden
from wearing uniforms, and when his friends all joined the Boy
Scouts, he had to settle for YMCA camp.

Soon after returning to the San Fernando Valley, Albert joined a
group of Quakers who had built a small community they simply
called The Farm. They had dreamed it up in Civilian Public Service

camp and, after the peace, had found some undeveloped acres in the northern part of the valley and built their houses with their own hands. On Sundays, the Joneses spent the day immersed in the Quaker way. The children were asked to sit in on the last fifteen minutes of the hour-long silent meditation. In the quiet of the room, outdoor sounds demanded notice: dogs barked and crunched gravel with their paws, cats climbed the wisteria vines outside the porch. After the circle of silence, the kids ran outdoors—uncontrollable and unreflective—to the rusting tractor or the Swiss Family Robinson tree houses suspended above a trickling stream.

Sunday evenings, Jeff was taken to visit his grandparents. Malcolm and Christine still lived in the house they had bought in the early 1920s and then lost and regained during the Great Depression. They had outlasted the village of Girard, which was now called Woodland Hills. At Christmastime, when the family made a tree out of silver-painted tumbleweed, his grandmother made heavenly hash: Jell-o with fruit cocktail and marshmallows. Malcolm was showing his age, and after he dropped his wife off at the store and then drove home without her, his family decided his driving days were done. Jeff watched as Albert snuck into the driveway, opened his father's hood, and removed the rotor from his distributor, so that the old man would no longer be a menace on the roads. Malcolm and Christine died within a few years of each other in the early 1960s.

•••

Even in California, Jeff was the blondest kid in every class photo. In junior high school, he was awarded for having perfect attendance. Away from school, he became a familiar presence in the community events section of local newspapers. He posed for a dozen photos commemorating some new activity, charity, or accomplishment.

In his first high school gym class, Jeff, skinny and unused to competition, was the fastest around the quarter-mile track—home in sixty-six seconds. When the boys were all back, panting, hands on knees, the coach blew his whistle, pointed to Jeff, and said, "You're not in this class anymore. You're on the track team." This gave him another chance to spend time outdoors. Family vacations always involved camping trips and long hikes. Even when he was home, Jeff spent many nights sleeping in the backyard. Zuma and Malibu beaches were a short drive, and though he tried surfing only a few times, with little success, he swam in the waves for hours.

In the winter of 1963, President John F. Kennedy came across one of Theodore Roosevelt's executive orders requiring all U.S. Marines to be able to march fifty miles in twenty hours. Kennedy mentioned it in a speech, and the entire nation started walking. There was a rush on pedometers and a spike in podiatry visits. As usual, the Russians scoffed. An American "walks 50 miles in one day—what of it?" asked the head of the Soviet track and field team. "Tomorrow, he catches a taxicab again to go four blocks."

Jeff's YMCA group joined in the walking craze. Before dawn on a spring day, about twenty of them were driven up Highway 99 to a stretch in the Tehachapis called the Grapevine. They walked all day, with hikers falling out of the bunch along the route. By the afternoon, only Jeff and two others remained. A local radio station got wind of the event and began to broadcast updates. Drivers, listening on the radio, honked as the kids walked past. Jeff jogged the last couple of miles, finishing up at the Mid-Valley YMCA headquarters. He told the radio reporter that he had done the walk because his president had told him to. It had taken less than sixteen and a half hours, easily good enough for the marines.

Shopping plazas and housing developments were encroaching on the Quaker farm by the mid-1960s. Still, few buildings rose above a single story, and the air was dewy with the scent of lemons, oranges, and eucalyptus. The Jones home was brand new, a one-story ranch house with a driveway, a garage, and a small yard. The San Gabriel Mountains began outside the windows, rising suddenly from the backyard and dominating everything.

In Jeff's senior year at Sylmar High, he was voted student body president and introduced the Beach Boys before they played at the school gym. He led the chants at pep rallies and boosted the school sports teams. "I feel it is my duty to let the member schools of the East Valley League know that there is going to be something different about Sylmar High School this fall," he wrote in a letter to *The*

Van Nuys News. "BEWARE, for Sylmar is on the move and we won't stop until we reach the top."

On yearbook photo day in 1964, Jeff avoided taking any fashion risks; he and nearly all his male classmates wore black suits and thin ties. His hair was as short as the day's technology could make it. His career plans involved a life in politics. And his bio, as it was presented in a newspaper story announcing his position as 1964's YMCA Boy of the Year runner-up, gave the details:

> Jones is student body president . . . and maintains a B-plus average in his studies. After graduation he plans to work either in Los Angeles or San Francisco and will later resume his studies at Antioch College in Ohio. A folk-singing enthusiast, he is a three-year letterman in cross country, was captain of that team for two years and received the "most valuable player" award. He was also class yell king. Jones has also applied for a Walt Disney Foundation scholarship, which can be obtained only by relatives of the Disney staff. Jones' father works at that studio.

Jeff's friends worried about the campus scene and made him promise not to let those easterners drag him into politics. In September, with all his possessions in a single duffel and a new twelve-string guitar in his hand, Jeff flew east on the Disney corporate jet. Antioch, with a commitment to work-study and an open curriculum, was one of the most progressive schools in the country. In 1964, a year before Jeff arrived, the campus had served as a staging area for white college activists busing to Mississippi to register black voters. One night, Antioch students had kept a line open to organizers in the South who were surrounded by armed Klansmen.

In dormitories, the sound of students learning to play Bob Dylan songs blew in the wind from every third room. For the first time, Jeff was surrounded by interesting young people who shared his vision of making a difference in the world. He let his hair grow a little and replaced his shirt and tie with an old army jacket. The most active group on campus was the chapter of Students for a Democratic Society, but that wasn't for him. When Jeff arrived in Yellow Springs, he was determined to keep his promise to focus on his class work. He held out for six weeks.

October 15 and 16, 1965, were the first International Days of Protest against the war in Vietnam. Intended to unite demonstrators in far-flung cities, more than 75,000 marchers participated in Oakland, Ann Arbor, London. In nearly every city, the antiwar crowds were outnumbered by countermarchers. In New York, 10,000 demonstrators walked down Fifth Avenue, pelted by eggs, tomatoes, and red paint. In Berkeley, Hell's Angels broke through a police line to attack the protesters.

In Ohio, Jeff climbed into the back seat of a Volkswagen Bug on campus and rode as part of a thirty-student Antioch contingent toward a "noisy but orderly" protest in Cincinnati. Roughly a hundred peaceniks stood in front of the Federal Building on Main Street. A small phalanx of cops stood between them and a large, angry counterdemonstration, including the former head of the National Association for the Advancement of White People. Starting at 11:30 A.M., the protesters stood on their side of Main Street with signs reading, "Evacuate Don't Disintegrate Vietnam," and "I won't fight." For about an hour, the pickets did their best to raise their voices above the angry opposition. Hecklers carried a wreath and a flag; they called out: "Communists!" As the vigil was ending, the students gathered together for a folk sing-along, sending the other side into a paroxysm of hooting and jeers.

Jeff piled back into the VW fleet and steered toward Yellow Springs. Compared to the battles that would be fought in the next ten years, the march didn't register even as a skirmish, but to Jeff it was D-Day. When he returned to Antioch that afternoon, he had decided to join SDS.

•••

At the time, SDS only had a few thousand members. It had organized one major march in protest of the war and had mostly been ignored in the press. To Jeff, the early leaders of the group—Tom Hayden, Carl Oglesby, Al Haber—were elders already. By 1965, when he signed up, they had overthrown their own mentors and accomplished the seminal transformation that created the New Left and led to the publication of its famous manifesto, the Port Huron Statement.

SDS was descended from the League for Industrial Democracy, a socialist group that had enjoyed early glory under the leadership of Upton Sinclair and John Reed. By the 1930s, the league was already moribund, its tepid liberalism infuriating to Annie Stein and her rival gang of radical students. During the reactionary 1950s, when even liberal groups had found themselves on the attorney general's list of subversive organizations, the league—and the Old Left in general— had grown increasingly defensive. In order to protect their positions as authors or professors, former activists chose to out-witch-hunt the witch hunters. By 1960, there was nothing left of the radical spirit of the Great Depression. The League for Industrial Democracy continued to exist, but in name only.

These veterans had attempted to pass on their doctrine to the founding generation of SDS, but their pupils were too young to remember the Old Left's infighting and mutual distrust. Sensing that a new doctrine was necessary, the students decided to hammer out a platform for the new decade. For the occasion, they retired to an empty vacation retreat in Port Huron, a town north of Detroit.

The statement they produced there would inspire college students around the country, but it infuriated the older generation. It was not that it was pro-Russian; "As democrats," they wrote, "we are in basic opposition to the communist system. The Soviet Union, as a system, rests on the total suppression of organized opposition, as well as a vision of the future in the name of which much human life has been sacrificed." But it refused to endorse America's own "unreasoning anti-communism."

"In such an atmosphere," the authors wrote, "even the most intelligent of Americans fear to join political organizations, sign petitions, speak out on serious issues." In the United States, anti-communism had become "an umbrella by which to protest liberalism, internationalism, welfarism, the active civil rights and labor movements." Red-baiting had dominated political discourse in America for fifty

years. When the founders of SDS decided anticommunism was irrelevant and brushed it aside like an annoying insect, they committed
the rebellious act by which the Fifties became the Sixties. When it
came time for Jeff to join up, the specter of anticommunism that had
haunted the Left was gone.

•••

The Antioch chapter of SDS met in campus common rooms and
held events such as a Speakeasy, promising, "dancing girls, beerbeer-
beerbeer, pickin & pluckin, feds and flappers and live, live music."
The local activists distributed literature and printed speeches in the
chapter bulletin. Jeff read everything he could find. He kept the Port
Huron Statement close at all times and spent weeks giving it a careful reading.

Inspired, he hitched a ride to Chicago during Christmas break in
1965 to attend a meeting of the SDS national council. He rode all
night, sighting the city just as the sun was rising out of Lake
Michigan. With no friends in town and nowhere to crash, Jeff went
to the national office on East Sixty-Third Street on the South Side
of Chicago. It was the first time in his life that he had ventured into
an urban ghetto. Upstairs, in a parody of the traditional office,
second-hand typewriters, telephones, printing presses, and an addres-
sograph machine were all operating at top speed to prepare for the
coming caucus. The elevated train rolled right by the window every
few minutes, rattling the castaway office furniture, none of which sat
flush to the floor.

Jeff told the first person he saw that he wanted to trade a day's
work for a ride to the convention. The man he asked was C. Clark
Kissinger, SDS national secretary during the 1964–1965 school year.
Jeff spent the rest of the day filing papers and preparing leaflets. That
night, in what would be the first of many, he slept on the office floor
using his coat as a blanket. The next morning he joined Kissinger in
his family's green Ford station wagon and rode to the University of
Illinois campus in Champaign-Urbana.

For Jeff, only a month and a half removed from his first demonstration, being at the national convention was like being on a movie

set. Nearly the entire pantheon of SDS stars was there: Al Haber, Lee Webb, Todd Gitlin, Steve Max, and Carl Oglesby. In November 1965, SDS claimed 3,000 members. At Champaign–Urbana the organization was shifting from the civil rights movement to protesting the Vietnam War. Its activities remained scrupulously legal. Burning draft cards was frowned upon.

As the meeting began, Lee Webb shocked his audience by announcing that Tom Hayden, along with Staughton Lynd and Herbert Aptheker, had violated a State Department ban and traveled to Hanoi. They were the first representatives of the American peace movement to set foot in North Vietnam since the war had begun. Jeff felt as if he had taken a college road trip to the center of world events. He immediately knew that these were the people and this was the organization he wanted to work with.

About four hundred students spent most of the daytime in workshops and the nighttime in parties. For Jeff, nineteen years old, a freshman in college, and one of the youngest participants in the convention, everything was new. The jargon of SDS made the simple seem complex and the complex utterly inscrutable. At his first meeting, Jeff had no idea what the others were talking about, but the political language was as heady to absorb as second-hand smoke. He mostly remained silent, keeping to the fringes and taking it all in.

Back in Yellow Springs, Jeff became an activist. It was natural after the way he'd been raised. Once he got a few facts about the Vietnam War, he knew it was something to fight against. In February 1966, a local newsletter reported, "Jeff has spoken at 7 colleges about Vietnam in the past six weeks." One campus he visited was Earlham where he met a young activist named Robert Meeropol, whose parents had been executed as Russian spies. On the ride home, one of Jeff's friends was astonished to learn that he had never heard of the Rosenbergs.

In March, as the term was ending, Jeff came home late at night after a few drinks, sat down, and typed a letter on yellow-pad paper to the "Joneseses" back in California:

I got a call Thursday from the acting national secretary of SDS. He asked me to check on the possibility of holding our national convention here next month and to assume responsibility for organizing it. It looks like I've got another project . . . I'll try and put together some of my newsletters and some SDS literature. Did I tell you I was in Chicago two weekends ago? . . . Next week will be my last official one, it goes like this.

On Sunday I can relax with only one meeting, the Steering Committee of the Yellow Springs Peace and Freedom Committee. Monday is open. Tuesday I'm going to Youngstown to talk about SDS. A professor friend has asked me to speak to some of his classes. I'll spend the night there and continue talking to people the next day. On Friday, Cleveland has the first of its activities for the International Days of Protest. Tom Hayden who is a founder of SDS and one of the three who went to North Vietnam earlier this year is speaking in the evening.

I've got a chance to buy a Volkswagen bus for $15. If it's registered in my name will your insurance go up? . . . Only thing is that it don't run. . . .

Dad, I wish you'd do something about those unions. . . .

My heart is in the ghetto. SDS is doing some fine community organizing in the ghettos of several cities. Listen for news of ERAP, Education Research and Action Projects. I have several very good friends in the Cleveland ghettos. If I had my choice of things to talk about, that's what it would be, but unfortunately I don't know anything.

When I was in Kentucky, I saw some stone walls that were built by slaves. It gives one a funny feeling to know that it was for real. . . .

My office is next to the tavern and my house is next to the bar. I really feel fine tonight. I hope the soul in this letter comes through.

My bed is calling me.

Love,
Jeff

Reading this letter gave Albert a good chuckle. It sounded almost identical to the work he had done as a member of the pacifism movement of the 1930s. He was impressed. Jeff, so upset by the war, seemed to have learned well the abhorrence of violence that he had tried to teach. If Albert had felt some concern that he was not focusing enough on his education, he could hardly have expressed it without feeling hypocritical. After all, it was he who had taken Jeff to Quaker meeting each Sunday and introduced him to community activism.

In the autumn of 1966, Jeff took a co-op job as a clerk at the law firm of Sipser, Weinstock and Weinman, with offices on Broad Street in Lower Manhattan. He had visited New York City once during his freshman year, riding, as usual, in the cramped middle of a VW Bug back seat. He had gone on a weekend whim, driving sixteen hours to get there and staying for just one afternoon. He was not the first to come over the George Washington Bridge and feel that he had found the center of the world. The girls were prettier. The radio stations were better. Anything you wanted was available at any time. When he moved into his tiny one-bedroom on Eighty-Fifth Street in September, the West Side was in decline; on every block, century-old brownstones had regressed into wrecks and boarding houses. Revitalization was just starting downtown. A month before he arrived, two jackhammers broke ground at the intersection of West and Cortlandt streets to prepare construction for the twin towers of the World Trade Center.

•••

Meanwhile, back at the ranch-style suburban home in Sylmar, all was not well. Millie had never fit in with the culture of the San Fernando Valley. As a young girl, she had hoped that her music would provide the escape she needed. When she met Albert, she hoped his politics, which she came to share, would give her spiritual relief. But in all the years of their marriage, Millie had harbored a tiny knot of worry. By trying to ignore it, by disciplining her mind, she had kept it tied tight. After twenty-five years with Albert, she felt unappreciated and passionless. He went off to work in the mornings, while she drove the 1964 Mustang all over the San Fernando Valley giving violin lessons. One of her students was an older man named Roger O'Donnell. Roger had only a high school education, but he was something of a charmer. He also had one attribute that Millie could not resist: he was a music lover. His father had taught him about opera as a child, and he had constructed his first violin when he was twelve. He was an amateur violin maker but could not play the instrument, despite the lessons from Millie.

In the 1960s, marriages were falling apart at an unprecedented rate, and Millie was proud that hers had lasted almost twenty-five years. At the same time, she looked at her friends and saw how they were changing their lives. It was not a women's liberation movement, yet there seemed to be some possibilities beyond an unfulfilling marriage. Millie had always followed the rules. She had gone to church and done her homework. She had been high school valedictorian. She had never gone out with boys before her marriage. She was now nearing forty and felt it was time to do something for her.

When Jeff's little sister, Julie, was seven or eight, Roger took her and her mother ice skating. Then, Julie noticed, he started showing up more often. For her eleventh birthday, Millie took her and a friend up to a cabin near June Lake. When they arrived, Roger was there waiting for them, and he stayed the entire weekend. Millie stopped attending weekly Quaker meeting. Suspicious, Albert was reduced to hiding behind bushes and spying on the couple, following behind Millie's car until he confirmed that she was meeting with Roger. He confronted her, reminding her of her duty to the children. "I would fight the world to stay with Roger," she told him. Still, they continued to live together.

In the autumn of 1966, Millie got the professional opportunity of a lifetime. She signed on with the orchestra that accompanied the Roger Wagner Chorale. The high point of the tour was a single show in New York City's Carnegie Hall. Albert dropped her off in Los Angeles and watched her board the chorale's chartered bus. That night, he was at the dinner table with Eric and Julie when the telephone rang. It was Roger's wife. She told Albert that her husband had quit his job and planned to follow the tour bus in his car. Julie it had been easy for Jeff to register as a conscientious objector when he turned sixteen. As a college student, he was exempt from the draft anyway, though he had reservations about this system. In school, he had written to Albert, "I'm questioning the validity of deferring students because they are students. Is it right to give students special privileges over the less educated, poor, Negroes, etc.?"

Having quit school, his CO status was particularly valuable, but in the past few months, Jeff's ideas about pacifism had shifted. He no longer believed it was the only course for protest. The Vietnamese had changed his mind; they were surely right to defend their villages against American soldiers. In 1936, Albert had taken a moral stand by denouncing violence and swearing that he would never fight. Now, in 1967, Jeff's own moral compass led him in the opposite direction: he forswore pacifism and determined that, at certain times, fighting was the only way.

His second letter was to Selective Service, the military bureaucracy in charge of the draft. He told the army that he no longer considered himself a pacifist and wished to have his status as a conscientious objector erased. He said he believed the Vietnam War was immoral and implied that if he was to be drafted, he'd prefer jail to serving in the army. Then he went down to the Whitehall Street Induction Center, Manhattan's draft hub, and spent the mornings "talking with guys going to their pre-induction physicals about the alternatives that exist to military service."

From his office in Union Square, Jeff met with the chapters in his region: Columbia, Fordham, City College, NYU. The general feeling was that they were on the cusp of something big. By mid-1966, the national organization had grown to 5,500 members in 151 chapters. *New Left Notes*, the SDS paper, was a spirited forum for rival ideas. Four times a year, delegates met in national councils or conventions. The leaders spent most of their time traveling between campuses. Jeff quickly learned that dogmatic speeches were not the best way to connect with the students. "Discussing the grinding meaninglessness of campus life at three in the morning with a little beer and the Stones on the stereo," one veteran of the process wrote, "has much more personal impact than lecturing people."

and Eric, their forks poised between plate and mouth, listened to Albert's half of the conversation.

"This thing has got so I can't take it anymore," he said to them, and asked if they thought he should go confront her. They wondered why it had taken him so long.

He arrived in New York City and telegrammed Jeff. Millie was shocked to find her husband was in town. Roger had brought his family down from Massachusetts and had tickets for them all to see the concert. Albert and Millie met for a parley in the Russian Tea Room. There, they agreed that after the tour, she would come back home and give the marriage another try.

On Sunday afternoon, at 3:00 P.M., when the crowd filed into Carnegie Hall for the concert, Jeff and Albert, not Roger and his family, were in the audience. The concert began with Victoria's "Ave Maria." For those in the audience feeling guilty about a failing marriage, the holy sounds were perfectly chosen to enhance the suffering. Millie, during what should have been her greatest moment, sat in her orchestra chair gently weeping on her viola. At the end of the concert, Albert packed at the hotel and flew home. Millie finished up the rest of the tour.

The agreed-on final attempt to save the marriage lasted only a few days. Then Millie and Roger disappeared again. Albert got a phone call at work and learned that the couple had driven down to Mexico and been married in Tijuana. Albert called his lawyer to start divorce proceedings. On April 5, 1967, the twenty-fifth anniversary of their wedding, Albert got the bill from Millie's lawyer.

•••

Students for a Democratic Society was looking for a new regional director in New York City. Jeff applied and got the job, which paid $12.50 a week, and moved to an apartment on 109th Street, near Broadway. He wanted to get started right away but first had to sit down and write two letters. He wrote to the trustees of the Disney Scholarship, telling them that he was leaving college to work full time against the war.

With a Quaker father, having been raised in the pacifist tradition,

From protest to resistance—that was the theme of the SDS national convention in the summer of 1967. From public display of opposition to cramming *sabots* into the sparking gears, closing down draft offices, chucking monkey wrenches, attacking the Pentagon: it was an escalation, a response to the administration's escalations in Vietnam. By late October, 13,907 U.S. troops had been killed in Vietnam. Within a few months, the combatant casualties would surpass America's total in the Korean War. This statistical horror was keeping Jeff from sleeping nights.

Everyone who came to see him at the SDS office in Union Square wanted to talk about the upcoming march against the Pentagon. Jeff represented SDS on a steering committee led by David Dellinger. In 1940, Dellinger had inspired Albert by choosing prison over the army. Now he was leading the next generation of activists, but Jeff, at least, was beginning to find Dellinger's way old-fashioned. After years of nonviolent protests, the war had only expanded.

Jeff was exploring another philosophy. In mid-October, Ben Morea, a Lower East Side anarchist who was always trying to goad SDS into militant action, arrived in Jeff's office waving two six-foot bamboo poles and said, "We're going into downtown Washington and bust up the place." Morea thought he had a surefire strategy to make this March on Washington a little less like a pleasant dream and more like a ringing hangover; he wanted Jeff to endorse a breakaway.

Japanese students used similar poles in their snake dances. Dozens of them would grab hold and, together in a tight mass, they would charge the police. Two thousand students of the *Zengakuren* league, the Japanese equivalent to SDS, had recently used their snake dance in a fight with the cops. They had burned police vehicles and nearly taken over the Tokyo Airport.

Jeff considered the tactic. The night before the action, he stayed with his counterpart in Washington, Cathlyn Wilkerson, in her house near Rock Creek. The SDS leaders were not optimistic about the next day's march and argued over the merits of a breakaway. In the end, they decided against it. SDS would not employ the street-fighting tactics of the snake dance. Not yet. Lying down at last on the night of October 20, Jeff need not have worried about taking part in another pointless parade. Before dawn, the opposing forces had congregated into their rival camps, and it was already too late to avoid a conflict.

Protesters had disembarked off chartered buses from Boston and New York and stepped off trains at Union Station. They hitchhiked and arrived in cars. That night they lay on church pews or hard on the floors of 4,000 homes whose inhabitants had volunteered to put them up. Across the river, the army was mustering too. Five hundred buses and trucks disappeared into a secret underground entrance in the Pentagon, unloading 2,500 troops inside to sleep in the Defense Department halls. Helicopters were fueled and readied down the entire length of the Atlantic seaboard, able at a minute's notice to carry thousands of troops into the capital to reinforce the Metropolitan Police, National Guardsmen, U.S. marshals, and a classified number of FBI agents posing as press or circulating among the crowd.

Though it was late autumn, the temperature on October 21, 1967, was in the sixties, and the sun was shining. Around noon, Peter, Paul and Mary performed in front of the Lincoln Memorial. Phil Ochs played his new song, "I Declare the War Is Over." Nearly 100,000 protesters—some estimates went as high as 318,000—were gathering around the reflecting pool and the grass that surrounded the Washington Monument. White pennants lay on the ground while their owners attached the poles and daubed in last-minute touches: Women Strike for Peace, American Friends Service Committee, CORE, Du Bois Clubs, Southern Christian Leadership Conference, SDS, the Student Non-Violent Coordinating Committee, the National Lawyers Guild.

The speakers were wrapping up. Monitors formed the crowd into lines and began the two-mile trek across the Potomac to the concrete pillbox that hid, as the protesters would have put it, the U.S. military establishment. Army, police, and television helicopters shaded the stretching line of marchers. Jeff walked beneath the enormous SDS banner. He was near the front of the procession. If there was an opportunity to cause some disturbance, he hoped to be right in the middle of the action.

Somewhere in the crowds behind him, Eleanor Stein marched with her mother, Annie.

The Pentagon was out of sight from the marching route. Then, coming around a corner, it loomed before them. The largest office building in the world, it was built with ramparts to defy a charge. Dozens of people, including Defense Secretary Robert McNamara, stood on the roof or looked out their windows, watching through binoculars. Positioned in a thin green line, military police, carrying rifles with affixed, albeit sheathed, bayonets, stood before the entrance to the building.

It was after five o'clock. An enormous parking lot lay between the bridge and the walls of the Pentagon. As Jeff neared it, he saw that the expanse of asphalt had diluted the moral force of the marchers. Spilling from the narrow bridge into the empty lot was like pouring red food coloring into a glass of water. They were losing their close ranks. Off to one side, the Fugs were playing, and a chanting coven was casting the peaceful spell intended to lift the building high into the air and turn it orange.

Directly in front of the SDS group was the Committee to Aid the National Liberation Front. Its members moved determinedly beneath a banner divided into horizontal blue and red stripes beneath a superimposed yellow star—the Vietcong flag. Instead of dissolving into the parking lot, this regiment charged across it in a brisk, disciplined trot. They crossed the four-lane Jefferson Davis Highway and trampled onto the grassy lawn before the Pentagon's Mall entrance. Before them, fourteen stone steps led to the fortress's columned main gate. There, a tense standoff had developed as hundreds of MPs held off thousands of protesters.

Jeff was separated from his friends; the SDS contingent that had marched as a body was disintegrating. He kept his eye fixed on the Vietcong flag and followed where it led him. Instead of staying straight toward the main confrontation, the flag jerked and veered to the left. Somebody in front had spotted a smaller side entrance, virtually unguarded. As he cleared the last hurdle, a flight of stairs, Jeff saw a few panicked MPs desperately trying to close the doors and bar the breach. The hard-charging leaders overwhelmed them and were inside the fortress. Jeff kept pressing forward. He was only a few yards from entering the belly of the beast.

Around twenty charging protesters actually breached a side entrance and entered the Pentagon. Seconds later, they were pushed back out onto the stairs by dozens of soldiers stationed in the corridor. The soldiers took their rifle butts to heads and chests, and the tiny invasion was repulsed in seconds, leaving blood stains on the floor and stairs. They hut-hut-hut-hutted outside, driving the fleeing, broken remnants before them, and formed a line until they had safely blocked the entrance and protected their own flanks.

Jeff shoved his way through the wedged-in crowd. No longer believing it possible to enter the building, he had one thought: to get to the very front. The soldiers were on the stairs, looking down at him and the others. There could be no doubt about who had the strength. Nothing in the world would have been easier than for these soldiers or their officers to surge into the crowd and start breaking heads. Someone in the march defused the situation, shouting, "Sit down, sit down." The near-violent turmoil of a moment earlier was transformed into a disciplined sit-down strike. Others joined until there were more than a thousand college students locked in a battle of wills with hundreds of college-age soldiers.

As the light began to fail, there was the first illumination of burning draft cards. The temperature dropped into the forties, and the cards were replaced by more substantial fuel; police line boards and picket sticks were piled up for bonfires. Food was distributed around the plaza. A girl carrying an aspirin bottle circulated asking, "Any headaches? Any headaches?" And the smell of pot smoke drove away the lingering hint of tear gas. There were no toilets and, turning "biological needs into a real symbolic gesture," demonstrators began to piss on the walls and lawn of the building.

When the sandwiches, the aspirin, and the reefer had dulled the marchers' pressing needs, a feeling of truce developed. Somebody found a bullhorn and turned it into an improvisational forum. Far past midnight, relayed speakers spoke continuously to the assembled crowd. Jeff took his turn to make a little speech, expressing his wonder at the moment. The marchers had gone to the most hostile place in the country and, using the tools of peace—words, pot, and good-will—had made it their own. Being a member of SDS had meant being a member of a minority. On some campuses, a chapter of 50 people tried to organize a student body of 15,000. In only a few instances had enough antiwar demonstrators come together in numbers that gave them a sense of security. Jeff felt it now—a togetherness and a solidarity in this temporary camp.

But they weren't secure. Any marcher who made contact with or interfered with a soldier in any way was pulled behind the line and handed over to the marshals, who often beat them with clubs before dragging them inside the building to be arrested. "An SDS girl from Boston was dozing about 2:30 A.M.," wrote a correspondent for *New Left Notes*. Someone near her was grabbed by a marshal. "She woke startled. In waking she must have brushed against a soldier—it isn't quite clear. She was then grabbed by a marshall *(sic)*, dragged through the line, whereupon the marshall started clubbing the hell out of her. We focused a spotlight and a camera on him. The look on his face could only have been that of someone having an orgasm. Pictures were taken. The girl, who ended up getting three broken ribs, was carried to a paddy wagon."

Late the next morning, after twenty-four hours, Jeff left the Pentagon, walking the two miles back to Washington. Crossing back over Memorial Bridge, an angry driver saw that he was a protester and tried to run him over. More than 1,000 arrests were made at the Pentagon. Almost 700 people had charges filed against them, and most had to pay a $25 fine to be released.

"It is difficult to report publicly the ugly and vulgar provocation of many of the militants," wrote James Reston of the *New York Times*. "Many of the signs carried by a small number of the militants, and many of the lines in the theatrical performances put on by the hippies, are too obscene to print. In view of this underside of the protest, many officials here are surprised that there was not much more violence." Jimmy Breslin elaborated in the *Washington Post*. "Taste and decency had left the scene," he wrote. "The kids went to the bathroom on the side of the Pentagon.... They turned a demonstration for peace, these drifters in raggedy clothes, into a sickening,

club-swinging mess. At the end of the day, the only concern any-
body could have was for the soldiers who were taking the abuse."
The most violent abuses of the marshals, coming hours after
Saturday deadlines, went unreported.

President Johnson enjoyed a brief double-digit spike in popular-
ity, and Jeff learned that the great masses of people would not follow
from protest into resistance. "A peace rally cannot become violent
without becoming self-defeating," the *New York Times* editorialized.
But to Jeff at least, it felt so right.

•••

On the morning of November 15, 1967, Jeff took a taxi to Kennedy
Airport. He, Cathlyn Wilkerson, and two others climbed on board a
707 and took off for Paris, the first leg of a journey that was supposed to end in Hanoi. Jeff knew he should call his father to tell him
where he was going. Albert might read about the trip in the newspapers. Few American civilians had been inside North Vietnam, and it
was considered big news. Still, Jeff put off phoning until the last
moment. Finally, he put in a call from a pay phone to the Disney studios. He broke the news as gently as he could, and both father and
son hung up worried.

Phnom Penh, Cambodia's capital city of half a million, was only a
hundred miles from tumultuous Saigon, yet the airport was clean
and calm, with no sign of security. It was not, however, air-
conditioned. Jeff paid four dollars for a seven-day visa and gathered
his bag for the trip along wide boulevards into the city. The modern
apartment houses he passed could have been in Manhattan, and
although rust-colored pagoda spires dominated the ancient town,
Jeff sensed the encroaching influence of the modern world. "Phnom
Penh was a beautiful city but it made me sad," he wrote. "The more
I got to know the Cambodian people the more it seemed to me that
this city—with its Times Square neon movie houses and teen-aged
prostitution—was not a truly Cambodian city, but an aberration created by Western cultural and imperialistic influences."

Pedicabs whisked the travelers through the streets. The drivers
received their payment with a bow and a *"merci, monsieur."* Jeff and

the others browsed the stalls of the Central Market: flowers and vegetables, comic books in French and Khmer, and Chinese fabrics. At dinner, he practiced his French on the waiters and ordered *ris cantonais,* Cantonese rice. The sidewalks, deserted in the heat of the afternoon, came alive at night. Shops were open and movie theaters jammed. In the darkness, Jeff thought he could see the flares of light as American planes bombed the countryside west of Saigon.

The flashes were a constant reminder that the small nation and its liberal dictator, Prince Norodom Sihanouk, were on the edges of a larger battle. "When two elephants are fighting, an ant should stand aside," went Sihanouk's diplomatic maxim, but the elephants had an annoying habit of stepping on the ant anyway. Within three years of Jeff's visit, the liberal prince would be toppled in a CIA-aided coup. Five years after that, the Communist Khmer Rouge would take advantage of the chaos and establish their murderous regime. "Our American friends," Sihanouk had said in the mid-Sixties, "are remarkable organizers, brilliant technicians and excellent soldiers, but their incontestable realism stops short of the realm of politics, where the attitude of the ostrich seems to them to conform to their best interests."

The only way to enter North Vietnam was to fly on one of the International Control Commission's rickety airplanes. These cartels kept diplomatic relations open between the combatants. Tom Hayden had gone this route in 1965, and *New York Times* correspondent Harrison Salisbury did the same a year later, when he filed the first reports about the civilian casualties caused by America's bombing campaign. Normally, there were one or two flights a week, but they could be turned back in midair or stopped for weeks or months when the bombings were particularly fierce. Jeff was eager to cover this final stage of the journey, but the flights were suspended. The air force was flying its Rolling Thunder missions, and Jeff was told that American bombings in the North had never before been heavier.

Stuck in Phnom Penh, he went to the theater for a performance by the NLF Dance and Song Troupe, which usually played to peasant audiences in the midst of the war zone. There, the actors and audience always kept rifles close at hand in case of surprise attack. Charred American tanks were used for stage scenery, and bomb craters served as amphitheaters. On another day, Jeff rented a car and drove to the Hindu and Buddhist temples at Angkor Wat. Jackie Kennedy had been to the temple a few weeks earlier and declared it "wonderful, marvelous."

Jeff rented a bicycle and rode alone on the narrow roads. "Cambodia is a beautiful country, a rice growing, fertile land," he later wrote. "It has dense jungles and rugged mountains. Looking across paddies and fields, one can see rising peaks and pinnacles, covered in soft mists and framed by the people working the water buffalo." His shoulder-length blond hair streamed behind him, and the children who ran beside his bike called after him, *"où vas tu, mademoiselle?"*

Alongside the dirt road, grass grew five feet tall and bamboo groves swayed and creaked with each breath of wind. He rode for miles past friendly villages and open faces. Then he must have passed some invisible line. He came to a muddy crossroads and felt implacable, hostile eyes following his passage. It was time to return to town.

Having traveled half a globe, he was just a few hundred miles from Hanoi, but there was no way to cover the remaining distance. After days of waiting, he had to sit down and write home, "Today the North Vietnamese ambassador called us and said he wanted to speak with us. It seems that the U.S. bombings are so heavy that they have cancelled all foreign visits. It's very sad to be so close and then not be able to go all the way. We'll be meeting with people from the North Vietnamese embassy and from the National Liberation Front for the next few days to learn as much as we can."

Jeff flew home through Tokyo. When he arrived in Los Angeles, there was a story about his delegation in the newspaper. Instead of writing that the trip had been turned back because of heightened bombings, the reporter accused Hanoi of shunting off the students as some kind of propaganda stunt.

Albert was waiting to pick Jeff up. They rode the highway through the San Fernando Valley. Jeff talked about the sights and smells of

Asia. As they drove, he was amazed by the changes that had come to the valley in the years he had been gone. They pulled into the driveway on Tyler Street. Millie was gone, and Albert was adjusting to life without her. Otherwise, the house had hardly changed. After two years of total upheaval in his own life, Jeff saw that the Joneseses had plodded along at the same old rate.

He lived across a continent from his family. He had just come from the far side of the world. But at the end of 1967, the distance that yawned between them could only be measured cosmically. This family, with all its comfort and loving acceptance, represented old hang-ups. Jeff had seen the new day in the crowd of righteous kids gathered before the Pentagon. Even the principle of pacifism that defined the spirit of this house was starting to seem obsolete. Before he had unpacked his bags, Jeff was already eager to leave, to get back to New York City and SDS.

CHAPTER 7

Class Struggle

MANHATTAN was having an English morning on April 23, 1968. Early fog hid the Hudson River, and hanging mist tangled tree branches in Riverside Park. Looking at the gray through her fifth-floor window, Eleanor Raskin, my mother, could have been back in sooty Manchester, where she had spent the previous three years studying and living in a coal-heated flat. She had left New York in August 1964, the morning following her wedding to Jonah Raskin, a graduate student she had met at college. Eleanor arrived in England only a few months after the Beatles made the same trip in the opposite direction to appear on black and white TVs around the country. When Eleanor returned in the summer of 1967 to begin law school at Columbia University, the United States had entered a new era. Everything had gone Technicolor.

She was twenty-two years old and had missed the rise of American student culture, but England had a youth movement of its own: a style of outrageous Day-Glo waistcoats, broad collars, and frilly sleeves. It was the fashion that the Beatles modeled on the record jacket of their newest album, *Sgt. Pepper's Lonely Hearts Club Band*. Eleanor affected a posh trace of accent and brought to New York an exotic echo of London's Carnaby Street, the mecca of Mod fashion.

For many classmates, her fame began on the first day of law school when she had worn a lime green coat and matching broad-brimmed hat, adding a splash of color to the aseptic three-piece suits and leather attaché cases of the class of '70. Eleanor proceeded to spend the rest of the school year as a rebel, helping to found a National Lawyers Guild chapter and complaining to professors about bias faced by the women students.

By this overcast day eight months later, her style had changed again. The green coat still draped off its hanger but it was tucked away in the back of her walk-in closet. She was dressing like a hippie now and her closet—stuffed with batiks, bell bottoms, and mirrored skirts from India—reflected the metamorphosis. On the floor was a stack of shoe boxes. Ignoring her knee-high snakeskin boots and her Charles Jourdan two-inch stacked heels, she wanted the red ballet slippers for Contracts B—Remedies, Third Party Beneficiaries, Assignments and Discharge.

Eleanor took a last sip of coffee—made with fresh beans from Schapira's in the Village. Her husband's empty cup was in the sink. He had left already, battling the Long Island Expressway to Stony Brook, where he taught Shakespeare and Dickens to his graduate students. She stuffed a thick casebook and some legal pads into her beaded shoulder bag, threw the weight across her back, turned the four doorlocks, and hit the button for the first floor. A heartbeat's hesitation before entering—she had recently been held up at knife point by two teenagers in her own elevator.

If 250 Riverside Drive had enjoyed a heyday, it was long past by 1968. Eleanor crossed through the lobby where once a doorman would have tipped his cap, came out onto 97th street, and turned left to catch an uptown bus on Broadway. Passing 100th Street she could look toward the park and the looming brick housing development where Annie, now fifty-five, lived alone. Eleanor and Jonah went to her mother's house at least once a week for dinner and political conversation. Annie, never shy, would express disapproval toward her daughter's wardrobe. When Eleanor insisted on buying a sheared lamb coat from Gimbel's—thigh-length with a zipper running all the way up—Annie was furious. At $200, the coat was way too expensive; worse, it was made from South African sheared lamb. The thought of her only daughter breaking the apartheid boycott for such a thing was more than Annie could stand. She brought out the family's most deadly insult for the occasion—the "B" word. But bourgeois or not, Eleanor bought the coat. She had been defying her mother for years.

The bus stopped at 116th Street, and Eleanor leaped off the last stair onto the sidewalk outside Columbia. The crowd on Broadway funneled toward the main entrance. There were few other ways to get onto the campus grounds, and Eleanor often thought that the university's architects must have expected trouble. In fact, the original master plan, designed by the well-known New York firm McKim, Mead & White, had called for open courtyards. Then Haarlem, a Dutch farming community, became Harlem, the world's most famous black neighborhood, and Columbia closed in on itself. During the years after World War II, when Dwight Eisenhower served as university president, he obtained a special permit from the police department to carry a derringer pistol on his walks around the campus.

The buildings formed a sheer wall to the neighborhood, and the lowest windows were guarded by black metal grilles. Eleanor passed the security guard's station and crossed under the wrought-iron gates to the tree-shaded brick path called College Walk. On her left were the broad stone stairs leading up to the administrative center at Low Library. On a nicer day, the steps would crowd with sunbathers. To her right were two manicured lawns and the sundial, a raised granite disc from which a speaker could stand above a meeting and reach a thousand listeners. The Columbia SDS chapter had scheduled a rally to protest a private gym that the trustees had voted to construct on Harlem's public land. There were signs all over campus publicizing it, but Eleanor was not a member and didn't expect much from the day's protest. SDS was for lowly undergrads, not worldly law students.

A few weeks earlier, after Martin Luther King, Jr. was assassinated, Mark Rudd, head of Columbia SDS, had put his group on the map by disrupting an administration tribute to the civil rights leader. In the law school, a professor examined whether this type of protest was guaranteed by the First Amendment. He and the class concluded that it was not.

On the far side of the sundial, Eleanor passed some of the oldest and most impressive structures on campus—St. Paul's Chapel, the classroom buildings Fayerweather and Avery—and then came to the newest and ugliest, the law school, which had opened in 1960. A gray rectangle with balconies suspended on the narrow sides, it was intended as a modernist monument to the future, "planned," according to a fundraising pamphlet, "to meet the needs of the next century." Students had instantly dubbed it "The Toaster."

As a Raskin, Eleanor was alphabetically remanded to the back of the lecture theater. Her closest friend at school, Gus Reichbach, sat next to her. In front of them were half of the students in her year. They flipped open their legal pads to the first blank page with a certain urgency. Many in the room sensed that their dream jobs with a Wall Street firm—starting at $15,000 a year—were slipping away. In a class of 312, there were only twenty-four women, the most the law school had ever admitted. Professors seemed to enjoy picking on them, and Eleanor sat in suspended dread of an instructor's looking down at his attendance sheet, adjusting his spectacles, and saying, "Now Mrs. Raskin, please explain . . ."

As Contracts B began and Eleanor started scribbling her illegible notes, hundreds of other students were gathering at the sundial. The administration had locked them out of Low Library, and the campus radicals huddled in a frantic caucus. It was hard enough for SDS to make a plan, let alone a contingency plan, and predictably they were at a loss for what to do. But the organization had made a political art form of confusion, and when a rank-and-file member yelled, "To the gym, to the gym site!" roughly three hundred marchers tromped off toward Morningside Park, leaderless and strong.

The university was badly in need of a gym and had plenty of property on which to construct one. Instead, the trustees had insisted it be built on city land in Morningside Park. Harlem residents could use a back door to access a separate, and presumably equal, swimming pool. The blueprint brought back memories of "colored only" signs on water fountains in the Deep South. Militant Student Non-Violent Coordinating Committee leader H. Rap Brown spoke for many when he said, "If they build the first story blow it up. If they sneak back at night and build three stories burn it down. And if they get nine stories built, it's yours. Take it over, and maybe we'll let them in on weekends."

The marchers came out onto Amsterdam Avenue, chanting and stopping traffic. Eleanor was in the back of the classroom, trying to hold her attention on the professor. Chants of "No Gym! No Gym!" started filtering in from the street below. She closed her books, got out of her seat, and slipped out through the back door to join them.

Three policemen, stationed at the construction site around the clock, failed to shut a gate against the students. Protesters poured into the hard-hat area. Someone took a running leap at the ten-foot-high chain link fence, and then others were working at it, bending and pulling it until forty feet of fence was trampled underfoot. More police arrived, leaving demonstrators at their second impasse of the afternoon. A rumor passed that hundreds of latecomers were gathered at the sundial. "Let's go to Low—that's where the power is," shouted one student. After a few minutes, the group turned and walked back to campus, trudging quietly this time and in single file up the steep slope of the park.

Eleanor had to laugh at the SDS people. This thing was headed toward disaster: if they kept marching back and forth, the crowd would split and wander off. Nearing the campus again, the marchers met the two hundred students who had been at the sundial and were now headed to join the main group at the gym site.

Back where it had started, the protest was collapsing into chaos until someone in the front row—participatory democracy again—yelled, "Seize Hamilton!" and hundreds of demonstrators marched inside Hamilton Hall, a main classroom building and home to many deans' offices, chanting together, "Racist gym must go, racist gym must go." One dean stood by packing his pipe, and another worried that the protest would disrupt his afternoon Phi Beta Kappa meeting. No one on either side realized the significance of what had just happened.

Annie Stein's father, Philip Steckler, poses with a guitar in Russian Army uniform. This photo was taken at Coney Island, where homesick immigrants could recreate nostalgic images of the motherland.

Annie as a toddler flanked by her two sisters. Frieda, on the right, was the eldest and most serious. Sylvia, the blonde, was always the most beautiful.

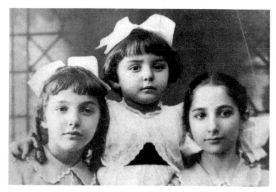

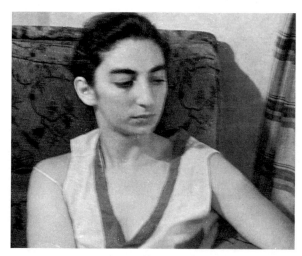

Annie during her Hunter College days in the early 1930s. Around this time she would meet her life-long friend Chavy Wiener, who introduced her to the Communist Party.

Malcolm Barton Jones lounges on the fender of the car in which he chauffeured Yosemite's important visitors. He would miss his first son's birth while driving Belgium's King Albert around the park on the morning of October 15, 1919. The child would be named Albert Leopold after the esteemed visitor.

Christine Tande with baby Albert shortly after his birth. When the Yosemite season ended, Malcolm and Christine took their son back to their winter home in Los Angeles. A few days after they arrived, the *Evening Express* ran the headline "King Hails 'L'Enfant' Jones" over a story about the baby born with a royal name.

Mildred Meyer as she was around the time she and Albert Jones met at Los Angeles Community College in the late 1930s. He noticed her noticing him, and he approved. Millie had a big smile and wore her hair shoulder length, as the styles from Hollywood dictated. The main thing that impressed Millie about Albert was his politics. She had never before heard of a pacifist.

Arthur Stein, holding a cigarette, shakes hands with Philip Murray, head of the Congress of Industrial Organizations, in 1946, around the time of his second heart attack and the year Eleanor was born. Arthur had been under FBI surveillance since 1941 for his alleged "subversive activities," an order that came directly from Secretary of Labor Frances Perkins.

Al and Millie Jones, the young married couple. So many wartime marriages were broken up immediately by the needs of military service that the full year they spent together after their wedding seemed generous. In April 1943, Albert was shipped off with other conscientious objectors to Civilian Public Service Camp #37 in Coleville, California.

In the winter of 1943, snow covered the low-slung bunkhouses of Camp #37. Albert would be confined there until well after the war's end. Eventually Millie would join him. They were the last to leave, in April 1946.

Annie, front row left, and the other leaders of the Coordinating Committee for the Enforcement of the Anti-Discrimination Laws of 1872 and 1873. Mary Church Terrell is in the center of the front row.

Mary Church Terrell with a statue of Frederick Douglass, who had escorted her to President Garfield's inaugural ball in 1881. By the 1950s, when she was in her eighties, she seemed to come from a different era. She was frail and had a romantic way of speaking. Her clothing was always fashionable, although the fashion was of fifty years earlier.

(*left*) Albert, on the far left, and the rest of the logging crew at Coleville. The truck was a converted snowplow. It rolled on ten tires and handled like a Sherman tank.

Arthur Stein had special plans for Valentine's Day 1956: he appeared before the House Committee on Un-American Activities. Like thousands of other progressives, he had been caught in the anti-Communist machinery. Once your name came before one of the congressional investigators, your professional life was ruined, your social circle limited to others who had been named.

Millie and Albert read bedtime stories to three-year-old Jeffrey in 1950.

Jeff, wearing a bow tie, and his younger brother, Eric, discussing the deeper meaning of *Mother Goose*. After school, Jeff would hurry home for a glass of milk and a few slices of Wonder Bread. He'd sit Indian-style in front of the TV and watch the *Mickey Mouse Club*.

Albert at his workstation in the Walt Disney studio. He made Jeff's birthday parties a sought-after invitation by lugging in his film projector and beaming the latest cartoon from a 16mm print.

The Joneses in the late 1950s: Albert, Millie, Julie, Jeff, and Eric.

Eleanor Stein was her father's pet, given unthinkable license to stay up late and get away with mischief.

Arthur and Annie Stein in 1960. His hair was white and his distinctive widow's peak had retreated even farther back on his forehead. By this time he had been out of work for years because of his appearances before HUAC.

August 1964. Eleanor and first husband Jonah Raskin doing the twist at their wedding reception at Tavern on the Green. The band, Jonah wrote later, "played out of tune, and they butchered the Beatles' songs, but they were drunk and happy. At the end they played 'The Internationale.'"

Eleanor with a raised fist salute in front of Columbia Law School, 1968.
Sometime during the course of the student uprising she had ceased to think
like a law student and identified herself completely with the movement.

(left) Jonah on the streets of Manchester, the original industrial city. Workers
lived along narrow, cobbled side roads in brick row houses, each peaked with
its own chimney pots. Friedrich Engels, coauthor of the *Communist Manifesto,*
had lived here for a time. He was certain that the sweatshops were manufacturing revolutionaries.

Eleanor in Havana in the summer of 1969. She went to the city of *revolución* in style with round, wire-rimmed glasses and hoops in her ears that she had fashioned out of bracelets—no jeweler made earrings big enough. It was there she met Nguyen Thai, a Vietcong fighter who had campaigned for decades against the French and American armies, and whose name she would remember when her first son was born eight years later.

Showing his solidarity with striking Levi's workers, Jeff took his jeans off on the sidewalk in front of Macy's in September 1967.

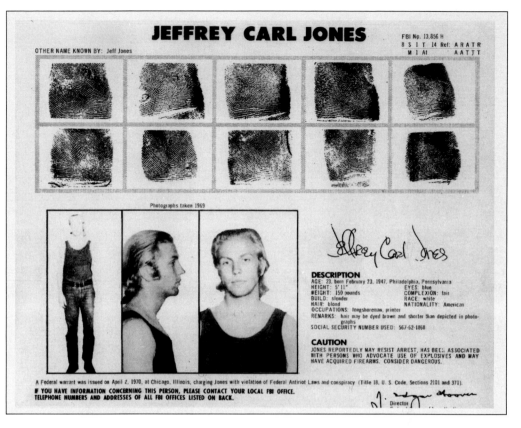

The mug shot for Jeff's wanted poster was taken during his greaser period in 1969. He and the other Weathermen always tried to look as tough as possible for the police photographers. The 1970 warrant for his arrest charged him with violation of federal antiriot laws and conspiracy, and said, "Consider dangerous."

Jeff and I pose in a photo booth, winter 1978.
His hair is dyed black—an impenetrable disguise.

Eleanor and Jeff's first wedding
photos, taken in a Woolworth's
photo booth in 1979. They were
married under assumed names and
used the certificate to acquire new
driver's licenses. Eleanor and Jeff
were Jean and James Hayes. I was
Timmy.

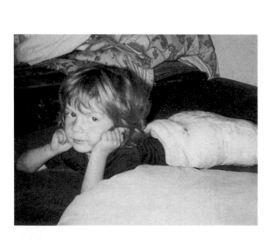

When I woke up after my surgery, I
had a steel clamp in place on my
bone and I smelled like wet
cement. A plaster cast ran from my
waist all the way down to the toes
on my left foot. Annie, who had
been battling cancer, was too weak
to walk by then. "I gave my legs to
Thai," she said. A week after my
surgery, Annie died.

On the run. I had watched my father with awe almost every morning for months as he returned home from a morning jog around the botanical gardens, slipped off his colorful sneakers, and peeled away his sweaty socks.

On December 11, 1981, a week before he was sentenced, Jeff Jones married Eleanor Stein at the Municipal Building in Lower Manhattan. They had wed before but not with those names. As they walked down the steps of the building after the two-minute ceremony, I reached into a bag and showered them with organic brown rice.

In 1966, when Jeff first joined SDS at Antioch, Millie left Albert Jones. She had never felt comfortable in the culture of Southern California, and after twenty-five years with Albert she felt unappreciated and passionless. When she moved to the Pacific Northwest she immediately knew she had found her home.

Chavy and Eleanor in the 1980s. In 1974, Annie and Chavy taught Marxism-Leninism to the new generation of radicals, now in hiding. By then, Chavy had transferred her allegiance from the Soviets to the Chinese, and was known in the underground as Comrade Wu. Together, Annie and Comrade Wu shared the lessons of almost fifty years of political activism that had begun when they met on a Brooklyn subway platform during the Roaring Twenties.

Gathering in the lobby, the marchers became sitters. Eleanor and the others started discussing their options, beginning a continuous meeting that would last for the next six days. Students outside beat on the door, wanting to go to class. Soon bananas, potato chips, and soda cans were circulating through the packed foyer of Hamilton Hall. The building took on the decor of a liberated zone, and posters of Lenin and Che, Malcolm X and Stokely Carmichael, went up amid red crepe paper and balloons.

In the evening, Eleanor left to go home to her husband and apartment. She passed back through College Walk, stepping over the camera cords of the press. Above her, students sat on the second-story ledge, watching the crowd outside grow and divide into factions. Here was a real lesson in contract law: the demonstrators felt there had been a breach, and now they were taking their restitution.

On Wednesday morning, Broadway looked like Piccadilly. Umbrellas were opened, and hard rain shined the sidewalks and rainbowed the oily streets. When Eleanor returned to campus, she learned that many protesters had stayed the night in Hamilton. Around dawn, the black students, wanting to make their own stand, had asked the whites to leave the building. Dejected, they had poured blinking into the light, while behind them chairs and tables were wedged against the doors. They looked out for another building to capture and with some hesitation had smashed a window in Low Library and occupied the office of the university president, Grayson Kirk. There they made themselves comfortable: reading files in his mahogany desk, smoking his White Owl cigars, tasting his sherry, and admiring his Rembrandt.

Outside Hamilton, the crowd had grown frayed and angry. Rain thinned the mass down to the zealots. Deans and faculty members kept an uneasy peace between two shoving, shouting groups: protesters and the conservative students. *Jock motherfuckers,* thought Eleanor. All the time, everyone kept a wary eye on the gates to campus, expecting an onslaught from Harlem at any moment.

Events had carried Eleanor to this point. She was sitting in her law school class. Then she was at the gym stomping on the chain fence and shouting at the police. Then she and hundreds more were occupying buildings, surprising even themselves. She was a law student with her mind on a career. Then she held a can of red paint in her hand and she was spraying a capital "N" three feet high on the side of Hamilton Hall. She made an "O," closing the circle with a flourish. She was writing "NO GYM!" on the limestone canvas, and before she finished, she saw several men moving out of the line of jocks.

They were almost on her as she dotted the exclamation point. One brawny arm grabbed her roughly. Then, in the role of *deus ex machina,* a black student on the second-floor ledge appeared with a fire extinguisher and sprayed the white foam all over her assailants. Eleanor was off, running through the crowd.

•••

Eleanor had learned to crawl, then walk, then march. She was in her mother's picket lines as soon as she could toddle. She had picked up the rudiments of socialism at the dinner table. Arthur, her father, had taken a lamb chop from the platter and placed it on her plate. Everyone in the world wants lamb chops, he said. But some people had no lamb chops while others ate two each night. There were even some greedy people who wanted more lamb chops than they could ever eat. Was it fair that they should acquire so many lamb chops, while others went hungry? No, Eleanor decided, it was not.

At school, she got a different lesson. One day her teacher taught her that all Communists were bad people. Annie and Arthur said, "No, that's not true." In fact, they told her, Annie's friend Chavy was a Communist. Of course, they couldn't tell her that they too belonged to the Party. Chavy's job was to indoctrinate Eleanor to the cause. She brought over a Soviet children's book, *The Story of Zoya and Shura,* which quickly became a favorite in the Stein house. "The crimson flag of our land, the land marching towards communism," the story began. "It bears the hammer and sickle, the symbol of peaceful labour and of the indissoluble unity between those who work, build and create. How many eyes, how many hearts are turned trustingly towards the Soviet Union—the hope and support of the working world!"

When Eleanor had finished, Chavy came over from the Lower East Side to discuss what she had read. Chavy explained to the girl that Communists were people who cared about the rights of blacks and the poor, who wanted peace in the world and more freedom to say what they believed in. "Oh," said the girl, "then my parents are Communists, too." Arthur and Annie burst out laughing; they couldn't even fool their own daughter.

Eleanor was a grade school crusader. When her music teacher passed out copies of Stephen Foster's "Dixie," the Confederate anthem, Eleanor took up a pen and wrote to America's leading black man, Ralph Bunche, a Nobel Peace Prize winner and the undersecretary general of the United Nations. Armed with his reply, she had Annie phone the principal and make an appointment. Eleanor went into his office and listened to him defend the song as an American classic. Then she whipped out her letter and said, "Well, Ralph Bunche agrees with me!" That was the fall of Old Dixie in P.S. 139.

When Annie moved to Brooklyn back in 1953, she had asked Mary Church Terrell for political advice. She was a little dismayed when the older woman suggested she join the local Parent Teacher Association. Annie had been a militant labor leader for decades and could not imagine herself hosting tea parties for the PTA. As usual, though, Mrs. Terrell had been right. School integration was the coming fight, and Annie would be in the middle of it for the next twenty years.

Eleanor never went to synagogue, but she spent a lot of time in the black churches of Brooklyn. Annie went and took Eleanor with her. In Brooklyn, and across the country, every church basement was decorated with a poster of the corpse of Emmett Till, the fourteen-year-old who had been kidnapped, shot, lynched, and thrown into a river in Mississippi. Till's mother had insisted on an open casket, and pictures of the body ran in black newspapers around the country. Eleanor, eight years old, saw it and had nightmares for months.

In Brooklyn, as in Washington, there were times when Annie's commitment was just too much. Vendors at Coney Island sold Confederate flags, and Eleanor was mortified by her mother's insistence on arguing about it with every single shop owner all the way down the boardwalk. Eleanor was closer to her father, who had gone through the ordeal of the witch hunt without losing his sense of fun.

With two uncooperative appearances before the House Committee on Un-American Activities on his résumé, Arthur had not had many job offers. Nine months after the family moved to Brooklyn, Annie had written to a friend that "Arthur is still looking for work, but he has many irons in the fire and is in good spirits." A typical FBI report from the late 1950s read, "[Arthur Stein] is at home during the day and night and apparently enjoys no steady employment." At times, he remodeled homes as a self-employed contractor and he even tried to market—unsuccessfully—a device called the Continental Bain-Marie, a European invention made from a candle and a metal box that kept food warm at the dinner table.

Finally, by 1961, Arthur was a working man again. He had a job in midtown Manhattan, conducting market research in an office filled with other Reds and run by the brother of Leonard Boudin, the famous progressive lawyer. Arthur traveled for his job and worked long hours, which made Annie nervous. She had spent thirty years worrying about the time bomb in his chest. Whenever he wanted to go for a swim or play catch with Philip, she reeled him back. Each time he was a few minutes late, she started to panic.

Arthur looked older than his fifty-two years. His hair was white, and his distinctive widow's peak had retreated even further from his forehead. He had gained weight and grown jowly in his cheeks and neck. He still smoked, gripping his cigarettes in fingers kept raw by constant nail biting. A stranger might have guessed that he was facing stressful days at the office.

He had spent his whole life shunning the corporate world, and being a capitalist depressed him. He cast around for a cause and embraced the Cuban revolution of 1959. He followed the victory of Fidel Castro and Ernesto Che Guevara and visited Havana with Annie in the summer of 1960. Back home, Arthur founded a Brooklyn chapter of the Fair Play for Cuba Committee. When Castro visited New York City in the fall, the Steins invited *El Presidente* to stay at their house in Brooklyn. "As you know," replied one of Castro's lieutenants, "the Prime Minister is already staying at the Teresa Hotel in Harlem, but we are saving your letter to show it to him when he returns, so that he will learn of your generous offer."

In early June 1961, Eleanor had final exams to worry about. She was finishing her sophomore year at Erasmus Hall High School in Flatbush. After dinner, she spread her assignments and textbooks on the kitchen table and her father helped her prepare for her math tests. He invented little formulas to enliven the subject. When Eleanor was studying geometry, he instructed her that "a slope is what you washed your flace with." Another one went, "The bases of the Pentagon circumscribe the hemisphere." While she clashed with Annie often, Eleanor remained her father's pet, given unthinkable license to stay up late and get away with mischief.

Eleanor was a fixture on the honor roll. She was editor-in-chief of the *Dutchman,* the Erasmus student newspaper. In junior high school she had written poetry with political messages such as these opening lines from a poem called "The North Star:"

A heavenly guide for refugee,
The way to freedom
For those escaped from the shackles of slavery,
And martyrdom.

Later, she read Blake and Shelley, and her poetry in the school literary journal was closer to the Victorian taste. She was captain of the debating team and secretary for the math team. She traveled to Manhattan during school days to take college courses in French. She studied painting at the Brooklyn Museum of Art. On weekends, she and her more daring friends took their guitars to play in Washington Square Park. Despite these accomplishments, the parents of Eleanor's friends were uneasy about the Stein family. Her school chums had brought home awed tales of her outspoken classroom defenses of socialism. After Annie and Arthur traveled to Cuba, Eleanor's best friend Naomi was told by her parents that she must never see the Steins again, ensuring the girls' lifelong friendship.

Each summer since grade school, the end of exams had brought Camp Lakeside, where Eleanor was sent with other leftist children to stay in a cluster of sagging cabins along a mosquito-rich pond in Norwich, Connecticut. To suppress class distinctions, campers were forbidden from bringing their own clothes. Instead, all were outfitted in blue jeans and T-shirts, and on laundry days the girls fought like fishwives for the best ones.

This summer, she was to be spared Camp Lakeside. The family had gone in April to update their passports for one month of touring in England, France, and Italy. In fact, they had other plans. For years, angry passersby seeing Annie and Arthur on the picket lines had yelled, "Why don't you go back to Russia?" The Steins were finally going to take this advice. The whole family—including Arthur's aging mother, Sadie—was returning to the shtetls from whence it had come more than half a century earlier. Their flight was leaving on July 15.

June 27, 1961, was a day of lasts for Arthur. He woke and ate his last breakfast. He saw his last newspaper: "Eichmann Testifies"; "7 Killed in Algeria"; "Khrushchev Adds to Berlin Threat." It was cloudy and cool for June. Annie drove him to the McDonald Avenue station, and he rode the subway to his office on Forty-Seventh Street. He had his last lunch at a place that he liked, Berger's deli. He went back to his office for the afternoon and then set out to meet his best friend, Al Bernstein, for dinner.

It was seventy-two degrees in Central Park. Midtown, where the steel and glass buildings reflected the heat, was a little hotter. It was a pleasant night, but as he walked downtown on Sixth Avenue, he must have known that something was wrong. Arthur knew the symptoms of a heart attack. It was a busy street—tourists and office workers sought the subways. In front of 1169 Sixth Avenue, he fell face forward. He did not put out his arms to brace the fall. He landed on his forehead and was dead. Arthur lay on the sidewalk for several minutes before anyone stopped to check whether he needed help.

Pedestrians parted around him, a lifeless island in a sea of strangers.

Eleanor and Annie were in the living room. Annie sat at her desk. Eleanor was perched along the backrest of the couch, lounging with a book, in an attitude that she knew annoyed her mother. At 6:10 P.M., the phone rang. Al Bernstein was on the line. He told Annie that Arthur was ten minutes late for their dinner reservation. She was pale when she put down the receiver. She whispered to herself, "Oh my God, oh my God, oh my God" as she walked into the kitchen to call the police. Eleanor hardly noticed. Her mother had taken leave of her senses again. She always acted like this. He was only ten minutes late.

The police called that evening. They had found him. Al Bernstein went to the city mortuary at Bellevue Hospital and identified Arthur's body. Annie came into the living room and hugged Eleanor. "Something terrible has happened . . ."

The funeral was in Brooklyn, and the seats were filled with Artie's comrades. Speakers talked about his work and about the sacrifices he had made for his principles. Driving home, Annie said to her fifteen-year-old daughter, "No one mentioned how handsome he was."

Eleanor's friends were always over; they took her for walks around the block and tried to make her laugh. She had a sudden realization—*my childhood is over*—and the thought itself made her feel like an adult. For two weeks, the house was filled with guests. Neighbors brought food and stayed to eat it. The phone was never quiet. Letters and telegrams of condolence rose in a pile on the hall table. Then the moment came when the last guest left.

Eleanor and Annie had been uneasy friends, and each had used Arthur as an intermediary—someone to whom they could complain about the other. Annie had collapsed when the police had called with the news that she had been expecting for all those years. Now that it had happened, at least her fear was gone. For Eleanor, whose parents had kept her father's health a secret, his death had come as a complete surprise. He had been her invulnerable man. She had not prepared, but then again, she had been given a childhood free of worry—about this at least.

Annie sold the house in Brooklyn and moved with Eleanor to Park West Village, a new housing development on the western border of Central Park. She liked to sit on her balcony and look out over the trees, though in twenty years of residence, she would almost never set foot within the stone walls of the park.

Around this time, she left the Communist Party by the most common means: she was expelled. The tiny, fragmented CP U.S.A. seemed always to be looking for new ways to trim its membership rolls. This time the issue was Maoist China, which had broken with the Soviets. Annie's sympathies were with the Chinese, and she was kicked out. Chavy, who had risen to become a leading organizer, was given a choice. One of her oldest comrades approached her and said, "You can either quit or be expelled." Chavy quit.

Annie was out of the Party but she was still a lowercase-"c" communist. She kept her sense of righteous indignation and passion for civil rights. She and Eleanor went to the capital for the 1963 March on Washington. There they heard Martin Luther King and Bayard Rustin, whom Annie disliked. They also learned of the death of W.E.B. Du Bois, whom she had adored.

Back from the crowds at the rally, they found themselves alone again. Instead of a whole house in which to tiptoe around each other, they now had only a two-bedroom apartment. Eleanor solved the problem by spending as much time as possible away from home. Annie, as always, brought her work home with her. She moved her filing cabinets, typewriter, and mimeograph machine to Manhattan and set up a new command post at the kitchen table.

•••

Despite all its problems, the adult world in 1963 seemed, Eleanor thought, to spend most of its energy ensuring that young, unmarried girls did not have sex. At Barnard College, where she was a freshman that year, students could have male visitors only during prescribed hours, and not too late. When a boy was present, the door to the room had to be left open, and both parties had to keep at least one foot in contact with the floor at all times. Any girl who violated these rules was expelled. Sex was the issue of the day between Annie and her daughter too, especially once Eleanor started dating Jonah.

She met Jonah Raskin, a friend of a friend, in her first week of college. Smoking a pipe on the steps of Barnard Hall, he looked cool—or at least the early-'60s version. He wore a tweed jacket with leather elbow patches and reminded Eleanor of Jean-Paul Belmondo, the French ex-boxer who had become a star in the coolest film of the time, Jean-Luc Godard's *Breathless*. Annie, meeting Jonah, was less impressed. "He looks like a heap of old clothes," she whispered to Eleanor as soon as he was safely out of hearing.

Eleanor and Jonah did the things all couples did. When Madame Nhu, sister-in-law of South Vietnamese President Diem, spoke on campus, they threw eggs at her, and Jonah chased her limousine and spat on the window. He was twenty-two—five years older than Eleanor, as Annie often mentioned—and a graduate student in the English department. His parents were progressives from Long Island, but he envisioned for himself a future life as a rebel professor.

They went together to Eleanor's mother's apartment after President Kennedy was assassinated. Annie and several of her black colleagues from the school integration movement watched as reporters speculated on the identity of the shooter. Annie's friends wrung their hands, repeating to themselves, "I just hope he's white . . . I just hope he's white."

Annie saw where this relationship was headed, and she didn't like it. She sat her daughter down and poured herself a scotch and soda. She told Eleanor about her experiences on April Farm, a free love commune she had visited in the 1930s. There had been promiscuity there, and everyone, men and women, was made miserable by it.

"I know you're passionate and he's a great guy," Annie said, "but a sexual relationship is a big commitment." She made her daughter promise to wait until her eighteenth birthday before having sex. As compensation, she attempted to bribe the young couple with theater tickets and keep them from temptation with dinners at the Russian Tea Room.

She tried to reason with them and quoted Lenin on the subject of sex. Some randy Bolshevik had compared having sex to taking a drink of water. "I do not consider the famous 'glass-of-water' theory as Marxist at all," Lenin had responded dryly. "Of course thirst must be quenched," he conceded. "But will a normal person under normal conditions lie down in the gutter and drink from a puddle? Or even from a glass the edge of which has been touched by dozens of lips?" Lenin's oratory had helped topple an empire, but Eleanor refused to listen. She found ways to dodge her mother's vigilance. She left early for school to visit Jonah's apartment. They went together to a doctor who specialized in such things and got a diaphragm.

Classes were an afterthought. Eleanor took Barnard's required freshman English class, "Reading and Writing." She got a failing grade on one essay in European history because she put Karl Marx in the footnotes. "Marx," her professor noted on the paper, "is not a source we use in this college." Jonah got a summer teaching job in Winston-Salem, North Carolina. The town was decorated with statues of Robert E. Lee and Jefferson Davis, and all of Jonah's students were black. He was supposed to teach basic grammar, but instead the class read James Baldwin and Richard Wright. Letters in the town paper suggested he "ought to go back North." In August, Eleanor joined him. To avoid scandal they posed as a married couple. After that, the decision to have a real wedding was easy.

On August 28, 1964, Eleanor put on her favorite green dress and went with Jonah to the Foley Square Courthouse. They sat waiting for the judge—Jonah and his parents, Eleanor and Annie. They both missed Arthur. The reception was at Tavern on the Green in Central Park. Most of the guests were Annie's friends. For Chavy, a permanent New Yorker, it was the only time in her life that she stepped foot inside the famous restaurant. Annie hired a band consisting, Jonah wrote later, of "friends from the 1930's who once played at Soviet-American friendship rallies, CIO dances, and benefits for the survivors of the Abraham Lincoln Brigade. They played out of tune, and they butchered the Beatles' songs, but they were drunk and happy. At the end they played 'The Internationale.'" The next morn-

ing, Annie drove the newlyweds to Kennedy Airport, where they
boarded a flight for England, where Jonah was going to earn his
Ph.D.

Manchester was the original industrial city. Factory stacks rose like a
forest beside the banks of the ship canal. Workers lived along narrow
cobbled side roads in brick row houses, each with its own chimney
pots. Friedrich Engels, coauthor of the *Communist Manifesto,* had
lived in Manchester for a time. He was certain that the sweat shops
were manufacturing revolutionaries. It was here in England, not on
the steppes of peasant Russia, where he and Marx expected the pro-
letariat to shed the blood of its masters.

Mr. and Mrs. Raskin found a flat at 68 Clyde Road, in Didsbury, a
neighborhood with a large Jewish population and the nickname
"Yidsbury." They had no refrigerator—only the wealthy in England
could afford that luxury. At night they turned on BBC radio and
tried to keep warm. Before bed, Jonah trudged down to the coal cellar and brought the briquettes up in a scuttle, dirtying everything he
touched. Neither of them ever mastered the art of starting the fire,
and even when the meager thing was lit, it provided heat only to the
side of the body facing the flames. They developed chilblains—
excruciating chapped skin between the toes—that came with constant cold and punished all the English alike, regardless of class.

Eleanor began taking undergraduate courses at the University of
Manchester. Administrators were dubious when they saw she had
studied "Reading and Writing" during her first year at Barnard. In
England, they told her, those skills were customarily taught prior to
entering college. She assured the admissions department that she had
mastered her ABCs and joined the school's nascent American studies
program. Later, at a sherry party, she found herself talking with the
head of the university's English department. He asked her what
course she was enrolled in, and Eleanor told him she studied
American history. "Oh," he asked politely, "what do you do in the
afternoons?"

Most days, she spent the afternoons picking up groceries in
Market Street or clothes shopping in St. Ann's Square. She went with

Jonah to the house where Engels had lived, and they worked in the Central Library, where he had written. In the evenings, Eleanor played guitar and sang in Manchester's pubs. The city that had once been known for its factories was getting a reputation for its music. Many groups of the British Invasion, including Herman's Hermits, the Hollies, and Freddie and the Dreamers, got their start on these stages. Eleanor played with a local band, performing a mix of Welsh standards and American blues. Some nights they earned as much as twenty quid. One day, a local paper listed her as Eleanor Raskin, from Harlem, U.S.A. That evening, dozens of African American GIs stationed in the north of England came to the gig expecting to see a black blues singer.

In February 1965, Eleanor and Jonah traveled to the London School of Economics. There was standing room only in the auditorium for the night's speaker, Malcolm X. For the international audience, Malcolm discussed imperialism. "They send the Peace Corps to Nigeria and hired killers to the Congo. What is the Peace Corps?" he asked. "Exactly what it says: Get a piece of your country." A week later Malcolm X was assassinated in Harlem.

•••

In April 1965, Annie visited her daughter in England. She was unaware of the frenzy of extra work her vacation created for the Federal Bureau of Investigation, but had she known, it would surely have pleased her. In March, the bureau's Washington office received the news from a source who "advised that the subject planned to visit her daughter in England." This startling intelligence activated the wheels of justice. On April 20, a special agent called the office of Yeshiva University where Annie was working as a statistician. "Under the guise of a personal friend seeking the subject," the agent learned that Annie had left at the start of the month and planned to stay in England for "25–30 days." The New York office requested that the Washington bureau review Annie's "requests to the Passport Office."

On May 5, after Annie had already returned, the requested information arrived. On February 4, she had indeed received passport number F-100343, valid for three years of travel to "all countries except Albania, Cuba, and those portions of China, Korea, and Viet-Nam under communist control." Concerning travel plans, "Mrs. Stein indicated she would leave New York City on approximately March 23, 1965, via the ship *Franconia* for a one month stay abroad."

On May 26, a special agent called Annie "under the guise of a fictitious travel agency" and learned that she had recently returned from a trip to England. The news was immediately relayed to London and the office of the director. America was safe again.

•••

After three years in England, Eleanor was anxious to return home. The war was escalating in Vietnam, and American students were in upheaval. In some ways, growing up around stories of the 1930s, she had lived her whole life in anticipation of a chance to join such a movement. She wanted to apply to law school at Columbia, the university her father and brother had attended. As a girl, Eleanor had been surrounded by progressive lawyers. She had seen the way they used intellect to further political causes and at the same time earned public notoriety and respect. Even the most radical lawyers had been able to earn a living and avoid serious persecution during the 1950s, when many other activists were out of work and facing prison.

Her thesis earned her first-class honors, the first American studies graduate at Manchester to earn that distinction—not bad for a Jewish girl from Harlem, U.S.A. In the summer of 1967, she and Jonah returned to New York City and got the apartment at 250 Riverside Drive. Soon after law school began, Eleanor went with her mother to the protest at the Pentagon. Annie was as militant as protesters one-third her age; she had had all that extra time to store up hatred for the military. Eleanor watched her mother scale a wire fence and shout wild curses at the building. Eleanor hung back. She was on her way to becoming a lawyer, and her mother's behavior seemed excessive, even unseemly.

•••

By sunrise on Thursday, April 25, 1968, Columbia students occupied four buildings: Hamilton Hall; the president's suite in Low Library;

Avery Hall, home of the school of architecture; and Fayerweather Hall. "I arrived," Eleanor wrote to friends in England, "to find that the white brothers—and by then, we were calling each other that, as we still are, and meaning it too—had taken . . . Fayerweather Hall, the main postgraduate classroom building, which was to be my home for the next five days." Its stone floors and wooden banisters had been polished by the passing feet and hands of seventy-one consecutive graduating classes, but it had never been designed to accommodate three hundred occupants. There was no soft surface in the building, only classrooms and offices with thin, unforgiving carpets that made for uncomfortable sleeping.

Shortly after midnight on Friday, students took a fifth building—Mathematics. This was where the real crazies stationed themselves. Outside agitators, drawn to the smell of action like sharks to blood, came to Mathematics, climbed onto the chest-high ledge, and wriggled through a narrow window into the stronghold. Among the most militant, stealing on and off campus with borrowed ID cards, was the SDS regional coordinator, Jeff Jones.

Eleanor had stood out from her law class by her clothes. Now she was completely isolated from most of her peers. There were more than 700 squatters in the liberated buildings but only a handful from the law school. Most of Eleanor's classmates thought that the participants in the rebellion should be punished. The whole campus was split, and armbands told the sides apart. The protesters wore red and the faculty white. Students who had not entered the buildings but were in favor of amnesty wore green. Baby blues were against the protests but also averse to police action. Medical students wore "medical presence" bands.

Eleanor, as a law student, had a white twist of cotton with the words "legal observer" in pen. Her status kept her from total commitment. As long as she wore her observer badge, she would always have an explanation for her time in the liberated buildings. She was thinking about her career—worried about the police, her law professors, future employers.

The band also gave her freedom of movement around the campus and earned her a position as runner, passing messages between the buildings. Hamilton had been temporarily christened "Malcolm X" Hall. In Low Library, students had taped "Liberated Area: Join Us!" on the president's window. The wild men in Mathematics had hung a giant portrait of Mao in the front window. On Saturday night, Eleanor was running across the central campus delivering a message. Red flags, spotlighted in the dark, flew from the flag poles on the roofs of the five liberated buildings. Eleanor was also part of the Building Defense Committee, in charge of blocking the doors. Overturned desks, chairs, sofas, all piled together like kindling for a bonfire, made the barricade. It wasn't as pretty as those built by the architecture students in Avery, but it would suffice.

Jonah slept in Fayerweather and drove to his job at Stony Brook in the mornings. Day and night, he was the lone professor among students. He wore his tweed jackets, shaved daily, smoked a pipe. In class he was Dr. Raskin, but in Fayerweather he was an outsider. Conversations seemed to cut short when he came around, and once, as he approached a group of students, one whispered, "there's a cop listening, cool it." Meanwhile, his wife was entirely wrapped up in being a part of the new community. The couple began to feel the strain. He and Eleanor took an afternoon off from the rebellion and walked to Grant's Tomb on 123rd Street.

"Do you want to leave me?" he asked.

"I don't know," she said.

"What do you know?"

"Sometimes," she said, "I want to take my guitar, say goodbye to everyone, get into a bus, and go away."

In the free society of Fayerweather on Sunday night, the citizens gathered in the main room. "The Pageant Players, a wonderful radical mime troupe, gave a very simple and lovely play," Eleanor wrote, "which turned into a beat bacchanal, with the whole audience of 300 taking part, everyone with a rhythm instrument, even if only a spaghetti tin. It became a real primitive rite, more unifying and inspiring than any political rally could have been." Amid the drumming, a bride and groom appeared in white at the top of the stairs. She carried a handful of daisies; he wore a Black Power button. The ceremony was held by candlelight. A college minister performed the simple catechism and, while the cheers and percussions started again, told the couple "I now pronounce you children of the new age."

On Saturday and Sunday, rumors of police action washed through the liberated halls every hour, soaking morale. By Monday, when more than one thousand New York City police officers were being gathered from all five boroughs and massed at Manhattan precinct houses, the students in the buildings had become inured to rumor and began to think the police wouldn't come after all. At the 24th Precinct on 100th Street, less than two blocks from Annie's apartment, police buses and paddy wagons lined up along both curbs as if they were forming up for a parade.

Hundreds of members of the city's elite riot squad, the Tactical Patrol Force, entered the campus and took up positions. Around each building was a cordon of sympathizers, professors, family, and friends, hoping their presence would prevent violence. Annie stood outside Fayerweather Hall as she had for most of the week, bringing food and organizing local support for the students.

At 2:10 A.M. on Tuesday, the water and phones were cut to all the occupied buildings. The black students in Hamilton had made a deal with the police, and they marched out willingly to be arrested. The other buildings were stormed one by one. The police emptied Low Library, then Avery. There, police dragged students instead of carrying them out, and then formed a hazing line, pummeling the arrested protesters with nightsticks as they were yanked down stairs.

The assault on Avery was visible from Fayerweather Hall, a few feet across a small quad. Inside, the students had split into two rooms: a classroom was designated for those who wanted to cooperate with the arresting officers and a student lounge was for those who planned to passively resist. It was a subtle distinction: the cooperators would walk out, the resistors would go limp and allow themselves to be carried. Eleanor was in the resistors' wing. Sometime during the course of the week she had removed her "legal observer" armband and identified herself completely with the movement.

Each classroom had a wall clock. Under normal circumstances, students would watch it tick off the last five minutes of class and then sprint from their seats. On the morning of April 30, 1968, as the hands marked 2:20 A.M., Fayerweather Commune watched and waited for their attackers to appear. Eleanor linked arms with Gus Reichbach and sang "We Shall Overcome," a song she had learned from her mother during her earliest days. They sang in quavering voices, especially when they came to the verse, "We are not afraid."

Outside, the Tactical Patrol Force crowded around Fayerweather. Annie and the other spectators linked arms, yelled, and pleaded for restraint. Fifty uniformed policemen and as many plainclothesmen in helmets started to work on the doors. "It took a long time for the cops to break down the barricades," Eleanor wrote, "and when they came in they were swinging pieces of furniture and blackjacks. . . . I saw my closest friend, a law student, who had been sitting next to me, carried out—he went limp, and a cop blackjacked him in the back of the head. All I could see for a couple of minutes was his huge gaping wound and his face and chest covered with blood. Then they picked me up to carry me out—four giant policemen. They kicked me, picked me up by the hair, pulled up my skirt and commented. I got mad, unwisely, and struggled—they dragged me down a gravel path and threw me into a heap of bloody brothers, to be put into the paddy wagons."

Eleanor was dragged face down over the pebble-embedded pavement and onto Amsterdam Avenue. Her knees scraped along the path, leaving scars that would never vanish. Time stretched while they pulled her along, and her senses grew more acute. She could hear her mother's voice. Annie was following the police, screaming at them. "You be careful with her," Annie shouted at the four cops. "That's my daughter. She's a law student. You be careful with her. I'll take your number."

Waiting for the transfer to jail, the battered students banged on the paddy wagon walls and continued to sing. The only doctor present, a volunteer who had lived in the buildings during the strike, told the cops to be careful with Eleanor, who had blood all over her legs. The plainclothesman who was supervising operations said, "We'll take care of her—she's a troublemaker." Then, Eleanor wrote, "Four more picked me up to put me into the wagon—I kicked the plainclothesman and he dropped me and handcuffed my ankles together, very tightly, cursing like mad. Then they threw me against the wall of the paddy wagon, and we drove off to court!"

More than 700 students and protesters were in Black Marias dispersing toward the city's jails. When the buildings were emptied, squads of plainclothesmen moved in. The halls had suffered from housing hundreds of squatters, but the communes had mostly kept good order, and when they were evicted in the middle of the night, the buildings were surprisingly clean and undamaged. Witnesses saw the plainclothesmen get to work: smashing furniture, opening locked doors and stealing cash and liquor, painting obscene or revolutionary slogans on the wall. By dawn, the damage was irreparable—all of it blamed on the students.

During the occupation, polls had shown a large majority of the campus against SDS, but the violence of the bust had turned most teachers and students around. A pariah group representing a small minority a week earlier, SDS captured the spirit of the campus in its new leaflet, posted on walls and buildings before the blood had dried on the steps of Low Library:

> At 2:30 this morning, Columbia University died . . . WE WILL AVENGE THE 139 WOUNDED MEMBERS OF THE LIBERATION. . . . DOWN WITH THE UNIVERSITY, UP WITH THE STUDENTS, UP WITH THE COMMUNITY, LONG LIVE THE FORCES OF LIBERATION AT COLUMBIA.

"It's a good lesson, I think, for every law student, to take it on the other side," Eleanor wrote, "eight hours in jail with no food, lights on all the time (after a sleepless night), forty sisters in one tiny cell." The prisoners maintained the spirit of the commune in the jails, singing solidarity and tipsy with victory. It was the busiest day in the history of 100 Centre Street, New York City's main criminal court. When Eleanor was finally brought before a judge, the courtroom was filled with hundreds of people. She was charged with criminal trespass, fined $25, and released without bail. Annie was there waiting, worried sick and proud as hell.

...

Eleanor and Jonah's Riverside Drive apartment still kept its English influence in the summer of 1969. The furniture was bright and mod. Aubrey Beardsley prints hung on the walls. They had a red telephone. On a late June night, it rang. Bernardine Dohrn, SDS interorganizational secretary, was on the line; she gave a number and told Eleanor to go down to a pay phone and call her back. The precaution made Eleanor uneasy, and as she placed her call from a booth on Broadway, she looked up and down the sidewalk for men in black suits and brown shoes. Bernardine told her that she was serving as cruise director for an American delegation that was traveling to Havana in a few weeks to meet with representatives of the National Liberation Front and the North Vietnamese government. Eleanor signed on immediately.

On July 7, she flew from New York City to Miami, where she met up with the rest of the group. There were thirty-four of them, a cross-section, as the Vietnamese had requested, of the American antiwar movement. Waiting in the Miami Airport for her flight to Mexico City, Eleanor had a fear that the government was watching her. It was. Her tension vanished in the air between Mexico and Havana as she left behind the specter of federal agents and the stewardesses served in-flight daiquiris. Ahead were Havana—the city of revolution that her parents had visited ten years earlier—and the Vietnamese.

They were her heroes, giants of world struggle. Fighting was not their choice, but until their country was free, no one would remain idle. She pictured a farmer ankle-deep in milky rice water with a basket of grain on one shoulder and an AK-47 on the other. One of her favorite photos showed a beautiful Vietnamese woman with long black hair lying on a reed mat in a city street aiming an old-fashioned rifle.

José Martí Airport, on Havana's fringe, was a low-profile terminal planted in a palm grove. The plane parked on the tarmac, and Eleanor stepped from the cabin onto the movable stairs that led to the steaming blacktop. The Vietnamese were waiting at the end of the steps. For giants, they were surprisingly tiny and raggedy-looking. The men wore cotton pajamas faded to a threadbare gray. The women were in traditional black *ao dai* dresses with slits at the neck and along the leg.

All the Vietnamese spoke English and inquired sympathetically about the trip. They commiserated over the difficulties the Americans had faced to come here. In the next few days, Eleanor learned how the Vietnamese themselves had traveled. Those representing the Hanoi government had flown the Iron Curtain local: Vietnam-Beijing-Moscow-Prague-Havana. The fighters from the South had walked; it had taken months for some to travel from the southernmost provinces of Vietnam, up the Ho Chi Minh Trail in wary stages to Hanoi, before beginning the long flight.

Havana was a time capsule from 1959. Since then, few major buildings had gone up, and almost no new cars had been imported. The colorful but crumbling stucco walls made the Old City seem like a pirate capital. The delegates were installed in an empty school in a suburban neighborhood. They ate stringy people's chicken and bland socialist rice and beans in the cafeteria. The official meeting lasted seven days and was led by the Vietnamese, who believed the war was in its final stage and that a strong antiwar movement in the United States could help end it even sooner. They had brought Eleanor and the others to Havana to try to teach them how to create that unified mass movement.

The Vietnamese teachers lectured in the mornings and afternoons. In the evenings, they all watched documentary films. At dinner, everyone mingled and mixed. Eleanor spent most meals with a National Liberation Front fighter from near Hue City. He was middle-aged and had been a soldier for twenty years. He had fought the French until 1954 and the Americans ever since. Somehow he did not hold the people of the United States responsible for the policies of their government. In 1968 he had fought in Hue during the Tet Offensive, one of the most intense battles of the war. He believed that his wife was alive but had not seen her in almost a decade. When the war was over, he said, they would meet again to build a new Vietnam. His name was Nguyen Thai.

One morning they sat in a classroom and learned about political slogans. A Vietnamese instructor stood at the blackboard with a piece of chalk. He called for examples that the Americans used in the movement. People shouted out responses: "No More Vietnams," "Two, Three, Many Vietnams," "No More Wars," "Bring the War Home," "Long Live the Victory of the People's War," "Make Love Not War." When the board was filled with slogans, the teacher asked his students if they recognized a problem. A revolution had stages, and each stage had a strategic goal. The entire population needed to be instructed of this goal through slogans. The contradictions in the American chants would only weaken and confuse the movement.

They went to the Bay of Pigs where the CIA had tried to invade Castro's island in 1961. Many of the bombed houses were left as a memorial to the American attack. Traveling with Thai and the others was like touring with movie stars. Cubans wanted to see and touch them. There was a museum of the People's War filled with guerrilla booby traps, weaponry, and other exhibits from Vietnam. Eleanor asked Thai what his favorite weapon was. He thought for a moment and said, "Bamboo." A sharpened bamboo stake was silent and light, there was no ammunition to carry, and if it rained, you could stick it into the ground, hang leaves from it, and make a tent.

The Vietnamese and Cubans were the vanguard of world anti-colonialism, yet they had different styles. The Cubans explained that their revolution was *con pachanga,* with pizzazz, but remained constrained and decorous in the presence of the Vietnamese. Luckily, most of them usually bowed and retired to bed soon after dinner. Then the rum flowed and Cubans started throwing Americans— fully clothed—into the swimming pool.

The Cuban government felt that it would be unsafe for the Americans to fly back. Instead, it offered a merchant ship to steam them home. It took two weeks for the *Miguel Ascunçe* to make its rusty way around Cuba and then up the coast to Canada. Its precious cargo was fish meal, processed marine entrails that could be used as fertilizer. The whole Atlantic wasn't big enough to disperse the smell. The Americans refused to sit idly as passengers. They insisted on working for their passage, and Eleanor, with a bandanna over her nose and mouth, shoveled the fish meal down in the hold.

During long meetings, they began to put the Vietnamese lessons to work. They drafted pamphlets and slogans, preparing for a new strategy of mass involvement. Instead of bickering over sectarian divisions, they would unify the movement around one strategic slogan, "End the War Now." When the *Ascunçe* arrived in St. John's, New Brunswick, everything was prepared. The posters were drawn. Leaflets were written and ready for the press.

Two representatives from SDS were waiting at the dock to update Bernardine on the changes she had missed. New leaders had been elected in June: Mark Rudd, leader of the Columbia uprising, was now national secretary; Bill Ayers, from the University of Michigan, was education secretary; and the new interorganizational secretary was a blond hippie from Los Angeles, Jeff Jones. In July and August they had turned away from a mass movement. Students for a Democratic Society was split, and instead of organizing demonstrations, many of its most committed members had divided into small collectives where they were out of sight to most Americans. In the fall, they planned a national action in Chicago that, rather than bringing in the masses who opposed the war, would be so militant that only a hard-core gang would participate.

Before Eleanor had even clanked down the gangway to the shore, Nguyen Thai's plan for an all-encompassing mass movement was sunk.

CHAPTER 8

Days of Rage

OULD it be possible that it was October 8, 1969, and Jeff was
back in Chicago? The Lake-fed wind was growing cold
again, blowing unwelcome gusts across the Loop. The leaves
had turned, and nights were getting longer. Autumn had arrived.

Only a moment ago, summer was beginning, and the leaders of a
splintered SDS were meeting to call for the violent demonstration
that would begin this evening. It had seemed like the distant future.
Each day in between had been crowded from rise-up to bed-down
with gut-checks and discipline. Time ran fast and slow together, and
Jeff ran with it, all the way back to Pig City.

The *Chicago Tribune* was still predicting the radical apocalypse and
playing rumors big across the front page. The previous summer, during the Democratic National Convention, it was the police who had
made most of the trouble, but this time the prophecies were true:
SDS was here to rampage. On October 6, a bomb exploded under
the police statue in Haymarket Square. Its bronze legs were blown
onto the northbound lanes of the Kennedy Expressway, while its
torso lay facedown at the base of its twelve-foot stone pedestal.
Haymarket Square, site of an 1886 riot where a bomb had been
hurled into a phalanx of officers, was the scheduled starting point for

SDS's final protest of the week. "We now feel," said the president of the Chicago Police Sergeants Association, "that it is kill or be killed."

Which is exactly how Jeff felt as he started getting ready for the evening's action. He had been one of the main organizers and had worked since summer to promote the march. "Bring the War Home" was the slogan for the demonstration, which would come to be known as the Days of Rage. It was a new kind of protest, and its genesis came from a new political party. Both had coalesced during oppressive summer discussions. No drugs or booze had been allowed around the table, just ice water and deadly, sobering rhetoric. After many all-nighters, the group had drafted and redrafted a 15,000-word manifesto. Signing it, they felt like communist John Hancocks: Karin Ashley, Bill Ayers, Bernardine Dohrn, John Jacobs, Jeff Jones, Gerry Long, Howie Machtinger, Jim Mellen, Terry Robbins, Mark Rudd, and Steve Tappis. Terry had suggested the title, "You Don't Need a Weatherman to Know Which Way the Wind Blows" from a speed-rapping Bob Dylan song with enough good lyrics to cull names for a dozen organizations.

Jeff walked into the bathroom and placed two bottles of powerful chemicals on the sink. He pulled the old-fashioned chain to turn on the light and faced his reflection in the grimy mirror. His trademark blond hair was trimmed down from the ponytail he'd worn in summer to the slicked-back style of a juvenile delinquent. He combed and greased it from his forehead and let it curl out below his ears. For years he had been the most blond among a dark crowd of angry easterners. Now he opened the bottles of Clairol hair dye. He poured one into the other, activating the ingredients, and brushed the combination into his scalp. The instructions said to leave the tingling mixture on for half an hour.

He looked at the time. There were hours still to go until nightfall. He tried to imagine what the park would look like at 10:00 P.M. He had been there during the Democratic National Convention in August 1968, but then there had been drugs, music, and a sense of fun. This night would be darker. He visualized the demonstration as it was about to begin. The park was filled with people, a strong group, disciplined and angry. Looking out over them he could see black and brown faces among the whites. The usual college students would be reinforced by younger, angrier high school kids. They would have come from across the country, responding to the bugle call, the chance to bust up some cops and bring the war home. Beyond their ranks, the police would sit and wait, making the classic error of preparing for the last war. This year, the protesters would not allow themselves to be attacked.

The people's army had fresh tactics and a new destination. All that remained to swing it into action was the word of Jeff's command and the surprise announcement of their objective. Only he and a few others knew the plan, and it was his task to stand before this army, give the signal, divulge the target, and lead them on to victory.

In the shower he rubbed out the dye. Dripping everywhere in his impatience, he examined his dark brown hair in front of the mirror. It was not the transformation, the rebirth, that he'd imagined. The night's events also would not match his mental image. Already he knew the crowds would fall far short of the "tens of thousands" they'd predicted in the summer. But there was still hope that the troops would come. He suspected his own failure at organizing but hoped that others had been more successful. The people might still arrive, Jeff thought, from Cleveland, Detroit, Cincinnati, New York, Seattle, San Francisco, Madison.

Well, he didn't expect many from Madison. He had driven there in September. Along with four other Weathermen dressed in combat fatigues and carrying National Liberation Front flags, he had burst into a meeting of more than a thousand students and faculty. Someone in the crowd shouted, "It's Jeff Jones! It's Weatherman!" Jeff ran toward the stage, leaped on to it, and shoved the speaker off to the side. The others lined up behind him striking karate stances. He shouted, "You don't see any motherfucking students at any mother-fucking college up here on this stage. All of us up here are stone communist revolutionaries."

In response, the members of Madison SDS turned their chairs around—all at once in a body—and, facing the other direction, con-tinued their meeting as if the hollow-eyed violence freak was not up there aiming curses at their backs. "Follow us," he yelled. "We're going to trash the Army Mathematics Research Center!" Then he and the Weathermen charged out of the room chanting. No one joined them.

He realized later, staring at himself in the mirror, that he didn't need the hair dye to make him a new man. He had become unrecognizable. The principles of his youth that had brought him to the movement in the first place were gone. He had abandoned his father's gentle teachings. That night in Wisconsin, he suddenly knew, was the low point of his political life.

Fuming, Jeff had led his tiny gang out of the Madison meeting and back to the car. He turned to the one person he didn't know, a rank-and-file member from Chicago named Bill Frapolly, and told him, "We're going to do something. But I don't know you, so you can't come." Then he and the others went to the Army Mathematics Research Center and hurled stones through the first-floor plate-glass windows. Later Jeff learned that the man he'd left behind in the car, Frapolly, was an undercover police officer. That was some vindication, but in the meantime, the Madison chapter of SDS had coined the slogan, "You don't need a rectal thermometer to know who the assholes are."

Jeff's clothes were spread out on the couch. Not since high school prom had he worried so much about an outfit. He had chosen a dark blue woolen sailor's cap, a heavy sweater under a leather jacket, a pair of blue jeans, gloves, and work boots. Others, he knew, would bring football or motorcycle helmets. He and Bill Willett, his best friend and bodyguard, had talked it over and decided not to wear them. If they were going to die tonight and have their pictures splashed all over the *Tribune* tomorrow morning, then, said Jeff, they should at least leave behind good-looking corpses. Besides, both knew that even in boots, they could still outrun any of Mayor Daley's potbellied pigs.

Jeff rode the elevated train to within a few blocks of Lincoln Park. It was after 9:00 P.M. when he walked through the station. Cops were waiting, just begging him for a misstep that would give them an excuse. He knew their game and kept his eyes forward as he stomped down the stairs to the street. The only people he could see were police, hundreds of them, lounging stiffly by their patrol cars underneath the street lights, radios crackling. Last summer they had waited until 11:00 P.M. and then marched in and cleared the park. They figured it would be the same this year.

Jeff passed the wall posters hung all around the city that afternoon. Along the top they read, "BRING THE WAR HOME." Then, in smaller print, "This is a war we can't resist. We've got to actively fight. We're going to bring the war home to the mother country of imperialism. AMERIKA: THE FINAL FRONT."

The park was a dark space against the city lights, a slightly rising blackness, getting nearer and larger. Jeff could pick out a few furtive shadows stalking in the same general direction as he. But too few. An orange glow appeared from the trees and steered him in. He had not pictured a bonfire in his imaginings of the scene, but now he thought it was the perfect touch.

The main group, 200 people, had arrived at 7:30 P.M. and torn out park benches to start the fire. They had trained all day, scrawled emergency phone numbers on their arms, and practiced fighting with wooden staves. Some had taped their wrists and ankles and bought goggles against the tear gas. The police kept out of sight from the fire, though many in plainclothes were mingling with the protesters. October 8 was the second anniversary of Che Guevara's assassination in Bolivia, and his picture was on the largest banner. A year ago, the sign might have read, "Never Forget," or "Never Again." Now, in block-lettered exhortation, it read, "AVENGE." Around 8:30 P.M., another 150 Weathermen arrived chanting and looking determined. Maybe 50 more came into the park after that. That was it.

Tom Hayden and Abbie Hoffman, who coined the phrase *Days of Rage,* came to the park. Two of the Chicago Eight, they were on trial for charges stemming from the previous summer's convention riots. Helped by the outrageously biased rulings of Judge Julius Hoffman, the defendants and their lawyers had transformed the courtroom into devilish political theater. Now Hayden took the bullhorn and told the crowd, "I want you to know that those reports in the establishment press about the eight of us not supporting your action this week are pure bullshit . . . We are glad to see people back in Lincoln Park." Then he and Hoffman beat a hasty retreat from the scene.

Was this all? wondered Jeff, as he arrived around 10:00 P.M. and saw a few hundred people beside the bonfire. If there had been a thousand of them, it might have seemed an army. This was a sacrifice, a play-acting troupe of soldiers armed with cardboard swords and shields. Then he made the mental adjustment that Weatherman had trained him for. There weren't many, he figured, but they were the right ones, the vanguard. He had known most of them for years. They had marched together, been arrested together, had their heads beaten in together. They had the same jokes, like the one about Marion Delgado, the five-year-old kid who, just for kicks, placed a twenty-five-pound slab of concrete across a railroad track to derail a passenger train. *New Left Notes* had printed his grinning picture, kneeling over the rails in overalls as he reenacted his heroic deed. For Weatherman, he had become a half-serious symbol of the damage that the small were capable of wreaking on the powerful.

Jeff took the bullhorn and faced the crowd. "I am Marion Delgado," he said, and cheers rose from those who knew the joke. Then he announced the goal of the march—the Drake Hotel, "where the rich people live."

"Judge Hoffman is up at the Drake," he said, "and Marion Delgado don't like him and the Weatherman don't like him. So let's go get him."

Jeff started to jog over the grass at a pace he thought the others could sustain. They fell in behind him, the hardest of the hard core. Vietnamese flags fluttered behind their running bearers, and the white fighting force chanted together, "Ho Ho Ho Chi Minh, the Vietcong is gonna win." Jeff pounded over the grass, past the shocked contingent of police who thought they had a half-hour to go before the action started. He left the park, and his boots pounded onto the hard pavement of Clark Street. Not a cop in sight.

They were marching ten abreast, walking fast, then breaking into a run, then walking again. Jeff was in the front rank. He blurred past the North Federal Savings and Loan, a building cursed with huge, irresistible plate-glass windows. A rock went through, and heart rates jumped. The alarms started, adrenaline music, and the marchers broke into a flat run. Every business or bank along their route—and houses too—became a target. Cadillacs and Volkswagens were destroyed. A Rolls Royce was demolished.

Jeff was still moving ahead as the tornado worked its magic behind him. He could hear sirens racing past on parallel streets as the Chicago force hurried to establish some sort of a barrier. The march was less than ten blocks from the Drake Hotel. Ahead, Jeff could see police organizing themselves at Division Street, more than a block away. Squad cars were parked haphazardly all over the street; their drivers had skidded to a halt, jumped out, and formed a line. About thirty cops were rowed up shoulder to shoulder, palming their nightsticks.

The marchers rolled their tongues in Arabic ululations and charged toward the line. Jeff ran as fast as he could, hoping the pure shock of the onrushing bedouins would surprise the police into retreat. He was one of the first to reach them, aiming to squeeze his way between two uniforms. One shoved with his club, and the other took a wild swing at his head but missed. Jeff was through. He turned right on Division Street and then ran into a dark, narrow alley. Six plainclothes detectives were there. He tried to run between them, but there wasn't room. The detectives tackled him, cuffed him, and kicked him in the side. One squirted Mace into his eyes from about an inch away, blinding him. *Who are you? Who are you?* they were yelling.

"I'm Jeff Jones."

Bullshit, they said. Jones is a blond. They reached for his wallet and checked his ID, then threw him alone into the blue and white paddy wagon. Outside, the fight continued. Officers shot eight protesters, and almost no one escaped without an injury, including a dozen cops with wounds serious enough for a hospital visit.

The paddy wagon swung into the street. Jeff watched through the porthole as a heavy, superannuated officer drove him into the medieval courtyard of the Division Street Precinct. The grandfatherly driver opened the back door and took a sorrowful look at Jeff. "It's too bad," he said. "You looked like a nice kid."

Soon, his words implied, you're going to look like a side of beef.

The doors slammed shut again. From outside, Jeff could hear the bolt lock into position. They let him stew in there alone for forty-five minutes. His vision started to return. In his mind, he rehashed every story about cop atrocities he'd ever heard of. The police were angrier tonight than he had ever seen them. They would be out for blood. He listened to every sound, trying to piece them into an idea of what was happening outside the closed-in truck. After midnight, several cars braked hard outside. He heard fast-approaching foot-steps. The door flew open, letting in the meager light of the lamps outside.

A city official, playing cop for a chance to wail on some hippies, climbed up onto the step of the vehicle and peered closely in Jeff's direction. The man had a growing welt on the side of his face where someone had landed a punch. Now he was out for payback. When he found the guy, there would be a free-for-all. In Chicago there would be no questions asked. Almost any injuries could be blamed on resisting arrest, an accident, or maybe, your honor, the suspect had just taken a nasty fall.

He looked Jeff over eagerly. One long-hair was indistinguishable from any other, and they all deserved a beating. Eventually, his face took on a disappointed look, as if he had made a decision and was unhappy with his own choice.

"Nah," he said, finally. "This ain't the guy." Then he got back in the car and raced off to continue the hunt.

•••

In early 1968, a year and a half before that lonely, chilly night in Chicago, the movement had flourished like a traveling festival. When the people went somewhere, they had gone in tens of thousands; arriving in a new town they made a splash, with placards on the walls and a big Main Street parade. The spectacle toured the country, stopping first in San Francisco's Haight-Ashbury. At the end of 1967 the whole carnival came to New York and the East Village.

Jeff lived at 109 Norfolk Street, just north of Chinatown. The neighborhood's old tenement houses had no elevators; some apartments had no hot water. There was little trash collection and no tourist attraction. Mayor John Lindsay had not brought slum clearance and urban renewal here. But there was a circus: deadbeat poets, flower children, methedrine freaks, plainclothes cops, suburban runaways, Hindu yogis, and motorcycle pagans. Two alternative newspapers, the *Rat* and *East Village Other,* listed "sitars for sale" and advertised the *Psychedelic Lighting Manual* containing, for two dollars, "complete instructions for building strobes, color organs, light machines etc." Ninety-eight percent of the *Other's* readers reported smoking marijuana. Most paid $21 for an ounce of grass, and only 25 percent could remember ever smoking too much. Seventy-seven percent had dropped LSD and 22 percent described it as a religious experience.

St. Marks Place, between Second and Third avenues, was the center ring. Walls and scaffold fencing were plastered layers deep with rock and roll posters. Head shops and secondhand stores outfitted a generation with the bongs and surplus army jackets that were suddenly indispensable for anyone under thirty. In the evenings, the crowds were so dense a car could take a half hour to drive the single block. The Velvet Underground played at Andy Warhol's night club. A few blocks away, the Fillmore East hosted Janis Joplin, the Doors, Richie Havens, The Who, Jefferson Airplane, and Jimi Hendrix, all in one two-month period in the spring of 1968. Jeff missed every concert.

There wasn't time in his day for frivolous things. He waded through the streets eager to be on his errand, annoyed at times with the thick crowds and wasteful apathy. Students for a Democratic Society and the hippies were never comfortable allies. Jeff visited Abbie Hoffman's apartment on St. Marks. Hoffman was the most flamboyant leader of the Yippies, the counterculture's most flamboyant group. His house was painted red, white, and blue and draped in American flags. He owned a twenty-one-inch color TV, the first one Jeff had ever seen. Since becoming a full-time organizer in 1966, he had never owned an appliance more advanced than a clock-radio or toaster. The furniture in his own apartment, which he shared with his long-time buddy Jonny Lerner, had either been constructed from cinder blocks or found on the street.

He was rarely home anyway. Most mornings, Jeff was awake at 7:00 A.M. The city woke up as he walked, past shopkeepers pushing aside iron grilles and hosing down the sidewalk, to the New York office of SDS. Complaining neighbors, worried about "bearded and unkempt people in the corridors," had gotten the group evicted from three buildings in less than a year. By the summer, the office was in a co-op on Prince Street. The loft space cost less than $100 a month and sometimes, as he was riding the elevator, Jeff could hear the free jazz rehearsal sessions of his downstairs neighbor, Ornette Coleman.

In the evenings, Jeff went to St. Marks Place and met up with Ben Morea, Tom Neuman, John Sundstrom, and the rest of the Up Against the Wall Motherfuckers. The Motherfuckers referred to themselves as "a street gang with an analysis," though they seemed to emphasize the street gang part. As for the analysis, a full-page ad in the *Rat* offered an example, "What is our program? We'll know we've got it if it makes us feel good. Is there any place in the revolution for incoherence? Incoherence is the only place."

In the mornings, they practiced karate at a rundown *dojo*. They trained to become protectors for the hippies, looking after their own against the police or predatory gang members. When they were mentioned in the newspapers, it was always as "a group with a certain unprintable name." Their most famous action, in late 1967, came when a garbage strike stopped collection on the Lower East Side. Gathering full trash bags from the sidewalk piles, Motherfuckers took subways uptown to Lincoln Center, newly built at the expense of a Puerto Rican neighborhood, and dumped some of the garbage into the fountain. The Motherfuckers called it "culture exchange."

Since the Watts riot in Los Angeles, summer had been a hot time in American cities. In 1968 summer came early, when Martin Luther King, Jr., was assassinated on April 4 in Memphis. Fighting started in Chicago, Washington, Baltimore, Buffalo, and Kansas City. Jeff went to Times Square to take in the mood of the city. It was ugly. Even there, angry vigilantes were smashing windows and grabbing TVs.

The next day Jeff rode to the National Guard armory on the Upper East Side. He opened a bottle of white spray paint and worked his way down a row of jeeps, marking each green canvas top with a painted peace sign. He was done drawing his third white circle and getting ready to add the cross-hairs, when two police officers grabbed him. Before throwing him into the back seat of a squad car, they smacked the paint out of his hand and punched him in the stomach.

Run-ins with police came almost every day, and neither side passed up an opportunity to raise the tension a little. It got so a Motherfucker could hardly show his face on St. Marks Place without being vamped on. They became so familiar that Jeff figured he could recognize most of the plainclothes cops from the nearby precincts.

One evening, after a whole day wasted in Courtroom C at 100 Centre Street, standing trial for redecorating government jeeps, he was back with the group on the Second Avenue end of St. Marks. It was late spring, so his surplus army jacket was at home. He wore his everyday uniform, blue jeans and a green T-shirt that he got for $1.50. With him were John Sundstrom and Terry Hanauer, an old friend from California. Usually they could see the cops coming, but this time half a dozen unmarked squad cars were right in front of them before they could react.

Members of the Lower East Side Red Squad, a tough detective group that spent most of its time trading blows with the Motherfuckers, leaped out, cuffed John, and threw him in a car. Terry started arguing, and soon he too was under arrest. Jeff rushed over and tried to open the door to pull John out. As he reached for the handle, he found himself looking down into the barrel of a revolver. Most of the police had their .38s drawn. One cop was leaning over from the front seat and jabbing John in the ribs with his billy club. Jeff backed away slowly as the cars took off down St. Marks. The street was crowded as always, and the police cars had to pick their way through. Jeff started running behind.

When a friend was arrested, movement people had learned that it was important to stay close by. If the police knew their prisoners were accounted for—that a lawyer was on the way—the chance of an interrogation-room beating seemed to decrease dramatically. Typically, someone arrested on St. Marks Place was driven to the nearby Ninth Precinct. The cars carrying John and Terry passed it and continued south. The detectives had other plans for them. Jeff knew that there was only one precinct in that direction. The old Seventh was a few blocks from his house, and he walked by it every morning. He also knew the quickest route there. As the police cars made their hindered way, he took the back streets, running as if he was back in Sylmar High School competing for the blue ribbon.

He turned the last corner just in time to see Terry and John being led inside. He had guessed right. Jeff ran up the steps and flung open the huge wooden doors. The desk sergeant and the undercover police stared at him, mouths open. Terry and John grinned like men reprieved from death row.

Jeff flashed them a closed-fist salute.

"Are you all right?" he asked.

"Yeah, I'm all right," John said.

"We'll be back," said Jeff, and finally one of the police officers recovered enough from his surprise to yell, "Get that guy!" and Jeff turned and ran back into the neighborhood.

A lawyer was dispatched to the Seventh Precinct that evening, and Terry and John were released with no further damage. At first, the police couldn't figure out how Jeff had gotten to the station so quickly. But they soon formulated a theory. The Motherfuckers, they explained to Terry, must have a network of lookouts communicating with each other from rooftop posts. How did they communicate? With walkie-talkies that had been donated to the group by the government of Red China.

•••

It had been years since President Lyndon Johnson had been able to leave the White House without attracting demonstrators. Gradually he had given up, and by 1968, he almost always spoke on army bases, or in other venues from which the electorate was barred. In January, he delivered the State of the Union address to Congress, safely inside the walls of the Capitol. His speech was a point-by-point explanation of how the United States was winning the conflict in Southeast Asia. Later that month, during the Vietnamese Tet holidays, the National Liberation Front refuted Johnson's speech point by point, launching its most dramatic offensive of the war.

The American troop level peaked at 542,000 in 1968, and by election day 29,184 U.S. soldiers had been killed, just over half of the eventual total. Opposition to the war was rising but was by no means universal: a Gallup poll in August showed that 53 percent of American adults believed that sending soldiers to Vietnam had been a mistake.

A peace candidate emerged, Senator Eugene McCarthy of Minnesota, and his message was aimed at the youth. His followers were called McCarthy Kids, and to counter the negative image of long-haired, unsanitary hippie teenagers, they were told to cut their hair, dress like normal adults, and "Keep Clean for Gene." In the New Hampshire primary, the media were shocked when Johnson and McCarthy came out nearly dead even. A few days later, Robert F. Kennedy, sensing that Johnson was weaker than anyone had imagined, joined the race as well.

With all this infighting, the Democratic National Convention, planned for August in Chicago, was emerging as the must-see event of the summer. The McCarthy Kids were expected to be there in the tens of thousands, Kennedy's youth base would be present, David Dellinger's Mobilization Committee to End the War in Vietnam was planning a demonstration, and the Yippies, calling themselves an alternative to the "National Death Party," had already secured Country Joe and the Fish, Arlo Guthrie, and Phil Ochs and had feelers out to Bob Dylan and the Monkees.

Certain strategists within Students for a Democratic Society, however, had doubts. Jeff coauthored a major article for the March 4 *New Left Notes* that ran along the top of the front page under the headline, "Don't Take Your Guns to Town." Already, months ahead of time, Jeff foresaw the result of the Yippie plan. "Their intention," he wrote, "to bring thousands of young people to Chicago during the DNC to groove on rock bands and smoke grass and then to put them up against bayonets—viewing that as a radicalizing experience—seems manipulative at best. The idea would not be bad, were it not for the Illinois National Guard and the Chicago Police." What he didn't foresee was that the strategy would lead to one of the biggest public relations victories the antiwar movement would ever win.

On March 31, Johnson shocked the nation when he told a prime-time audience, "I shall not seek, and I will not accept, the nomination of my party for another term as your President." Long-distance phone lines immediately jammed, and in New York a jubilant demonstration emerged from nothing and arrived at Washington Square Park numbering hundreds.

During a celebration of his victory in the California primary in early June, Robert Kennedy was shot twice, once in the head, and died hours later. Students for a Democratic Society had backed neither peace candidate. In May, *New Left Notes* had printed McCarthy's Senate voting record, noting that he had "voted for every appropriation for the Vietnam War, voted for the Tonkin Gulf resolution, voted in 1966 to kill a proposed amendment that would have prohibited the use of draftees in Vietnam unless they volunteered." McCarthy had little chance at the nomination anyway. The favorite was Johnson's hand-picked successor, Vice President Hubert Humphrey, whose war policy, dictated by the president, promised only more fighting.

Jeff flew to O'Hare Airport in late August to attend the convention. One billboard alongside the freeway into the city read, "Mayor Daley Welcomes You to Chicago," although certain recent actions implied that the mayor's welcome did not extend to SDS. Another sign was more relevant to Jeff's plans—a warning of what he was getting into. "You have arrived," it said, "in Daley Country."

Richard J. Daley had been mayor of Chicago since 1955. He ran the largest political machine in the land but basically remained a neighborhood guy, and that neighborhood was an Irish-dominated enclave on the South Side. He made decisions that he knew would be popular there, because he knew that most of the constituents he cared about lived in such neighborhoods. In the weeks leading up to the convention, when he refused to give Abbie Hoffman and Tom Hayden the permits they needed to march to the International Amphitheatre, or when he forbade the protesters from sleeping in Lincoln Park, he did so confident that the people of Chicago wanted them there about as much as he did—that is, not at all.

When blacks rioted following the death of Martin Luther King, Jr.—whom Daley had called "a rabble rouser, a troublemaker . . . a dirty sonofabitch, a bastard, a prick"—he gave the order he knew people in his neighborhood would have given. "I have conferred with the superintendent of police this morning," he told reporters:

> I said to him very emphatically and very definitely that an order be issued by him immediately and under his signature to shoot to kill any arsonist or anyone with a Molotov cocktail in his hand in Chicago because they're potential murderers, and to issue a police order to shoot to maim anyone looting any stores in our city.

To the rest of the country Daley sounded like a Wild West sheriff. But as usual he was thinking like his constituents. Of the 1,100 letters and telegrams that poured into city hall, the people of Chicago—at least the white people—supported his shoot-to-kill order by a ratio of fifteen to one.

The voters loved him, but to the antiwar protesters, Mayor Daley was born to play the villain. He was the kind of man who would machine-gun a mosquito. When Yippies Jerry Rubin and Abbie Hoffman got the convention week activities started, coming to Chicago's business district and nominating a pig as their candidate for president, Daley had his police arrest not only Hoffman and Rubin but Pigasus, the pig, as well.

The civic unfriendliness scared away the bands and most of the crowds. But a few thousand were still coming, more than enough to start a panic. The Chicago papers seriously reported the most far-out movement threats: nails would be spread on the expressways, gas lines dynamited, LSD slipped into the water supply. The amphitheater was surrounded by a half-mile of barbed-wire fencing, and all nearby manhole covers were sealed with tar. Inside the convention, sodas would be served without ice cubes to prevent them from being hurled at the delegates. In total, Daley assembled 40,000 armed men to ensure that his convention would proceed normally.

Before the action started, Jeff had breakfast with his father. Albert was in Kansas City that week at the annual convention of his union, the International Association of Theater and Stage Employees. As the very active president of the Disney local, he rarely missed a national event. The conventioneers had listened to rip-roaring speeches and then enthusiastically endorsed Hubert Humphrey. Albert had not seen his son since December, when Jeff had returned from Cambodia and spent a few restless days at home. When Albert learned that Jeff was in Chicago, he had booked a round-trip flight. It seemed like a waste to be so close and not meet up.

They hugged at the gate and sat down for breakfast at an airport restaurant. They avoided talking politics for about ten seconds, and then Albert started pushing the benefits of Humphrey. His logic was simple: the Democrat wasn't perfect, but he was a hell of a lot better than Richard Nixon, even if the Republican was a California Quaker. A vote against Humphrey was a vote for Nixon.

To Albert's way of thinking, the McCarthy Kids were the irresponsible ones who had gone too far to the Left. But Jeff was way past that. He was not interested, as his father was, in saving the Democratic Party. He was in Chicago to smash it. As for supporting Humphrey, demonstrations rang all week with the chants: "Dump the Hump, dump the Hump."

The restaurant was crowded. Silverware rang off china plates, and outside the planes took off and landed. Albert watched over his eggs and potatoes as his son denounced the Democrats, demeaned the unions, and talked like a violent revolutionary. Father and son had never been further apart. Albert could see the gap becoming unbridgeable, and he didn't want that, not if they only got to see each other once or twice a year. He busied himself with eating and let Jeff finish his rant. Afterward, on the flight back to Kansas City, Albert wondered if meeting up had been such a good idea after all.

·

On Sunday night, August 25, Daley officially opened the convention. TV cameras beamed out the red, white, and blue bunting of the crowded hall. Delegates shook their state signs with gusto. Outside, the police worked over the crowds in the streets, flinging their batons around like orchestra conductors. Noses were mashed, teeth spit out onto the sidewalk. Medics kneeled over the bodies in the Loop, bandaging and salving eighty serious scalp wounds. The Chicago police must have been reading the newspapers because when they stormed into the crowd, they didn't see soft-bodied, unarmed teenage Americans. They believed the long-hairs were in Chicago to spread communistic plots, undermine the American family, and assassinate every politician above the rank of ward heeler. They saw a real threat to Our Way of Life.

For Jeff, the nights blurred together as the battles were fought over the same terrain. At 11:00 P.M., the police enforced a curfew and drove the people from the isolated, self-contained Lincoln Park, where they would have bothered no one, out into the busy streets of downtown Chicago. There the protests acquired a new choreography. At the Pentagon in 1967, the marchers had basically performed a sit-in, allowing themselves to be arrested, sometimes brutally, by the federal marshals. During the takeover at Columbia, they had resisted passively when the bust came, offering no more protest than going limp and forcing the police to drag them away. But in Chicago, demonstrators for the first time, fought police in the streets, running and chasing, dispersing and regrouping, refusing to back down.

Wednesday, August 28, was apotheosis day. Inside the amphitheater, the convention voted down an anti–Vietnam War initiative. As the news spread, a small protest gathered along Michigan Avenue, across the street from the Conrad Hilton Hotel where the delegates were staying. Humphrey himself was in his suite, waiting for the time later that evening when his nomination would be put to the vote.

A cordon of police stood before the hotel entrance. Both sides reinforced. People came running to the front lines as busloads of police arrived and formed up into squads. The cops snarled and stared coldly, waiting for the order to charge. Against them, the demonstrators shouted curses, chanted, and hurled bottles and rocks. The confrontation, like hundreds of others in the past few years, was set. This time, though, there were television cameras. Daley had taken elaborate steps to limit the networks' ability to film his police in action, but there were cameramen near the lobby and in the streets, while others poked their lenses through the hotel windows.

The police charged around 8:00 P.M. One troop rushed out of its bus chanting, "Kill, kill, kill." They made arrests, sprayed Mace indiscriminately, and launched tear gas that rose up into the air and filtered into the delegates' hotel rooms. For almost twenty minutes, the fighting continued. The crowd was not pacifistic; it screamed curses and voiced the rage created by the week's fighting, but, in the end, it was unarmed. The police attacked protesters and bystanders, used their clubs and tear gas and motorcycles as weapons, and every punch and kick was burned into the video tape. Cameras panned and flung wildly out of control, losing the action, and then returned to the frantic street fighting.

Jeff dodged in and out of the melee, chanting and shouting along with the chorus of angry voices right and left. He allowed the police to get close to him but always kept his eye on a line of retreat and managed to stay out of the reach of clubs.

After the cops had cleared the avenue, cameramen unloaded their tapes and handed them to couriers, who sped to the amphitheater and sneaked the footage inside the barbed-wire fencing to the network control rooms. More than half an hour after the violence was over, the first images of the fighting were broadcast on television to portable sets scattered around the convention hall and to the nation's living rooms, where 89 million viewers couldn't believe their eyes.

Neither the Pentagon nor Columbia had produced these kinds of images. It was a scale of violence that American TV audiences had seen only in the Deep South or on the battlefields of Vietnam. There was no protective filter, no anchorman to provide a balancing perspective. The video was allowed to speak for itself, and what it showed was a police force completely out of control and a political system in crisis. Jeff and dozens of others, in the midst of the violence, started chanting, "The whole world is watching. The whole world is watching." And, finally, it was true.

In the convention hall, Abe Ribicoff, senator from Connecticut, denounced the "Gestapo tactics on the streets of Chicago." Daley rose from his seat, his jowled, purple face a raisin of rage, and shouted what lip-readers later translated as, "Fuck you, you Jew son of a bitch, you lousy motherfucker, go home." After 11:00 P.M., the voting began. Humphrey had showered to rid himself of the tear gas that had seeped into his room. Amid echoing boos and catcalls, he was nominated as the Democratic presidential candidate.

By Thursday morning, no one in Chicago had any clean clothes left. No one had slept much. No one had eaten an unhurried meal. It was a bedraggled, hung-over town of disappointed and disillusioned people. An exodus began: back to work, back to school. The remnant, a few thousand who still had not had enough, gathered in Grant Park, across from the Hilton, and listened to speakers. McCarthy spoke and was applauded when he said he would not support Humphrey.

Jeff had hardly slept in days. His hair was mussed and shaggy like a wrong-way carpet. He threw a loose-fitting jacket over his dark T-shirt and went to the park to represent Students for a Democratic Society. "The power belongs to the young people and the black people in this country," he said, holding the microphone like an ice cream cone. "We're going to remake this country in the streets," he yelled, emphasizing the word *streets*. "Don't get hung up on this fourth party bullshit. Don't get hung up on peace candidates. Come on! We gotta fight it out where the only power we can build is. That's at the base. We gotta build a strong base and someday we gotta knock those motherfuckers who control this thing right on their ass."

Then, as the raised fists flew up in the audience, Jeff turned, with relief or disgust, and dropped the microphone. It was one of the angriest speeches he ever gave.

During convention week, the Chicago police made almost 700 arrests. In Vietnam during the same period, 308 U.S. troops were killed, and more than 1,000 were wounded. Liberal shock, the kind expressed on newspaper editorial pages, denounced the behavior of the cops. The obligatory commission made its report and called the convention violence "a police riot." But Daley, as always, knew his constituency better than any editorial writer or blue ribbon panelist. Only 10 percent of white people polled afterward believed that the police had used too much force.

Hubert Humphrey probably suspected as much when he said, "The city of Chicago and the people of Chicago didn't do a thing that was wrong. . . . There are certain people in the United States who feel that all you have to do is riot and you can get your way. I have no time for that." His campaign, after the least promising beginning in American political history, started way behind Richard Nixon's but slowly closed the gap until the election, which Humphrey lost by less than 1 percent.

Jeff returned to the Lower East Side to find that he was no longer on friendly terms with the Motherfuckers. They had always considered SDS, with its conventions and proposals, a little too much like Latin club. SDS, they were fond of saying, "should talk less and drink more." By the winter, the Motherfuckers were reduced to squabbling with the owner of the Fillmore East over his capitalist insistence on charging hippies for admission to his concerts. Ben Morea, attacked by a group of marines during a protest march in Boston, had put the knife he always carried to good use and was facing charges of assault and battery, which he would eventually beat. The East Village scene had gone dark and dangerous, and Jeff abandoned it for San Francisco. He had always viewed his time on the East Coast as temporary. He was back in California to stay, or at least that was the plan.

•••

The Chicago Coliseum was not the leadership's first location choice for the SDS summer national convention in 1969—roughly, it was the sixtieth. There wasn't a campus in the country that was willing to host the organization, now that Nixon was in the White House and the heat was on all radical groups. SDS had held conventions, the major annual event for the organization when policy was set and a new slate of national officers elected, each summer for the past seven years. But this was Eleanor's first, and she had high expectations.

The business end of a policeman's billy club had been a radicalizing agent. Eleanor and thousands of other students joined SDS at the start of the autumn semester in 1968. Official membership rose to 100,000 in 350 chapters, and the leadership believed that almost half a million students were participating locally and had access to *New Left Notes*. SDS, as a tiny clique of a few thousand students, had exerted influence far beyond its numbers. Now, there was no limit to its potential.

Eleanor heard rumors of dissension—that the national office was fighting to maintain control—but she didn't give them much thought. Her focus, like almost all of the other new members, was on her own campus chapter. And the Columbia chapter was vigorous and world famous. In her mind, the only problem was that the leadership was made up entirely of men—and undergraduate men at that who, to a law student, were little more than boys.

Nevertheless, Eleanor had done what she always did and completely dedicated herself to the project of the moment—in this case, smashing the bourgeois state. In March 1969, she made a name for herself by leading more than two hundred students in pickets of Columbia buildings. The *New York Times* quoted the fiery new leader on campus:

> "We've effectively shut down the college and cut down attendance at the university by half," said Mrs. Eleanor Raskin, an SDS spokesman who is a second-year law student at Columbia. "This strike is the opening gun. This strike is our first blow." . . . At a news conference, Mrs. Raskin . . . warned that if Columbia failed to act on the demands before the end of the spring vacation, which begins Friday and ends April 6, the SDS chapter would "take further action."

For a law student, it was a pretty martial press conference, with its opening guns, first blows, and further actions.

•

The SDS convention began on June 18. Buses lined up on Wabash Avenue in front of the Coliseum, a rundown theater with a blank marquee and a burned-out neon sign. Eleanor came in style. Her curly brown hair was kept back—tenuously—by a patterned silk headband. She wore a miniskirt, knee-high boots, round wire-rimmed glasses, and hoops in her ears that she had fashioned out of bracelets—no one made earrings big enough for her.

Security kept the capitalist press on the sidewalk until they paid a twenty-five-dollar fee. Otherwise, anyone who looked hip, including plenty of undercover police, was allowed in. By the evening, two thousand delegates and observers were inside. Eleanor found an empty seat and joined others from her chapter toward the rear of the main floor.

As the national officers were gathering near the front, one of Eleanor's Columbia sisters whispered, "There's Jeff Jones." Eleanor had never seen him in person, although she knew his reputation and had even worked on his legal team. Jeff, who had been arrested almost a dozen times, kept several of New York's liberal law firms busy getting him safely from one legal jam to the next.

She turned and looked as he walked past her down the aisle in blue jeans, a leather jacket, and cowboy boots. His hair was long and the blondest in the room. As he approached the stage, he started walking faster. It had stairs on either wing, the kind that everybody would worry about tripping over during a high school graduation. Speakers had climbed the steps carefully before making their presen-tations. From a few yards away, Jeff broke into a run and leaped straight up on to the four-foot stage.

He was part of a new faction that had announced its presence with a manifesto published in this day's issue of *New Left Notes*. In the chatter and buzz before the program started, Eleanor noticed that many delegates were leafing through the six-page "You Don't Need a Weatherman to Know Which Way the Wind Blows."

The Port Huron Statement, published seven years earlier, had been widely and eagerly read. College freshmen had stashed it away like a bag of grass, locking their dorm rooms and savoring the state-ment's attack on materialism and its call for personal responsibility.

Weatherman was into gut-checks, and so it was fitting that only a true stone communist revolutionary could read the party's founding statement in its entirety. Jeff, who sat through its tortuous birth, had read it from beginning to end once. Eleanor picked it up but couldn't finish. It was rumored that a thorough reading would leave you blind.

"We are within the heartland of a world-wide monster," the preamble warned, "a country so rich from its world-wide plunder that even the crumbs doled out to the enslaved masses within its borders provide for material existence very much above the conditions of the masses of the people of the world." Then came the most shocking revelation: "All of the United Airlines Astrojets, all of the Holiday Inns, all of Hertz's automobiles, your television set, car and wardrobe already belong, to a large degree to the people of the rest of the world." *My TV set?* the typical reader wondered. *Give my TV set to the Third World?* That was revolutionary commitment indeed.

A movement came of age when it published its own manifesto of garbled Marxist doctrine. The leaders of Weatherman were no longer content with the student movement; they wanted to be revolutionaries. Standing in their way was classical Marxist theory. The obstacle that had stymied Annie and Arthur Stein and the American Communist Party thirty years earlier now faced Weatherman—the working class. Elusive and coy, idealized and alluring, the working class that Marx, damn him, had insisted would foment the revolution remained stubbornly resistant to its own best interests.

Weatherman's solution was to show that "most young people in the US are part of the working class. . . . Most kids are well aware of what class they are in, even though they may not be very scientific about it. So our analysis assumes from the beginning that youth struggles are, by and large, working-class struggles." Therefore, the Weathermen weren't college-educated middle-class youths who could rely on their families for financial support. Not at all. They were working-class revolutionaries. Having performed that uncomfortable feat of political yoga, no ideological barriers remained to block the path to Marxist struggle.

·

From start to finish, the first night's programs showed the divisions in the convention. The opening piece of business, establishing the week's agenda, was attacked so loudly that within five minutes, the chairman was frantically beating a rock against the table on stage to gain order. The evening ended with the same sour tone: As the last panel left the stage, half of the audience chanted, "Bullshit, bullshit . . ."

Every SDS chapter with more than ten members had representatives of the different tendencies. If you thought that white youth should defer to the Black Panthers and Third World revolutionaries, then you gave at least some loyalty to Weatherman. If you believed white youth had to defer to white factory workers, then you subscribed to Progressive Labor. If you thought that white middle-class students could contribute in their own right, then you were really far off. If you didn't care about any of that stuff, then you weren't a member of SDS in the summer of 1969.

Eleanor had not realized how far things had degenerated. Most of her friends belonged to either Weatherman or its allies, but they had been outorganized by the Progressive Labor Party. Students for a Democratic Society thrived without discipline. Members came and went as they pleased. They showed up for conventions or stayed away. Meanwhile, Progressive Labor had spent weeks ensuring a high turnout for the convention, so although they represented a small minority of the total organization, they made a voting majority at the Chicago convention.

At stake were the positions of leadership: national secretary, education secretary, and interorganizational secretary. These three officers controlled the national headquarters and the printing press, and they set the agenda in *New Left Notes*. The organization was in trouble, Eleanor realized as she left the Coliseum and headed toward a friendly church, where she spread out a blanket and settled in to sleep on the floor. Before drifting off, she wondered which of the factions she would support if it came to a decision.

On the third day of the convention, with insults and jeers still flying around the room and Progressive Labor in the ascendancy,

Bernardine Dohrn, the outgoing interorganizational secretary, declared that Weatherman and its allies were going to leave the convention and meet separately before returning to elect the new national officers. Only the Weatherman collective was prepared. To the audience it was a surprise, and as Bernardine left the stage and marched down the aisle, the delegates had to locate their loyalties quickly. Many followed her out.

Eleanor, dismayed, watched them leave the hall. She hadn't spent a lifetime in a Communist Party household without hearing about factions, political lines, and purge trials. But this wasn't supposed to be 1930s Moscow. This was the New Left, and those things weren't supposed to happen here. Yet SDS, an organization founded as a welcome place for the country's deviants, was now charging members with the crime of political deviation.

The next day, Bernardine and the others returned to the Coliseum. She stood on stage behind a wooden podium decorated with a painted fist and purged the members of the Progressive Labor Party. To cries of, "Shame, shame," she led another walkout. This time Eleanor joined 800 others in the long march to the First Congregational Church, where they elected a new slate of national officers. Mark Rudd, head of her own Columbia chapter, won the position of national secretary. Bill Ayers, from Michigan, was elected as education secretary. Jeff Jones, acceptable to all, ran unopposed and became the new interorganizational secretary. The split in SDS, an overwrought Jones remarked to a reporter for the *Guardian,* was "perhaps the most important thing in left history in 30, maybe 200, years."

"It's not what they say that counts. It's what they do when they put their theory into action that counts," Jeff told television reporters after the convention. "What they do contradicts what they say and on that basis we had to expel them from the organization."

It was not speeches that made Eleanor go with the Weathermen. She went because they were the scariest choice. The group demanded the biggest sacrifices and represented the strongest challenge to the status quo. She felt—and everyone who joined agreed—that with the current state of the world, it would be impossible to do too much. It was normal to want to participate in violence, to fight and be arrested, to leave the comforts of life behind. It was staying inside the middle-class cocoon that sounded crazy.

Progressive Labor elected its own slate of officers. But the Weathermen held the national office. They made clear their power to shape opinion the next week, when the front page of *New Left Notes* was dominated by a single headline, "NATIONAL CONVENTION EXPELS RACIST PL, AND ELECTS NEW OFFICERS." Eleanor's first convention would be the last one ever held. Weatherman had destroyed SDS in order to save it.

•••

Eleanor was finding it difficult to abandon privilege. After casting her lot with the righteously far-out Weatherman faction, she still came home to a comfortable apartment on Riverside Drive, a husband, and a promising future as a lawyer. Her mother still lived nearby, and they met for dinner and politics. Annie believed that the ground had never been more fertile for organizing the masses. Between the crisis of the inner cities, the war in Vietnam, and the bitter generational divide, 1969 should have been the first year in the reckoning of a new history, the year of revolution. Instead, she thought, SDS and particularly Weatherman had its theory backward. It was abandoning the masses at exactly the wrong moment, hiding away in isolated cadre groups at a time when the charismatic leaders of the left needed to be in the streets inspiring massive demonstrations. As Annie talked, Eleanor was only half-listening, anxious to shed this old lady and enter some more exciting conversations.

Her third year at Columbia Law School was supposed to begin in a few months. She was almost a lawyer, yet was considering throwing away her education, and the tangible aid it could provide the movement, in favor of becoming just another foot soldier. She had already proved that a movement lawyer had services to offer. That year, Eleanor had coauthored *The Bust Book: What to Do Until the Lawyer Comes,* with Kathy Boudin, Gus Reichbach, and Brian Glick. "This book is not a substitute for a lawyer," the title page warned, "it's legal first aid."

It was first released as a fifty-cent pamphlet in July, but a later ver-

sion printed by Grove Press eventually sold more than 50,000 copies. The chapters traced a demonstrator's path from protest, through arrest and arraignment, to bail and trial strategy. Eleanor put in a lesson that her mother had taught her about how to prepare for a demonstration. *"The New York Times,"* she wrote in the chapter on self-defense, "although not useful for any other purpose, makes a very hard object when rolled up lengthwise and folded in half, and unlike other weapons, is inconspicuous and not incriminating."

Her relationship with Jonah was ending. He had been arrested at Columbia and was fired from his professor's job at the university in Stony Brook, but Jonah was a writer and a thinker, not a revolutionary. It was possible in America to be a radical and also have a good career, a nice house, a healthy marriage, wealth, and even fame. Many lawyers, authors, doctors, and labor leaders had done it. But Weatherman said this was wrong. These options were not available to the Black Panthers or the Hispanic Young Lords, and they certainly were not possible for the people of Vietnam. A white revolutionary had to be willing to abandon these things, which Weatherman referred to as "the enemy within." She had to take to the streets; fling up the cobblestones into barricades, as the students had done in France; pick up the gun, like the blacks were urging in the ghetto, and bring the war home.

That's how Eleanor found herself in Pittsburgh at the beginning of September 1969.

The Steel City was the type of working-class town that SDS was attempting to woo. Eleanor and about seventy-five other women arrived on September 3 and spent the night, as usual, holding a meeting in a church. During the discussion, someone told the group that the spiritual and political leader of North Vietnam, Ho Chi Minh, had died.

The next morning, the women drove toward the neighborhood of Mt. Washington and parked their cars. With fists full of leaflets and carrying the flag of the Vietcong, they marched to South Hills High School. At 12:30 P.M., when they arrived, many of the white working-class students were on a lunch break. Some of the women

passed around their literature, most of it advertising the Days of Rage that had been called for October. Eleanor and some others burst into the hallway of the school. Someone shouted, "You must be communists," and the women yelled, "Right on, damn right."

Eleanor and about a dozen others crashed through the door of a history class. The teacher's face turned as white as chalk dust at the sight of the intruders: this was not the glee club. Eleanor glared out over the rows of students and started hollering, "Schools are bullshit! This school is a prison! The history you're learning is a bunch of lies! The real history is that this country is waging an illegal war in Vietnam. Come with us! We're going to have a demonstration in Chicago, October 8 to 11, come bring the war home. COME ON! IT'S JAILBREAK TIME!"

The women behind her chorused, "Jailbreak! Jailbreak!" and then they ran from the classroom, followed, to their surprise, by a handful of the students. They met up together outside the school, which now had the words "Ho Lives" painted on its walls, and started to march back toward their cars. Word about the invasion spread, and soon the women were surrounded by crowds of angry construction workers. The police started to arrive, and scuffles broke out around the fringe.

The women chanted and the men screamed insults. Eleanor was in the front row, face-to-face with a youngish-looking construction worker in a hard hat and jeans, exactly the kind of tough guy SDS was supposed to appeal to now. He looked her right in the eye and said, "Fuck Ho Chi Minh." This was provocation beyond endurance. Eleanor reached back and threw her right fist upward toward the man's jaw. He turned his head slightly, and she hit him square on the chin with the hardest uppercut she had in her. He staggered backward into the arms of his buddies. Then all hell broke loose. The women punched, kicked, bit, and shoved any man they could reach. Police moved in, arrested Eleanor and twenty-five others, and dragged them off to a musty brick fortress called the Allegheny County Jail. She was fitted for an orange jumpsuit and placed in a cell. That night, she ran her fingers over the knuckles of the punching fist. Her hand felt terrific.

Reactions to the jailbreak were mixed. *New Left Notes* called them

the Women's Militia and claimed that "the action in Pittsburgh attacked imperialism and racism, and because it was carried out by women alone, it dealt a particularly strong blow to male chauvinism." Local radio stations reported that the SDS women had run bare-breasted through the hallways of the high school like avenging Valkyries. (This was an exaggeration. The most that could be said was that most of them were braless.)

Eleanor was charged with rioting, inciting a riot, and disorderly conduct, told to pay a $25 fine and $11 in court costs; and held on $1,500 bail. She had wanted to experience a life without comforts, and she got her wish and more during her three weeks in the jail. She also missed the start of the semester at the law school. Finally, back in New York City in early November, Eleanor wrote a letter to the dean:

> Dear Sir,
> I would like to apply for a leave of absence for the year, 1969–1970. I am sorry to apply so late, but I have been in jail in Pittsburgh, Pa., for political activities.
> I would like to use this critical year to employ my legal skills in aiding in the defense of political prisoners, such as the Conspiracy Eight and others in Chicago. The shortage of lawyers doing this kind of work, and the need for it, makes me feel the urgency of helping in these major criminal defenses.
> I would be glad to give more details if necessary. Thank you very much,
>
> Yours,
> Eleanor Raskin

While Eleanor was breaking the ties to her old life, she decided to leave her husband. As Jonah wrote, she "packed a suitcase, threw away her jewelry, miniskirts, long evening gowns, her shoes, sold her law books, and moved to a Weatherman collective."

•••

After the June convention, the Weathermen had begun working on the National Action. They jogged in city parks and practiced karate. They went to working-class beaches and picked fights to show how tough they were, thankful for once that there were plenty of police around. The July 8 *New Left Notes* dedicated the front page to a boldfaced call to arms. "BRING THE WAR HOME! Occupation troops out of Vietnam, Latin America, all other foreign countries, black and brown communities, and the schools. Chicago, Oct. 11 All Power to the People!" was the headline, and beneath it Jeff wrote the article. He criticized the old SDS for failing to rally around minority movements and for not participating in the organization of the Democratic National Convention demonstrations of the previous summer. "We must move swiftly and effectively to rectify our mistakes," he wrote. "The Vietnamese and the black and brown struggles for liberation here need the support of a militant fighting anti-imperialist youth movement."

The SDS newspaper took on the mania of the leadership. *New Left Notes* became *Fire!* and the old forum for irreverent debate became a party organ filled with attacks on political rivals. It is not difficult to imagine the tens of thousands of SDS members, college students who had looked forward to the next issue of *New Left Notes,* getting their copy of *Fire!* in the mail and wondering about the lunatics in the national office. The drive of Weatherman to create a white fighting force was not shared by the mass base. The leadership collective had turned into Casey Jones, the speeding locomotive conductor. At the front, they were feeding coal into the fire as fast as they could shovel. They picked up speed in a rush and assumed the whole train was moving with them. Actually the sudden jolt came when the passenger cars unhooked themselves, leaving the locomotive to hurl itself, alone, toward Chicago and the Days of Rage.

As interorganizational secretary, Jeff was mobilizing other groups to support the protest in Chicago. This work took him to college campuses and to speak with GIs in South Carolina, where the SDS office was boarded up and had bullet holes in the windows. Inspired by the Black Panthers, Jeff asked Bill Willett to be his backup. They had bodyguards and guns, so SDS wanted them too.

Bodyguards as a rule tended not to be graduates of Williams

College, but Willett was a street fighter and, by SDS standards, a tough guy. He had grown up in Alabama and after college had caught on with the Washington, D.C., regional office. Jeff and Willett smoked the most pot, dropped the most acid, and considered themselves the organization's Lifestyle Wing. As bodyguard, Willett's job was to look scary during Jeff's speeches and to carry the .38 special that they rarely left behind. They may have looked tough—and they sometimes took target practice with the revolver—but neither would have known what to do with it in an emergency.

In San Francisco, Jeff and Willett tried to buy motorcycles from a pair of Hell's Angels chicks. They each borrowed one hundred dollars from their girlfriends and went to pick up the hogs. Jeff knocked on the door with a sinking feeling; looking inside, he could see several dangerous-looking Angels lounging around.

"We've come to pick up the motorcycles," he said.

"I don't know what you're talking about," said the biker chick, "Get the hell out of here." Then she stuck the tip of an ice pick into the skin on his neck. Jeff and Willett beat a hasty retreat, worried about how to tell their old ladies they were out a hundred bucks.

When he wasn't traveling, Jeff spent most of his waking hours in the national office on West Madison Street in a Chicago slum. The white radicals were eager for the goodwill of this community but they were plagued by neighborhood kids who would hang around the office looking for things to steal. Jeff had his wallet taken, but there was nothing he could do. He wasn't about to call the cops, and the kids knew it.

The Illinois Black Panthers had their headquarters up a steep flight of stairs in an office a few blocks away. In Chicago, they were led by Fred Hampton who, at the age of twenty-one, was quickly becoming a national figure. Hampton was a natural orator with a wicked sense of fun. He once hijacked a Good Humor truck on a hot summer day and passed out free popsicles to the children of the South Side. Fred lived with the knowledge that he was a hated and vulnerable enemy of the state. "You can jail a revolutionary," he told the large crowds that came to a Chicago church to hear him speak each weekend, "but you can't jail a revolution. You can run a freedom fighter around the country but you can't run freedom fighting around the country. You can murder a liberator, but you can't murder liberation."

Students for a Democratic Society and the Black Panthers were supposed to be allies. A Chicago Panther had spoken at the June convention and demanded the expulsion of the Progressive Labor Party. But in daily practice, SDS found the Panthers difficult friends. At the same convention where they had supported Weatherman, a Panther had shouted "pussy power" into the microphone and earned hoots from the audience. On several occasions, the Panthers arrived unannounced in the SDS office to demand use of the press. Once, in the middle of a printing run, Hampton and his bodyguards stormed in and demanded to use it immediately. When they were asked to be patient, one of the Panthers pulled a handgun. Negotiations continued at gunpoint until finally they agreed to wait their turn.

Chairman Fred opposed the Days of Rage. He was sure the march would only infuriate the Chicago police, who would then take out their anger on the black community. In one of his highest oratorical flights, Fred denounced the plan to reporters:

> We believe that the Weatherman action is anarchistic, opportunistic, individualistic, it's chauvinistic, it's, uh, Custeristic, and that's the bad part about it. It's Custeristic in that its leaders take people into situations where the people can be massacred, and they call that revolution. That's nothing but child's play. It's folly. . . . We think these people may be sincere but they're misguided, they're muddleheads and they're scatterbrains.

A week before the action started, Jeff, Bernardine, and Terry Robbins made a final attempt to convince Hampton that the strategy was a winner. They showed up at the Panther building, and walked up the narrow, creaking staircase. Inside, they went past the guard—there was always one on duty—and sat down in Fred's office. The conversation lasted a few minutes, with Fred, as usual, doing most of the talking. When his patience was finished, he ordered his men to throw these white people out of the office. Terry was kicked and rolled, elbows over knees, down the dangerous staircase. Jeff and Bernardine, just managing to keep their balance, hustled out behind him.

•••

Before dawn on the morning of Thursday, October 9, Bernardine came to the Cook County Jail to bail Jeff out. His eyes still stung from the Mace spray, and his sides were sore. Almost one hundred protesters had been arrested with him on the first night of the Days of Rage. It had been a disaster, and most of the other demonstrations planned for the week were cancelled. But that afternoon, a group of women charged police lines and were arrested. At night, Walter Cronkite reported that the Illinois governor had ordered more than 2,000 National Guardsmen to "standby emergency duty in Chicago."

Then a reporter described the scene. "They smashed countless windows on the city's near north side," he voiced over the wild images. "It seemed to be violence for violence's sake. With the radicals making no specific demands."

The entire national leadership and just about everyone else left in the organization would be arrested during the Days of Rage, which culminated in a final melee on Saturday. Jeff knew the costs meant there would never be another action like it. The press, which had nervously sided with protesters after the police riots during the Democratic National Convention, was relieved to pile its invective on Weatherman. The left was split, but mainly it felt that the protest had been a disaster, a massacre, as Fred had predicted, if not of the people then at least of the good karma that the movement had been building up for years.

Daley took the opportunity to look like Mr. Reasonable. "What right has anyone to walk down the street with a chain in their hand?" he asked. "Or a club, which we saw last night used against the police. Or an iron pipe? We know very well they're not playing hockey in those kinds of outfits. Unless they're playing hockey with somebody's head."

In the next few weeks, the Chicago police tailed Jeff and the others. The Red Squad followed him until he and most of the police were on a first-name basis. He was pulled over on Lake Shore Drive and the cops discovered a .22 pistol in the trunk of his car and arrested him for illegal possession of a firearm. The constant scrutiny made it almost impossible for the leaders of SDS to organize; wherever they went, they brought attention with them, and who among their contacts wanted that? They began talking about building a clandestine infrastructure and going underground.

The street fighting of the National Action seemed to have softened Chairman Fred Hampton's position on Weatherman. The police had been furious, but they kept their attention on the white protesters and had momentarily lifted the heat off the Panthers. White and black organizers were constantly being harassed, which added some sense of solidarity. In late November, Jeff and Fred appeared together on a radio call-in show. Jeff noticed that Fred seemed frustrated with his own people. He gave curt answers to the callers. They challenged him, claiming the Panthers were too violent or that the police were in the ghetto to protect people. To Jeff, Fred seemed disillusioned with Chicago's black community. Jeff disagreed, but it was a curious argument to be defending black people to the local chairman of the Panthers.

Jeff drove Hampton home after the show. They'd had their disagreements in the past but, one-on-one, they were friendly together. It was almost winter, and the night was cold. Fred wrapped his long coat around him as the car's heater warmed up. He had once talked to an audience about the relationship of the leaders to the people. "We're not going to be dealing in commandism, we're not going to be dealing in no tailism," he had put it as only he could. "Just as fast as the people can possibly go, that's just as fast as we can take it." Jeff urged him not to give up on that plan. The car pulled up in front of 2337 West Monroe Street, the faded tan and green building where Fred had a first-floor apartment. Jeff watched him head up the decaying wooden stairs that led inside.

Less than a week later, on December 4, fifteen officers of the Red Squad gathered before dawn outside that same building. The Federal Bureau of Investigation had provided the Chicago police with a detailed map that showed where Hampton usually slept. They entered through the front and back and fired almost one hundred bullets into the apartment. Hampton, lying on a bare mattress, stayed fast asleep. Earlier that evening, an FBI informer who had infiltrated the Panthers had slipped him phenobarbital, a sleeping pill. The police knew where to find him. They put a bullet in his shoulder and pumped two more through the back of his head.

Hundreds of mourners trooped through the apartment or filed past Hampton's coffin. He was the twenty-eighth Panther to meet a violent death in the past two years. Black militants were risking their lives to be political. The Weathermen felt they should be doing the same. It was only a matter of time before the police started blasting predawn raids into their own apartments. Walking past Chairman Fred's casket in the South Side funeral home, Jeff and the others knew that it was time to build an underground.

•••

The decade was ending at the wrong time; the finish was coming too soon or too late, but none of the questions that had wracked the years with conflict had been resolved. In spite of poverty programs and civil rights laws, the ghettos were growing larger and more violent. Despite the efforts of the movement, there were still almost half a million American soldiers in Vietnam, and the war was about to spread into Cambodia. The youth rebellion, the counterculture, had gathered 250,000 kids at Woodstock in August, reviving for three days of peace and love the dreams of a new communal society. Then in December, police arrested Charles Manson and his "family" for ritual murders they had committed more than a year earlier. It was the murderers in hippie clothing who had the final word on the Sixties. Manson, taking the same drugs, digging the same music as the Woodstock kids, had ruined the last of the decade's hopeful dreams.

This made for a dark mood when hundreds of Weathermen met together in Michigan on December 27 in the Giant Ballroom, a dance hall in Flint's black neighborhood. The meeting was called "a gathering of the tribes—a war council," and people were frisked for weapons at the door. Inside, they found a twenty-foot-long card-board machine gun dangling from the ceiling. In one corner was a pool of blood from a knife fight that had broken out the night before. The walls were posted with photos of Ho Chi Minh, Che, Fidel, and Fred Hampton. There was also a picture of Sharon Tate, one of Manson's victims.

The dance hall's sound system shook the floors as the Weathermen threw a party. There was a songbook and the gathered tribes sang, "We all live in a Weatherman machine, Weatherman machine, Weatherman machine," to the tune of the Beatles' *Yellow Submarine*. They sang "I'm dreaming of a white riot" and "Ho Ho Ho Chi Minh the NLF Is Gonna Win" to the tune of "Heard It Through the Grapevine."

At Flint, there was a feeling of desperation and a need for self-purgation, confession and absolution. Observers wondered at the change that had come over them. Jeff and Eleanor—and almost the entire organization—had missed Woodstock; now they were singing and dancing. What almost nobody knew was that this would be their last public appearance. The leaders were ready to disappear. They had collected safe houses, false identifications, untraceable automobiles. Flint was in part the final fling of an army marching off to a battle. It was also a distraction, a puff of smoke to engulf the stage; when it cleared, the magician would be gone.

Jeff's old friends—the comrades who had been with him through Antioch, the Pentagon, the Democratic Convention and the Days of Rage—were alienated and abandoned. His relationships were casualties of the Smash Monogamy movement. Jonny Lerner and Bill Willett had suffered through torturous criticism and self-criticism sessions, grueling interrogations that were supposed to help the leaders decide who had the strength and discipline to go underground. For hours, peoples' weaknesses and inconsistencies were thrown in their faces. Jeff's friends had waited in vain for Jeff to come to their defense. After an entire night of being attacked, Jonny had looked over and seen that Jeff had fallen asleep in his chair.

The ballroom was dark. Blankets, sleeping bags, pillows, and trash were piled into the corners to make room on the floor. The

Weathermen slept for an hour each night, and in the days, found time for meetings and work. Eleanor dropped acid for the first time in her life. But Flint was mostly about dancing. The last night of the War Council ended in frenzy. Weathermen frolicked until morning, with three fingers raised in imitation of the fork that Manson had stuck into the body of one of his victims. "He made people afraid," they said, "that's what we have to do."

The stereo speakers rattled the walls, playing Sly and the Family Stone's "Thank You (Falettinme be mice elf Agin)" in an endless loop. When the chorus started, the frantic revolutionaries replaced the lyrics with the words, "Che . . . viva . . . viva Che." Over and over, they hypnotized themselves and found release. Many there, they assumed, would meet Fred Hampton's fate within the year.

The next morning, Jeff woke up and cleared out, leaving the wreckage behind. Michigan was buried in snow as he left the ballroom for the next stop. It was time for a new beginning. He was going underground.

It was January 1, 1970.

CHAPTER 9

In the Forest

HELLO. This is Bernardine Dohrn."
A disembodied voice. A slow, careful enunciation of a prepared message.

"I'm going to read a declaration of a state of war."

At 7:30 A.M., on May 21, 1970, the early morning crew at radio station KPFK in Los Angeles had discovered this hidden audiotape in a nearby pay phone booth. Typed transcripts of the declaration were also delivered, in blank brown envelopes, to the Liberation News Service and the Chicago bureau of the *New York Times*.

"This is the first communication from the Weatherman underground."

In fact, that was not quite true. The March 6 explosion in the basement of James Wilkerson's Greenwich Village townhouse had been the underground's first communication. Since that warm pre-spring day, the American government had gone the limit looking for them. But the Weathermen had evaded capture. Not only that, they weren't running scared. They were declaring war. This low-tech missive, recorded on a store-bought cassette player, signaled the start of their offensive.

"Within the next fourteen days we will attack a symbol or institution of Amerikan injustice. This is the way we celebrate the example of Eldridge Cleaver and H. Rap Brown and all black revolutionaries who first inspired us by their fight behind enemy lines for the liberation of their people.

"Never again will they fight alone."

Fourteen days. The declaration was quoted at length in the *New York Times,* and in its entirety in the *Old Mole,* the *Liberated Guardian,* and the *Berkeley Tribe.* Their readers and, surely, agents of the Federal Bureau of Investigation began counting the days. Two weeks were nothing to the people whose job it was to find the Weathermen. The government had already waited five months—ever since the group's last public appearance at the War Council in Flint, Michigan—for a chance to get them into custody.

In their absence, the antiwar movement had grown even stronger than it had been in 1968. Nixon announced the American incursion into Cambodia on April 30, and protesters launched their own invasion into the streets. Within a week, National Guardsmen had shot and killed four white students on the campus of Kent State University in Ohio. Ten days after that, police in Mississippi used shotguns to kill two black students in a crowd at Jackson State University. In that time, more than 500 colleges had been shut down, and 100,000 marchers had swarmed through Washington, D.C.

At the end of the specified fourteen days, all of America's symbols and institutions remained intact. "Raising people's hopes that high isn't a good way to build trust in the underground," complained a reader's letter to the *Tribe.*

Then, on the evening of the twentieth day, an anonymous telephone call was placed to New York City. "There is a bomb set to go off at police headquarters," a man told the switchboard operator. A quarter of an hour later, at 6:57 P.M., a time bomb with the explosive force of ten to fifteen sticks of dynamite detonated inside the second-floor men's bathroom of the police building in Lower Manhattan. Windows shattered down into the streets below. Mortar and brick collapsed, and files were scattered inside the offices. Seven were hurt, mainly by the falling glass, and three were taken to the emergency room.

Early the next morning, hand-written copies of a note arrived by special delivery at the *New York Times* and the Associated Press. "The pigs in this country are our enemies," it said. They "try to look invulnerable, but we keep finding their weaknesses. . . . They look for us— We get to them first."

The city offered a $25,000 reward for information leading to the radical bombers. Mayor John Lindsay stood in the rubble and vowed to reporters that the "police investigation now going forward will be relentless." If these "cowardly bombers," as a *Times* editorial dubbed them, wanted war, war is what they would get. The only problem was that bombs had been exploding around town for months, and the previous investigations, all equally "relentless," had done nothing to diminish the attacks. No other city suffered more from the flames of political violence. In the previous sixteen months, 121 bombs, mostly prepared and detonated by antiwar activists, had exploded around New York.

And at least one went off before it was prepared. Of all the bombings, none had been as spectacular as the townhouse explosion. It had made for fascinating news stories: self-destructive Ivy Leaguers, upper-class levelers, dynamite in a fashionable neighborhood. "Convinced that only violence can change society," *Life* magazine reported in late March, "a small group of fanatic young radicals has taken the dead-end road of terrorism. Some call themselves Weathermen." They had never received so much press. They topped the nightly news broadcasts. A photo spread of the victims and survivors in one national news magazine included a picture of Cathy Wilkerson and Jeff as they had boarded the plane together on their way to Cambodia in 1967.

Late in March, several Weathermen were scheduled to appear in a Chicago courtroom to face charges of rioting during the Days of Rage. No one showed, and a few days later, the federal government charged twelve leaders of the group with conspiracy. Mark Rudd, Bernardine Dohrn, Jeffrey Jones, Kathy Boudin, Bill Ayers, and John Jacobs were among a dozen defendants. They had all been accused of "crossing state lines with the intent to foment a riot and conspiring to do so," the identical charge leveled at the Chicago Eight a year earlier. Julius Hoffman, the same judge who had ordered Black Panthers leader Bobby Seale bound and gagged in court and whom Jeff had named as the enemy during the Days of Rage, was assigned the case.

But the defendants were nowhere to be found. Bench warrants were issued with "unlawful flight to avoid prosecution" added to the list of charges. The Federal Bureau of Investigation launched a national manhunt for the Weathermen, whom J. Edgar Hoover referred to as "the most violent, persistent and pernicious of revolutionary groups." No one doubted that they would be brought to justice shortly. The FBI was on the case, and its agents always got their man.

Summer dragged on with no results. Congress convened hearings in July to study the rise in political terrorism. Over the course of five days, dozens of politicians, analysts, and lobbyists expressed bewilderment at this new enemy of the state. "What kind of person," one congressman asked, plays "with highly volatile explosives as casually as a 10-year-old youngster builds a model airplane?" The old days began to look surprisingly rosy. At least with the Commies, you were dealing with people who had a system. These Weathermen had no historical materialism, no motive at all. "There is no real reason and logic to exactly what and why they bomb," a congressman complained. "It is bomb for bombing's sake against the establishment," and, he added a little nervously, "I guess we are all the 'establishment.' "

But nothing said by any expert could equal the eloquence of the large chart of printed numbers that the Treasury Department had compiled to track the terror epidemic. The Weathermen were the most notorious, but they were not the only group to use violence as a protest tool. From the start of 1969 to mid-April 1970, there had been 40,934 bombings, attempted bombings, and bomb threats, leading to forty-three deaths and almost $22 million in damage. Out of this total, 975 had been explosive, as opposed to incendiary, attacks. This meant that an average of two bombs that someone had planned, constructed, and placed had detonated every day for more than a year. Nothing like it had ever been seen before.

The FBI had 9,000 special agents. Their top priority was to bring the "well-known New Leftists . . . Mark Rudd, Bill Ayers, Jeff Jones, and Bernardine Dohrn" to justice. The G-men contacted their informants. They traveled to Flint. They made unannounced visits to friends and family, pinned mugshots to post office walls around the country. Dohrn, the most charismatic of all the fugitives, was placed on the Ten Most Wanted list. The world-famous FBI laboratory was equipped with everything a sleuth should need to crack this case: machines to analyze microscopic clues, a serology lab to study blood samples, a petrography wing to match shoe patterns, and a hair and fibers team that was second to none. Yet all these resources failed to produce the band of lunatic hippies who were making a mockery of the bureau. Memo after memo reported "negative results." Disheartened field agents inked up their hand stamps and marked "unknown" in the spaces reserved for addresses and whereabouts.

Perhaps the best clue was supplied by the Weathermen themselves in the declaration of war they had sent before the detonation at New York City police headquarters. "If you want to find us," they had said, "this is where we are. In every tribe, commune, dormitory, farmhouse, barracks and townhouse where kids are making love, smoking dope and loading guns."

•••

If you wanted to find one of them—a blond whose hair was dyed an almost convincing chestnut brown—he could be seen most evenings arriving at the Sausalito piers, just north of the Golden Gate Bridge. Jeff never parked in front of where he lived; instead, he left his pickup truck a few blocks distant and walked toward the bay. The waterfront had its own sounds, a whipping wind, and a certain smell. The boat basin was a floating trailer park that for years had been home to beatniks, widows, and anyone else with a reason to avoid the encumbrances of terra firma.

Jeff swung through the wooden gate and stepped out onto the solid planks that led to the moorings. He walked along the boards of Pier Six, between the slowly rotting boats and gulls perched on almost every post. Two-thirds of the way down the dock, almost fifty yards from shore, he entered the pale pink houseboat from which he and Bernardine Dohrn handled affairs of the newly created West Coast underground.

The houseboat had its own slight motion except for twice a day, at low tides, when it settled on the muddy bottom. There was a fireplace in the middle of the main room and a metal ladder leading to a rooftop patio where Bernardine sunbathed. Rent was two hundred dollars a month, and it was worth it for the view alone. Out on the water, there was no street noise, no television sets, no ringing phones. There was only one way to get there, so Jeff could never be taken by surprise.

He had not come to San Francisco just to become a floating hippie. He had an explicit political goal, and a congressional report described it accurately when it referred to Weatherman's "intention to build a small, tough, paramilitary organization designed to carry out urban guerilla warfare to bring about the revolution."

A daunting project, perhaps, but not as harrowing as what Jeff had just been through in Chicago. SDS was finished and the office abandoned. The movement had split until every member was a political faction, and every two were a political argument. The hardest core was disgusted by the milder shades. Total sacrifice was the only sacrifice that was acceptable; resting was frowned upon, and complacency was treason.

Leaving this and arriving in San Francisco had been like stepping out of a darkened movie theater and finding that it's still afternoon and the sun is shining. Here, the police were not watching his movements. At least he hoped not. His days of street fighting with the cops were over. As long as he was careful and made each decision with its long-term consequences in mind, the underground would offer him protection. So he parked his car a few blocks from home and took a hundred little precautions. Straight paths and candid conversation were gone from Jeff's life. He had exchanged them for diagonals and curlicues, tangents, oxbows, and elliptical trajectories.

He got started immediately with the cloak and dagger. In January 1970, Jeff went to a restaurant in Chinatown to meet a man in a trench coat whom he had never seen before and would never see again. They had dim sum, drank Chinese tea from little cups, and talked about the war. The man belonged to a different underground, helping draft dodgers flee the country. At the end of the meal, he reached into the pocket of his coat and handed over an envelope. Inside, Jeff found a miscellany of blank documents: birth and baptismal certificates and half a dozen draft cards. All he had to do was fill them in and become someone else.

A new persona was built like a pyramid standing on its head—the thin capstone went at the bottom. Each additional piece of ID added weight and scope until the base, a legitimately issued driver's license, completed the structure. An inverted pyramid was not a steady construction, and neither was a false identity.

Jeff took his draft cards, rolled one blank copy into the typewriter and keyed in a name. He usually stuck to the J's: John, Jake, Jason. He classified himself 4F and signed on the line. The draft card would not get him a phone bill or satisfy a police officer, but along with a birth certificate or library card, it would get him into a three-hour driving course. In the next few years, he would take the course more than twenty times. Each time he watched the gory instructional film of horrific crashes and he became, of necessity, a very safe driver. The three-hour certificate was another building block, and for an extra twenty bucks, most instructors would allow him to use their car to take the road test.

Jeff always tried to have a valid driver's license on him, another one stashed away, and a third that he was building up. He learned which states required the least information and spent much of his time in small-town Department of Motor Vehicles offices, always arriving with his forms perfectly filled out. When his number was called, he would walk to the counter, place the neatly typed sheet and exact change in front of the teller, and make as little conversation as possible. That almost always worked. Once he listed Portland, Maine, as his place of birth. The woman behind the counter flashed a smile and said, "I'm from Portland too. What part did you grow up in?" Jeff thought about grabbing his forms and bolting for the door. Instead, he said, "You know, I don't remember." She might have found that odd, but she gave him the license anyway.

With that, he could buy a car, and good sense seemed to urge an inconspicuous one. But practicality was no competition for true love, and that's what Jeff found in a forest green 1954 Chevrolet pickup truck. So that no law enforcement officer should ever mistake the truck, he lined the roof with paisley fabric, covered the floor in thick Persian carpeting, and replaced the gearshift handle with a cut-glass doorknob. He called her Suzie Q.

Everything he did went toward creating a secure network in California. He had little contact with the other groups in New York City and Michigan. In Manhattan, one of the autonomous collectives had a different agenda. Far from finding safe houses, they moved into the family home of a well-known Weatherwoman. To prove themselves the heaviest of the factions, they planned to start the revolution with a big bang—only their nail-packed antipersonnel bomb had exploded in their own basement instead of in the midst of an Officer's Club dance at Fort Dix, New Jersey, where dozens of young military couples might have been maimed and killed.

It took days before Jeff began to sort out the implications of the townhouse explosion. First, he grieved. Then he worried about the timetable; his plan had always been to disappear at the end of March after he missed his scheduled court appearance. Now, nearly every person in the organization—hundreds of members and supporters— had unexpectedly become fugitives overnight.

Close friends were dead, and across the country, their survivors were trying to make sense of the accident. For Jeff, it was a political question. He realized that a strategy that demanded human casualties would not spare the strategists themselves. Others had taken a different lesson. People in New York City, especially John Jacobs who, with Terry Robbins dead, was now the East Coast leader, were arguing that the inexperience, not the politics, of the townhouse group was to blame for the disaster. Jacobs, known everywhere as J.J., believed the people in the townhouse had simply been careless with their weapons and had activated the wrong connection or incorrectly rigged the timer. As in the movies, they had cut the blue wire instead of the red.

Shortly after the explosion, Jeff decided to see his dad in Los Angeles. Every little comfort of home was a revelation: a couch to recline on, a cold beer, TV. He wandered the San Gabriel foothills that rose straight out of his father's backyard. How had he chosen a life of constriction, of urban alleys and dingy warrens, when he was so much happier outdoors? Underground was exactly the place that his temperament most demanded he avoid. If there was to be an underground, he decided, it would be a tribe, wild and free, rather than an army.

He remembered a warning Albert had given him before the Days of Rage. In his sternest voice, his father had said, "Son, I believe very strongly in your goals. But if you set out to hurt somebody, I would hope and pray that you are hurt first." Jeff decided that he no longer wanted anyone to get hurt. He had argued with J.J. and the others, but now he was done arguing. He went to the houseboat and sat on the roof with Bernardine. Together, they began to plan a national meeting on their turf in northern California. The two of them would be the only ones who knew where to go. They would gather people and drive them to the site. They would set the tone and the agenda. In other words, they plotted to take over the organization.

They found a house in Mendocino, a coastal town 150 miles north of San Francisco. Windswept and salt-breezy, it had long been a refuge for hippies, and a few more could arrive without arousing any suspicions. The waves pounded the shore with a music that Jeff hoped would soothe his troubled party back to sanity. The meeting house had two stories and large bay windows facing the sea. It had wide lawns and no close neighbors—the perfect place for a dozen or so freaked-out revolutionaries to spend a week without attracting notice. They put out the call, and late in the spring of 1970, Weathermen from across the country headed west.

Eleanor was in New York City. She lived inconspicuously but under her own name. Since the explosion, she had kept to herself as much as possible. She traveled to California with Bill Ayers and J.J., who started arguing his position as soon as they left the City and kept it up during the entire trip. He sensed that he was speeding toward a clash of wills and a struggle for moral superiority. It didn't help his cause that he was traveling in a rented car purchased with a stolen credit card. When Jeff found out, he demanded they ditch it and take a bus the rest of the way.

J.J. was a master propagandist and a dazzler with words. He spoke in monologues and emphasized his points with frantic gestures. He had been at Columbia and the Days of Rage. More than anyone else, the decision to go underground had been his. At Flint, he and Eleanor had taken acid together. His dark hair and pointy beard had made her feel as if she was in the presence of a wolf, predatory and dangerous.

Arriving in San Francisco, Eleanor walked to Geary Boulevard and looked for her contact. Then she saw Jeff coming toward her. He wore boots and a leather cowboy hat and warmly welcomed her to the West Coast. San Francisco was a revelation. At a swimming hole outside the city, she saw dozens of stark-naked flower children frolicking in the water. Even the hippies didn't do that back in Brooklyn.

When everyone was settled in, Jeff outlined the rules for the conference. There would be no group discussions for a few days. For now, they were to relax and share each others' company. Everyone agreed to this but J.J. He was eager to argue and looked everywhere for an audience.

Meanwhile, Jeff and Bernardine allowed the scenery to take its effect. In the evenings, everyone pitched in cooking huge spaghetti and salad dinners. It was treatment by normalcy. A revolutionary laughing over a bowl of noodles was less likely to kill or be killed than one haunted and alone, eating scraps in a city cellar. Jeff and Bill strolled out onto the cliff. Jeff said to him, "Bill, your best friend just killed your girlfriend, and it's okay for you to be angry about that and mourn." Jeff and Bernardine made converts and then threw open the discussion. For days they argued, sitting in a circle on the thick shag carpet in the sunken living room. At night, they scrunched up onto the sofas, spread out sleeping bags, or just lay where they fell.

Steadily, the opposition lessened until only J.J. and a few others insisted on military action. He had grown increasingly frantic as his support vanished. He saw the underground, his idea, being taken from him. But he couldn't admit a mistake.

"All right," Jeff said, "we're not going to be able to work with you." Then Bernardine, who had the ultimate authority to say it, told him he was out of the organization.

Jeff and Bernardine returned to San Francisco. Only at the Mendocino meeting, where they had argued down the most bellicose strategists of the left, could theirs' have been the position of moderation. In the larger perspective of the antiwar movement, Jeff still inhabited the lunatic fringe. A few weeks after the meeting, Weatherman released its Declaration of a State of War that promised to attack a symbol of Amerikan injustice within fourteen days. It was difficult to view it as a document created by the group's peaceful wing—it certainly would not have satisfied Albert's concept of pacifism—but that is what it was.

The declaration incorporated Jeff's ideas at Mendocino. It advocated political bombings and the creation of a revolutionary underground. From then on, Weatherman's targets would be symbols of American power rather than the bodies of American humans.

•••

No middle-class white American was educated for a career in constructing and operating an underground network for the purpose of overthrowing the government. Such a course was absent from the curriculum at even the best colleges, which many Weathermen had attended. This was true even at progressive Antioch, where Jeff had spent two years.

Training came from the veterans of Third World revolutions. Weathermen watched *The Battle of Algiers* and read guerrilla manuals by Carlos Marighella from Brazil and Amílcar Cabral of Guinea Bissau. In 1971, Random House published the scrapbooks of a woman freedom fighter in *Tania: The Unforgettable Guerrilla*. Tania, who had died with Che Guevara in Bolivia in 1967, became a heroine to Americans, including Patty Hearst who adopted the name as her own after being kidnapped by the Symbionese Liberation Army in the mid-1970s. The original Tania taught the lessons of becoming a new person. "I was able to practice sustaining a personality image," she wrote. "As the days went by, I found it necessary to tell anecdotes of my life and talk about my family problems and my aspirations. It reached the point that I convinced myself I was talking about my real life."

The Vietnamese, of course, remained the dominant inspiration. The theories of General Vo Nguyen Giap—the man whose armies defeated the Japanese and French and were on the verge of adding the Americans to his list—were available in *The Military Art of People's War.* The struggle of the Huk guerrillas in the 1950s Philippines had been recorded by William Pomeroy. "It has been said that a guerrilla army is like a fish in the sea of the people," he wrote. "It can also be like the leaves in the forest, hardly stirring in the still air, blown about when a storm rages."

Fish in the sea, leaves in the forest: these became Jeff's metaphors for the underground. They implied a naturalness and harmony that was central to his politics. He would blend in and disappear, not in tropical jungles as the Huks had done, but in northern California's flourishing counterculture. "They have learned to survive together in the poisoned cities and how to live on the road and the land," the Weathermen wrote of these tie-dyed utopians. "They've moved to the country and found new ways to bring up free wild children. People have purified themselves with organic food, fought for sexual liberation, grown long hair." The underground members would be fish in this sea of hippies.

In 1970, one of the biggest fish was in the tank: Dr. Timothy Leary was a prisoner of the state of California. An icon of the 1960s, Leary had cast off a career as a Harvard researcher to proselytize for the liberating power of psychedelic drugs. He urged young people to abandon the strivings for political and material gain in favor of his own recipe: tune in, turn on, drop out. "He did for LSD," a government agent once said, "what Henry Ford did for the motor car."

In January, Leary had been caught with two joints and a few flakes of marijuana that police vacuumed from his jacket pocket. The government made an example of the good doctor and sent him for a ten-year sentence to a minimum-security prison near San Luis Obispo, where the inmates were kept behind a fifteen-foot chain link fence topped by two strands of barbed wire. Leary noticed a telephone cable that ran over the fence. It was above the level of the floodlights so that, in theory, a man crawling along it hand-over-hand would be invisible to the guards. He decided to try an escape. All he needed were helpers on the outside, people with experience in clandestine operations who could get him from Highway One, just beyond the fence, to freedom in another country.

The Weathermen were contacted by members of the Brotherhood of Eternal Love, an organization that believed it was a good thing to provide the masses with high-quality drugs and an even better thing to make a fat profit for doing so. The Brotherhood offered a fortune to have Leary transported safely across the border.

A casual observer could have watched the entire exchange without noticing it. A woman carrying a brown paper bag filled with clothes walked along the Santa Monica Pier in Los Angeles. Nothing could be more natural. She rested for a minute on an unoccupied bench and set the bag on the ground beside her feet. Here came another tired person, also carrying a brown paper bag. He sat down on the same bench and placed his package next to hers. They chatted for a few minutes. Then the man got up, grabbed a bag, and walked away. She sat for a moment longer, then left, taking with her the remaining bag. Only now, instead of clothes, it was filled with hundred-dollar bills.

Fifteen minutes later, Jeff was counting the money to see if it was all there. It was: $50,000. As an added perk, he got a few doses of Owsley acid, the Chateau Rothschild of psychedelics, to be saved for celebration when the deed was done.

The evening of September 12, 1970, was cloudy: perfect jailbreak weather. Leary, a few months short of his fiftieth birthday, pulled himself across the wire. He ran through the woods bordering the highway until he found a tree with three trunks growing from a single root. He waited there. Ten minutes later, a car approached, its right blinker flashing. Leary ran to the road and the car door flew open. "Nino?" asked one of two young women inside. He climbed in and they drove off at high speed.

In the back seat, Nino changed from his prison-issued blue denim shirt and jeans and was handed a wallet with a new set of IDs. His old clothes were transferred to another car headed south—they would be stashed in a gas station bathroom closer to Los Angeles. After a few miles, Nino himself was moved from the car into the back of a camper driven by a middle-aged couple. They continued north to San Francisco. The next morning, Leary and the middle-aged man, code-named Frank, prepared to continue alone together: just a couple of fishermen out for a few days in the woods. Frank removed the camper's California plates, revealing a set from Utah that had been hidden underneath. He left the bumper sticker: "America, Love it or Leave it."

Frank, whose real name was Clayton Van Lydegraf, was older than Leary and one of the few members of the underground who could have passed as his fishing buddy. As a traditional Marxist with no sympathy for the guru of acid, he wasn't thrilled with the assignment. Facing a drive of hundreds of miles with only each other for comfort, Van Lydegraf turned to Leary and said, "I was against this whole thing from the start and if it was up to me you'd still be rotting in jail."

By the time they set up at a campground in the redwoods, they had been arguing for hours. When Jeff, Bernardine, and Bill Ayers arrived after dark, Nino and Frank were both eager for their company. Jeff had seen Leary once before, when he had given a speech at Antioch in 1965. Now the doctor looked old and worn out from his escape. The climb along the cable had taken all his strength.

They talked around the campfire and drafted a communiqué, writing until the embers in the pit were black. Two days later, they released their statement to the press. "The Weatherman Underground," it began, "has had the honor and pleasure of helping Dr. Timothy Leary escape from the POW camp at San Luis Obispo." They arranged for his passport and moved him around the country. Before he left, they grieved together over the news that Jimi Hendrix had died. A month later, Leary surfaced in Algeria as a guest of exiled Black Panther Eldridge Cleaver. They were jubilant fugitives. Stew Albert, a Yippie, and Eleanor's ex-husband, Jonah Raskin, visited soon after Leary and his wife, Rosemary, arrived. "He was disguised as a completely ordinary pig businessman," Stew wrote. "But the twinkle in his eyes was a dead giveaway. Fortunately the F.B.I. isn't trained to read twinkles."

" 'Hey Leary, did you spend much time with the Weathermen?' Eldridge inquired."

" 'Yes, we turned on a lot and Rosemary and I went to see Woodstock with Bernardine Dohrn and Jeff Jones. We were stoned out of our minds."

Television reporters hurried to Africa. Wearing a floppy leather hat and twinkling away, Leary told them, "I escaped with the help of the Weatherman underground. Twenty-five of their crack underground operators came to California for six weeks before my escape and it was a very complicated operation. They not only helped us escape they spirited us to several of their underground stations with great efficiency."

Leary quickly alienated both Cleaver and the Algerian government by smuggling 20,000 hits of acid into the country and trying out his philosophy on the people of Africa. A few months later, he was on the run again—first to Switzerland and finally Afghanistan, where American forces negotiated his capture. Facing serious jail time in the States, Leary suddenly became pragmatic. "I want to get out of prison as quickly as I can," he told FBI agents. His new comrades, the Weathermen, were the first to be sacrificed.

He identified them from photographs and led investigators to the safe houses they had used to get him out of the country. "I'd like to use this as step number one in seeing if I can work out a collaborative and an intelligent, an honorable relationship with different government agencies," he said, as the tape reel wound around its spokes, recording his testimony. The FBI followed up the leads, but word of Leary's intentions had leaked out and agents found the trail cold, the operators vanished, and the buildings long abandoned.

•••

It was autumn 1970, and dusk came early, bringing ocean fog and San Francisco damp. Jeff and Bernardine avoided the city's trendier neighborhoods, sticking instead to working-class districts where they would be unlikely to run into old friends. The tenements and warehouses of the Tenderloin, where they had just concluded a meeting, were adequately unfashionable. Bernardine opened the door to Suzie Q and sat behind the wheel as Jeff climbed into the passenger's side. They had a date to meet some contacts at a Chinese restaurant near the beach, but first they needed to pick up some money.

Revolution was Jeff's day job, and it didn't pay. Most of the Brotherhood's $50,000 had gone to spring Leary. Afterward, he was back to surviving on handouts. Jeff's collective operated on roughly $1,200 each month and kept to a strict budget. A few weeks earlier, he had used almost $300 to buy a brand-new engine for Suzie Q. She had never run better; that big six-cylinder motor was good for another 200,000 miles.

Bernardine parked in front of the Western Union office. This was only the second time Jeff had come personally—usually a subordinate was sent to pick up money—but he was in the neighborhood and needed the cash to pay for dinner. He was expecting a payment from an East Coast supporter. Less than a thousand dollars, it would still come in handy.

Jeff got out of the truck. This was the risky part. Before he pushed open the glass door to the office, he ran through his mental checklist: *who am I, where do I live, what is my social security number, why am I here*. Then, after a second's hesitation, he pushed through and got in line.

Immediately, he sensed trouble. Three men, two whites and an Asian, dressed in costume-room hippie outfits, were lounging on the far side of the office. One of them leaned his foot up against the wall, the very image of nonchalant relaxation. Jeff calculated quickly. If they were FBI, they could grab him at any moment. If they knew who he was, they would have arrested him already. Nothing would draw more attention to himself than turning around and fleeing the building without his money. He decided to wait.

Often when he was going on a mission like this, he'd bring the *Chronicle* sports section. It would serve as cover and also help him pass the time and banish nerves. He missed it now. The people in the line ahead were taking forever. He stood patiently as, one by one, they stumbled through their transactions. Finally, he reached the counter and gave his name, sliding his license to the teller through a slot in the bullet-proof glass. He got his money and hurried out, leaping back into the truck.

Bernardine had left the motor running. Jeff said to her, "There were three guys in there, and I didn't like the looks of them." She told him a man had just walked up next to the truck and checked the license plate number. As she pulled out into the street, Jeff peered into the extra-large side mirrors he'd installed especially for this type of chase. As soon as Suzie Q pulled out into traffic, a black car parked on the other side of the street hung a U-turn and started to follow.

Through four or five intersections, their tail stayed half a block back. Up ahead the streetlight turned yellow. Bernardine slammed her foot down on the accelerator; the brand-new engine fired gasoline to the pistons, which exploded into action. The pickup sped under the light just as it turned red. Behind them, their pursuer was trapped by a stream of traffic. Bernardine didn't let up, navigating in zigzags out of downtown and toward the beach. They parked the truck on a deserted street and walked to the restaurant where Bill Ayers and the rest of their friends were waiting.

In the safety and warmth of the restaurant, Jeff began to doubt if anything had actually happened. Were those men really suspicious looking? Had that car been following them? This was always a problem: you were never sure what you had seen. As dinner wound down, he began to feel a little embarrassed. Paranoia had finally caught him. Just in case, though, he switched cars with others at the table. They weren't fugitives and had no reason to worry about being seen in the truck. After dinner, Jeff drove their car back to the houseboat while they went downtown in Suzie Q to catch a movie.

The next morning, he went to a pay phone and made contact with the people who had borrowed his Chevy. They told him that after the movie, they had gotten into the truck and started driving. Moments later, they were surrounded by police cars and unmarked vehicles. Agents grabbed them, took them into separate cars, and interrogated them. After answering the questions, they were brought back and allowed to drive off. It was clear what had happened: the FBI had bugged the pickup and were now waiting to be led to the Weathermen. The night before, they hadn't grabbed Jeff in the Western Union office because they weren't expecting a leader to show up. Waiting for a bag man who would lead them to the leaders, they had blown a golden opportunity.

Jeff listened on the phone to the end of the story. They had driven to the most deserted place they could find, parked the pickup in a ditch, thrown away the key, and run like hell.

He had lost Suzie Q.

Then he began to realize the greater loss. He had registered the truck with the same name he used to pay an electricity bill at a San Francisco apartment; someone else had used that address to receive a driver's license. As he hurried back to the houseboat, the repercussions branched and spread. The entire network was interconnected. Everything he had spent the past eight months building was gone.

•••

On October 5, 1970, 364 days after it was first destroyed, bombers again blew up the Haymarket police statue in Chicago. A caller identifying himself as "Mr. Weatherman" gave warning ahead of time, and when the explosion occurred at 1:15 A.M., nobody was hurt. For the second time in a year, the stern bronze cop lay helplessly on the ground, his legs blown off in either direction.

The next day, a letter was given to Chicago newspapers. It announced the beginning of a "Fall Offensive" and was signed by Jeff, Bernardine, and Bill Ayers. "Last night we destroyed the pig again," they wrote. "We are building a culture and a society that can resist genocide. It is a culture of total resistance to mind-controlling maniacs; a culture of high-energy sisters getting it on, of hippie acid-smiles and communes and freedom to be the farthest-out people we can be." This was a departure from the dour Marxist-Leninist language of the pre-Mendocino days. But it wouldn't have been a Weatherman message if it didn't include some threats, and this one ended with a warning to President Nixon: "Guard your planes, guard your colleges, guard your banks, guard your children, *guard your doors.*"

In fact, the president was safe from the Weatherpeople. Their network was in disarray. Jeff had told only a few people where he had been living, so he hoped that the houseboat remained secure. Still, after the near-miss at Western Union, he was clearly no longer safe in San Francisco. He packed lightly and set off for the East Coast.

When the California network was blown, the whole organization had trembled. Back in New York, Eleanor had hurried to figure out if there were links that could stretch across the country. There were. A New York fugitive had received a speeding ticket in a West Coast car. Eleanor bought a roll of brown wrapping paper and spread it out on the floor of her apartment. With the others, she connected all the IDs, houses, and vehicles and realized that everything they too had collected was gone.

They fled Manhattan and rented a house in Hampton Bays, on Long Island, where they were joined by Jeff and the others. Their landlord told them that the previous tenant had been Jimmy Breslin, who had just spent the summer in the house writing his novel, *The Gang That Couldn't Shoot Straight*. With his entire network ruined, Jeff ruefully felt that his own gang was starting to fit that description. It was Thanksgiving season, and the Weathermen were also using the house for writing. They were working on a statement that would summarize, once and for all, the metamorphosis in their thinking.

By late 1970, the nature of the Vietnam War had changed. Nixon's strategy of Vietnamization—pulling out the infantry and escalating the aerial bombardment—had decreased American casualties. Despite the continued atrocities, the mass movement to end the war began losing its force as U.S. troops started returning home. In November, though, there were still 360,000 American soldiers in Vietnam. During Thanksgiving week, 65 of them were killed and 335 more were wounded. Total American deaths had climbed above

44,000, while the army reckoned enemy deaths at almost 700,000—and that was counting soldiers only.

On Long Island, the writing collective worked at their statement in the mornings over coffee. Jeff distributed the last of the Owsley acid and took Bernardine, Bill, and Eleanor on a wild seashell gathering expedition along the area's Atlantic beaches. On Thanksgiving Day, Eleanor cooked a turkey while the boys played touch football in the yard—just a typical All-Amerikan family.

They listened to Bob Dylan's latest album, New Morning, and when it came time to name their communiqué, they remained faithful to tradition and used him as inspiration. The New Morning statement was released to members of the underground media in December. It was a self-critical analysis of the underground's early mistakes and never could have been written in the gung-ho atmosphere of the previous spring. Taking fire from the growing women's movement, the Weatherman Underground dropped its gender-insensitive syllable and become the Weather Underground. It also unveiled a new emblem, evocative of the counterculture: a rainbow shot through with lightning.

Nine months had passed since the explosion on Eleventh Street and the tragedy was still shaping their decisions. "The townhouse," they wrote in New Morning, "forever destroyed our belief that armed struggle is the only real revolutionary struggle."

The deaths of three friends ended our military conception of what we are doing. It took us weeks of careful talking. . . . But it was clear that more had been wrong with our direction than technical inexperience (always install a safety switch so you can turn it off and on and a light to indicate if a short circuit exists). . . .
At the end they believed and acted as if only those who die are proven revolutionaries. Many people had been argued into doing something they did not believe in, many had not slept for days. Personal relationships were full of guilt and fear. The group had spent so much time willing themselves to act that they had not dealt with the basic technological considerations of safety. . . .
This tendency to consider only bombings or picking up the gun

as revolutionary, with the glorification of the heavier the better, we've called the military error.

For as long as Jeff was associated with it, the Weather Underground would never again hurt another person.

•••

A bomb's purpose is to kill. It is far easier to build a bomb to kill a hundred people than it is to construct one that will harm none. Once the Weathermen decided that their bombs would never hurt people, constructing and placing them became far more complex. Some members became expert at demolitions, and precious copies of the *Blaster's Handbook* were passed around and hidden beneath closet floorboards. They perfected safe and dependable timers. When they calculated the number of sticks of dynamite to use, they aimed for the least power that might be effective. They did not try to destroy the American government or disable its war machine. "We have obviously not gone in for large scale material damage," they admitted in New Morning. "Most of our actions have hurt the enemy on about the same military scale as a bee sting."

Over time the police came to recognize the fingerprints of an authentic Weather action. There was always a warning ahead of time and a communiqué claiming responsibility afterward. The underground had a penchant for setting off bombs inside bathrooms, and over the years, the nation's toilets and sinks paid a particularly heavy price for the government's war policies.

Other groups planted larger bombs that did more damage, but only the Weather Underground built an organization capable of conducting a long-running campaign that could attack effectively and still avoid capture. From 1970 through the end of 1975, the group claimed responsibility for detonating more than twenty bombs around the country.

•••

In February 1971, South Vietnamese armies, backed by American air support, invaded the neighboring country of Laos. While Nixon's

Vietnamization was pulling troops back home, this latest invasion proved he was still committed to expanding the war.

At 1:00 A.M., on March 1, 1971, an anonymous caller spoke to Norma J. Fullerton, a switchboard operator at the U.S. Capitol Building, in what she would describe to reporters as a "low, hard tone." What he said terrified her: "This building will blow up in 30 minutes. You will get many calls like this, but this one is real. Evacuate the building. This is in protest of the Nixon involvement in Laos." Half an hour later, a bomb exploded inside a little-used men's bathroom in a restricted area of the Capitol's lower floor. The force of detonation ruined a congressional barber shop, upset tables in the senators' dining room, and heavily damaged a painting of three famous Revolutionaries: George Washington, the Marquis de Lafayette, and Baron Von Steuben.

"We have attacked the Capitol," read the subsequent statement, "because it is, along with the White House and the Pentagon, the worldwide symbol of the government which is now attacking Indochina."

•••

Black revolutionary was a dangerous calling. Malcolm X, Martin Luther King, Jr., and Fred Hampton had learned that in the hardest way. At any given time, most of the leaders of the Black Panthers were in prison, and those who remained free were targeted by the FBI with its entire bag of dirty tricks.

But black revolutionaries kept fighting. George Jackson had spent most of his life in prison. First arrested at the age of fifteen, he had been given a one-year-to-life sentence for robbing $71 from a gas station in Los Angeles. For the next ten years, he was juggled around California's prisons. He went to Soledad, where he was involved in a fight that led to the death of a white guard. His letters from prison were published in the best-selling *Soledad Brother*, and Jackson became a hero to the people and a threat to the government.

"They've pushed me over the line from which there can be no retreat," he wrote. "I know that they will not be satisfied until they've pushed me out of existence altogether." Jackson, thirty years old in

1971, was transferred to San Quentin. On August 21 he was shot to death in the yard by prison guards. The warden claimed he had pulled a gun and tried to break out, but few believed his story; it was too transparent, too crude. "We may never know exactly how he died," wrote the *Berkeley Tribe*. "But we damn well know why he died."

A week later, Weather bombs exploded in the Sacramento Office of California Prisons and the Department of Corrections building in San Francisco, causing more than $100,000 in damage. "Two small bombs do not cool our rage," said the communiqué. "We nurture that rage inside us. We view our actions as simply a first expression of our love and respect for George Jackson and the warriors of San Quentin."

•••

By May 1972, the United States and North Vietnam had finally met at a conference table in Paris to discuss peace when President Nixon, in the middle of an ugly reelection campaign, escalated the air war again. He sent planes to drop mines in the enemy's major harbors and intensified the bombing campaign against Hanoi, knocking out bridges and railroads, as well as hospitals and sidewalk cafés.

On May 19, Ho Chi Minh's birthday, a bomb exploded inside a women's bathroom in the air force section of the Pentagon. Flooding from broken pipes temporarily inundated a global communications computer and ruined a top-secret archive.

•••

In the autumn of 1970, the people of Chile, South America's most mature democracy, elected a leftist government headed by Dr. Salvador Allende. In Washington, Henry Kissinger remarked that American policy could not allow a country to "go Marxist" just because "its people are irresponsible." American corporations, especially Pepsi-Cola, the Chase Manhattan Bank, and International Telephone and Telegraph, had millions of dollars in the country; they expected the U.S. government to protect these investments. The

people of Chile were irresponsible for naming a Marxist in a fair election, but it was okay because Richard Nixon and the responsible people of the Central Intelligence Agency would do all they could to destabilize and topple this legally chosen foreign regime.

On September 11, 1973, after years of intrigue, President Allende was ousted and murdered in a coup d'état supported by American secret agents and financed by American business. The coup led to worldwide outrage. ITT offices were bombed in Rome and Zurich. At 2:00 A.M. on the morning of September 28, the night telephone supervisor at the *New York Times* received a call from a man who spoke in a "radio announcer's" voice. "Take this down," he said, "because I am only going to say this once. I am the Weatherman Underground. At the I.T.T.–American building, a bomb is going to go off in 15 minutes. This is in retaliation of the I.T.T. crimes they committed against Chile." The *Times* employee immediately dialed 911.

At 2:19 A.M., a bomb—consisting of dynamite, a detonator, a battery, and a watch—exploded in the closet of a ninth-floor reception area in ITT's Manhattan office. The room was left "a mass of twisted metal strips, overturned furniture, acoustic tiles and shattered partitions." Five window panels crashed down onto the empty sidewalk of Fiftieth Street.

No one was ever convicted for these or any other Weather Underground bombings.

•••

Jeff, like his father, had a healthy American fascination with car engines unaccompanied by any particular facility with them. In the spring of 1971, having lost Suzie Q to the FBI, he had spent a few hundred bucks on a 1956 Chevy, green over white. She had a hand-painted red rose on the trunk, which was a nice aesthetic detail though, perhaps, not ideal for keeping a low profile. Jeff fiddled with Rosie's carburetor on weekend afternoons and nursed her back to something like health. With his pickup gone and the West Coast lousy with agents, he was going to steer his Chevy east to help establish a new network. Eleanor was visiting San Francisco and agreed to ride with him. As long as they stopped every two hundred miles to pour water in the radiator, Jeff thought Rosie might just make it.

Each time Jeff and Eleanor got into the car, they paused for the Conspiratorial Minute. Together, they ran through their crucial information: names, addresses, social security numbers, where they came from, where they were going. Once while they were driving, Eleanor was applying lipstick in the passenger seat when a police cruiser's sirens flashed behind their car. The cop had mistaken the white lipstick applicator for a joint. He and his partner took Jeff and Eleanor to opposite ends of the vehicle and interrogated them separately. Because of the Conspiratorial Minute, their stories matched.

It was dawn when they arrived, after three thousand miles of driving, in the Catskill Mountains. They turned from the interstate onto the twisting local roads. Dew-drippy eastern forest trees formed a tunnel of branches, and morning mist rose off the Pepacton Reservoir as they pulled up at the house where they would fall in love.

It was nondescript, remote, and surrounded by hills. On a clear day, they could sit on the porch and see seven ridge lines disappearing into the distance. The house had four bedrooms, but Jeff chose to sleep on a metal bed on the back porch. Down a path from the front door, he turned the soil over and planted a garden of cucumbers and carrots. He stuck stakes in the earth for tomato vines and pole beans. His housemates were easterners, and they had lived here for months without planting a thing. But Jeff had been in cities for too long. He was going to hike and wander among the old stone walls that farmers had stacked a hundred years earlier. When he found a nice flat rock, he was going to sit and smoke a joint. He was doing what many burnt-out Sixties survivors were attempting: retreating from politics and getting back to the land.

In the mornings, he woke in his outdoor bed to a chorus of birdsong: warblers, flickers, and a friendly scarlet tanager. He began to fall in love with upstate New York. If the vistas of the West were ecstasy, then here was comfort. A Catskills mountain was old and mellow. Erosion had ground it down and it was green from base to peak, mossy and ivied like a lived-in stone house.

And he began to notice Eleanor. They went shopping together in Delhi, the nearest town with a main street, a general store, and a grocery. There was a post office there too, where Jeff's wanted poster hung conspicuously on the wall. He could go and feel safe, knowing that the dark-haired and bearded man would never be connected with the rebellious blond kid in the photo. The Catskills had survived the Woodstock festival, and hippies were a common sight. In New Paltz, a college town, they turned the streets into a place of dogs and ponchos, pot and music. Jeff and Eleanor went often, sat in bars and felt comfortable for the first time in years.

To Eleanor, he seemed reserved and even shy. It was hard for her to connect him with the macho persona of his SDS years. He thought she was strong and funny, the heart of the household. She was amazed at his green thumb, his knowledge of birds and the outdoors, his sense of direction that would never in any circumstances leave him lost. He was dazzled by her singing voice, her wide reading and political sophistication. Products of their upbringings, the only experience they shared was the years of political struggle. Otherwise, they had almost nothing in common, and so each had what the other lacked. They grew closer every day. And one night he came in from the back porch and moved to her bedroom.

After that, he had to meet her mother.

Visiting the house was not a simple matter of popping in whenever it was convenient. Guests weren't exactly blindfolded and led, disoriented, as to a bandit's lair, but they were expected to take precautions. Annie rode a bus from Manhattan, making sure she wasn't tailed to Port Authority. She bought a ticket for New Paltz or Kingston, where she was met and driven to the house more than an hour away.

Jeff dreaded her arrival.

She knew she was visiting the country, so she packed her polyester "outdoor wear," but once installed at the dining room table, she was a fixture until she left to go back to Manhattan. She sat surrounded by a cloud of her own cigarette smoke, drinking one cup of coffee after another and lecturing on politics. When she was around, Jeff had to walk on tip-toes and creep outside to sneak a joint.

Annie and Jeff represented the Old and New lefts. She had a library of Lenin, Marx, and Mao at her fingertips from which she could provide irrefutable arguments on any subject. He had read the Port Huron Statement and hadn't bothered with the rest. Annie had to be polite because her daughter was involved with these people, but she conversed with them through gritted teeth. Realizing that the best way to protect Eleanor was to guide the group toward the nonviolent politics of the mass movement, Annie tried to become mentor to the Weathermen. Perhaps the best way to do this would have been to soothe, not taunt; to ease, not prod. But that was not how Annie talked politics.

The first thing she noticed was the garden. It reminded her of a line in New Morning that she had found especially outrageous. The Weather authors had achieved raptures in describing the hippie culture of raising "free wild children" and living on "organic food." This line had all the hallmarks of a Jeff Jones contribution. When Annie came to the house and saw the garden she said, "I see you revolutionaries are aiding the struggle by growing free wild carrots." She could never see the counterculture as political. She would say, "You can have every hippie in the world raising all the free veggies they can grow and smoking all the pot they want and you still won't have a revolution. Only the workers can control the means of production."

If Jeff said something that sounded particularly naive, she didn't gently suggest alternatives. She said, "You couldn't be more wrong" or "These ideas have been considered and rejected by every revolution in the world." Jeff's suspicion that she was probably correct hardly helped ease the unpleasantness of being scolded.

But Jeff and Annie had points of agreement too. He had always believed in the power of the masses and known that an underground acting alone could not be effective. It hardly seemed likely from their early meetings, but in the next few years Annie would become Jeff's most committed ally.

•••

In Times Square, at 7:00 P.M. on the evening of January 27, 1973, the word "PEACE" lighted up in letters ten stories high on the side of the Allied Chemical Corporation Building. For a full minute, "PEACE" also scrolled around the building's famed news ticker. The previous night, Richard Nixon had made a short speech on national television, announcing, finally, that a cease-fire agreement in Vietnam had been reached. He called it "peace with honor" and promised that the remaining American soldiers—fewer than 30,000—would be coming home within the next sixty days.

Jeff was about to turn twenty-seven. He was a wanted man, a disguised fugitive, who had not seen either his mother or his father in almost three years. The army's first acknowledged casualty in Vietnam had occurred in 1961. At that time, Jeff had been a student at Robert Fulton Junior High School in Van Nuys, California. For most of the intervening years, the deaths in Southeast Asia, the crimes of the war, had tormented him. Vietnam was his cricket chorus; it could recede into the background, but the din was always ready to return, forcing itself into his conscious thoughts and ruining his mood.

At the end of June, the army cancelled the draft, although men would still have to register with Selective Service when they turned eighteen. There were still two years to go before the fighting would stop in Vietnam, but ending the draft effectively ended the antiwar movement. It had implicated everyone in the war—sons who might fight, as well as their sisters and parents. With the draft gone, most Americans just added Vietnam to their list of other people's problems.

Jeff had become an adult while he was underground. Fighting the war had been his primary purpose. With it over, he could have claimed victory and abandoned militancy. He might have surfaced, held a press conference, copped a plea bargain, and gone on to pursue politics in the evenings like the rest of the movement people. But neither he nor the others considered it. They had gone too far down the path to turn around and come home. In fact, they would become more fanatical, study Marxist-Leninist theory, and talk more seriously than ever before about toppling the government, though the chances of succeeding were now slighter than they had been at any other time since 1968.

A businesslike revolutionary party had to have an acronym, so the Weather Underground changed its name again, to the Weather Underground Organization, or WUO. A new manifesto was written collectively and in great secret. Fewer than ten copies were printed, and Jeff carried one in his backpack to fugitives all along the eastern seaboard. He would sit while they read it and then ask, "So, are you in or out?" It was a crossroads: if anyone wanted to abandon the project, this was their opportunity. None took it.

Everyone contributed to the project. It was "chewed on and shaped in countless conversations." It "traveled around the country, developing." Jeff drafted the section on Vietnam and drew many of the maps in the book. By the time the manifesto had been approved and was ready to be printed and released to the public, more than two hundred people had affiliated themselves with the WUO.

The Red Dragon Print Collective bought a multilith offset printer and stashed it in the basement of a brownstone. The thing sat like a torture instrument in a dim and curtained room while the printers scrambled around it, turning levers and pressing buttons, covering themselves in ink. In the next room they built a phony front office with a desk, a phone, and a filing cabinet just in case any curious neighbors chose to stop by to see where all the noise was coming from. "A half a million pieces of paper went through that press," Jeff said later. "We kept the press running the way people used to keep Model-T's running. It's a 156-page book. We did 5,000 copies and every page was collated by hand—gloved hands."

Three-quarters of all the copies were distributed in a single night to alternative bookstores in San Francisco, Chicago, Madison, New York, and other friendly cities. On the morning of July 24, 1974, when the book was released, Jeff was as nervous and excited as he had been before the Days of Rage. They called it *Prairie Fire: The Politics of Anti-Imperialism,* taking the title from Chairman Mao, who once said, "A single spark can start a prairie fire." The inflammatory book came in two editions. One had black flames and writing on the front. The other, for those who wanted to remain inconspicuous, was hidden behind a blank red cover. Inside, both said "printed underground in the U.S. for the people." The original 5,000 copies sold out immediately. The authors urged others to reproduce the book themselves, and eventually more than 40,000 were printed and passed around.

After the book, the WUO put out *Osawatomie*. a quarterly newsletter named after a nickname for John Brown, the insurrectionary abolitionist. Jeff contributed short stories under the pen name Sparrow Hawk, "the only North American to become a short order cook at a truck stop on the Ho Chi Minh Trail." In his serial adventures, Sparrow Hawk dodged U.S. Marines and served tea and fried bananas to high-ranking Vietnamese Communists.

Having isolated themselves from the rest of the left, the Weathermen were once again reaching out. "We hope the paper opens a dialectic among those in the mass and clandestine movements," Bernardine, Bill, and Jeff had written in the introduction. "We hope people will take PRAIRIE FIRE as seriously as we do, study the content and write and publish their views of the paper as well as their analysis of their own practice. We will respond as best we can."

One person who read it was Emile de Antonio, a documentary filmmaker who was well known in political circles for his films: *Point of Order,* about the Army-McCarthy hearings; *In the Year of the Pig,* on Vietnam; and *Millhouse: A White Comedy,* about Richard Nixon. As he leafed through *Prairie Fire*, de Antonio asked himself, "What the hell is an essentially white, middle-class revolutionary group doing in America in the year 1975?" He contacted Robert Friedman, who had edited the *Columbia Spectator* in 1968, and got a message to the underground: let's make a film together.

In the spring of 1975, de Antonio traveled to Sheepshead Bay in Brooklyn. He walked for several blocks until he came to a phone booth. He stepped inside, and the phone immediately started ringing. He picked up after the first ring and was told to go to Lundy's, a nearby seafood restaurant, and look for a woman holding a copy of *Newsweek*.

The Steins had often celebrated birthdays and graduations at Lundy's, which was a huge and busy place occupying a full city block. When de Antonio arrived, Eleanor was there, reading

Newsweek, and beside her was Jeff. In his journal, the filmmaker would call them "bright, streetwise, pragmatic and uneducated." Jeff, whom de Antonio described as the "Leninist All-American boy," was excited about making the film. But he had some reservations and made the director promise not to cooperate with the government, even if he was subpoenaed. Jeff also insisted that the faces of the fugitives could never appear clearly on the film. Once the shooting was finished, he would be allowed to view all of the negatives and destroy any frame that could be useful to police.

In late April 1975, de Antonio, Mary Lampson, and cinematographer Haskell Wexler, who had shot *One Flew over the Cuckoo's Nest* and won an Oscar for *Who's Afraid of Virginia Woolf?* entered a dark alley where Jeff was waiting in a station wagon. He handed each of them a pair of sunglasses, painted black, so that they wouldn't know where he was taking them, and then drove around for half an hour. They found the safe house empty and remote. The windows were boarded over.

Along with Jeff, Bernardine, and Bill, Kathy Boudin and Cathy Wilkerson were participating in the project. Everyone was nervous—so many Weather people were almost never in the same place together. Jeff told the director that this was the most dangerous thing they had ever done. To protect their identities, a thin gauze was hung in front of the camera.

Filming lasted three days. Afterward, Jeff and Eleanor went to Wexler's Malibu beach house to view the film. They snuck in by lying on the floor of his car. Outside, "a couple of guys looking so much like cops, you wouldn't believe it," watched the windows through binoculars and snapped Polaroids. As the FBI agents staked out the house from the street, Jeff and Eleanor stayed in the basement where Wexler kept his Oscar. They examined the negatives frame by frame and, whenever they saw a face, they threw the celluloid image into the fireplace.

In spite of all the precautions, word of the film leaked, and de Antonio was served with a subpoena. He called a press conference and had a petition signed by thirty-two celebrities, including Jack Nicholson, Warren Beatty, Mel Brooks, Terence Malick, and Daniel

Ellsberg, who had stolen the Pentagon Papers and given them to the *New York Times*. Facing this publicity, the government backed down and withdrew the subpoena. The film benefited from the controversy, and when it was released as *Underground* in 1976 theaters billed it as "the film the FBI didn't want you to see."

Jeff had asked de Antonio to get in touch with Albert. The filmmaker called him at home and invited him to a private screening in Hollywood. Albert had not seen his son in more than five years. In that time, he had been under continual pressure from the Federal Bureau of Investigation. Agents had regularly knocked on his door at home. They made "pretense calls," posing as travel agents or insurance salesmen to make sure that Albert was still living at the same address. They had talked to his neighbors and his bosses at Disney, so he knew there were always eyes on him. A certain Agent Martin came down to the Burbank studio and asked to see him while he was at work. It was intentional harassment, an attempt to embarrass him and call attention to the fact that he had a wayward son. They had stood outside in the lot, and Albert answered with clipped and short responses. "I sense resentment from you," Agent Martin said. Damn right. At that moment he was lucky to be dealing with a pacifist.

Albert drove into Hollywood, uneasy with the sense of doing something surreptitious. He met de Antonio, who told him Jeff was well and sent his love. It was a small room and Albert settled into his seat as the beam of light traveled above his head. He was about to see his son on screen and that was as close as he could hope to get. The date appeared: May 1, 1975. Then Albert's heart skipped. Jeff's voice, his son's unmistakable voice, began the narration. "We're five people from the Weather Underground Organization," Jeff said, as the camera panned across to a shadow behind a flimsy screen.

"We're in a house, you could call it a safe house." Jeff's voice was nervous and breathy, he sounded scared, and Albert felt the urge to find him and protect him. "We're here with a group of filmmakers and together we're going to make a film. We're underground in this country. We've been underground for five years. Those of us here

today are fugitives. We've been asked to come here by our organization to speak for the organization. My name is Jeff Jones.

"You can say that this screen that's between us is a result of the
war in Vietnam, or is a result of racism in this society. It's an act, it's an
important act, to overcome this barrier and we're going to try to
reach through it, talk through it." Jeff reached out from behind the
gauze and touched it, pressing his fingers against it and, to Albert, it
was as if he was reaching out to him in the theater. He could see
Jeff's outline clearly behind the fabric; he wore a dark shirt and a
wool cap with tufts of blond hair sticking out beneath it.

The film moved on to the other people, and Albert relaxed. Then
there was footage of Jeff from the Democratic convention in 1968.
He was standing on a stage with a microphone, promising, "Someday
we're gonna knock those motherfuckers who control this thing right
on their ass." Albert cringed. He hated that word, the M-F word, and
had raised his son never to say it. Then, later, another jolt, as Jeff outlined his beliefs. "The imperialist power will fight as long as it can
with the most advanced technological weapons that it has," he said.
"And I feel that pacifism and non-violence becomes an excuse for
not struggling." There it was, as if he was speaking directly to his
father, repudiating everything he had been taught.

There were images of Vietnam. Ho Chi Minh looking frail.
Cluster bombs falling silently, beautifully, toward a carpet of trees.
"Just think back two months. Think back two years. Think back five
years," Jeff told the camera. "We used to chant, 'Right on, take
Saigon' or 'Ho Ho Ho Chi Minh, the NLF is gonna win.' Who
believed it? Who could believe it? Who had been educated, who had
the tools to believe it? . . . It just happened."

On April 30, 1975, the day before the crew had started filming,
North Vietnamese tanks entered Saigon and accepted the uncondi-
tional surrender of the South's regime. American helicopters picked
up the last refugees from the roof of the embassy and evacuated
them to nearby aircraft carriers. The war was finally over, having
claimed more than 58,000 Americans, 1 million enemy soldiers, and
millions more civilians. Other men's sons would be coming home.
And Albert had a right to wonder if this film, and the peace, and

Nixon's Watergate disgrace, and all the progress, meant that maybe his boy would be returning soon too.

Then he heard Jeff's voice again from behind that impenetrable divide, confirming the worst: that he was not going to be reasonable, accept this victory, and abandon the rest of his impossible platform. Tens of millions of people had been waiting for the fighting to end.

But, Jeff told the camera, and his father sitting in the theater, "We are not going to let the war in Vietnam be over."

CHAPTER 10

The Bust

I was born on April 30, 1977. My name, according to the birth certificate filled in by an administrator at Park City Hospital in Bridgeport, Connecticut, was Ty Emerson. It was my first alias.

My mother had not chosen my real name until the day I was delivered. She and Jeff had discussed possibilities for months; they considered nature influences such as "Hudson" and "River," as well as "Gaviota" for the mountain pass in California where they first agreed to start a family. But my birthday had a special meaning that made these all irrelevant. The final day in April was when Saigon had fallen to the Communists; it was the official end of the Vietnam War. I was born on the second anniversary of peace, and that is the meaning of *thai* in Vietnamese.

The name also had a second significance for Eleanor. She bestowed it in honor of Nguyen Thai, a Vietcong fighter who had campaigned for decades against the French and American armies. When Eleanor met him in Havana in 1969, Nguyen and his wife had not seen each other for years. They fought in different sectors and had sworn not to meet again until victory. Peace and protest, family and politics: it was all in the name.

·

Eleanor had led a wandering life for more than seven years when she arrived in Bridgeport four months before I was born and decided to stay. A depressed New England city, it was a former mill town, a former port town, and, by the late 1970s, a dreary, spreading slum. Eleanor moved there at the start of one of the worst winters in memory and took the name Anna Margaret Emerson. If anyone asked, she said she was running away from a bad relationship. Months had passed since she had last seen Jeff. In her Lamaze class, Anna was the only unmarried woman. She dressed in hippie clothes and posed as a sculptor. The other couples found it natural that an artist would end up in such a sad predicament: pregnant and alone.

Eleanor lived by herself in a cheap apartment, cut off from what was left of the underground. In March, she celebrated her thirty-first birthday and could hardly account for the previous ten years of her life. She had nothing to show for them: no family, no money, no accomplishments. All she had was secrets. During the day, she worked as a secretary in the art department at the University of Bridgeport. In the evenings, she was a telephone solicitor for a shady company. She worked in an undecorated room with twenty other women, all black. One evening Eleanor arrived to find the office doors padlocked shut. As she stood on the sidewalk wondering what had happened, a coworker came over and said, "Honey, you just missed the FBI." Agents had come, arrested the boss, and carried away all the files.

On the evening of April 29, Eleanor went to see *Rebel Without a Cause* at the university. After the film, she walked to her apartment to drink a bottle of red wine and pass out. When she woke up a few hours later, she was in labor. With no other friends to take her, she called the elderly landlady who lived downstairs and asked for a ride to the hospital.

Anna Emerson flashed her Medicaid card and was put to bed in the maternity ward for what she hoped would be a natural delivery. Giving birth was political, and refusing to take drugs made it wholesome and radical and, most important, different from how her mother had done it. She had practiced her breathing and brought a focal point for concentration: a swatch of Vietnamese cloth that she hung on the wall opposite her bed.

She labored all through the night and the next morning while I practiced noncooperation. My head was pointed the wrong way—toward my mother's back—making the birth process far more painful and difficult. During the afternoon of April 30, my heartbeat grew erratic, and doctors sensed I was choking and in distress. Around 4:00 P.M., they rushed Eleanor into a brightly lit delivery room, turned her on her side, and injected a horrifying needle directly into her spine. Instantly, all sensation fled. She remained conscious but it was as if her lower body belonged to another patient. The staff set up a small screen to block her view and the doctor made the cuts for an emergency cesarean section. During the operation, they talked about ordering pizza.

Then I was born. A doctor held me upside down by one foot and said, "It's a boy." I weighed seven pounds, one ounce, but had contracted pneumonia in those first stressful moments and steadily lost weight over the next eight days, which I spent in a hospital bassinet. While I was there, Eleanor received a visit from the hospital pediatrician. He lay me on my back, took both feet and brought them up until my knees rested on my chest. They did not touch at the same height and he told her that my left femur was significantly shorter than my right one. It was not an immediate problem, but soon, he said, it would require surgery.

Eleanor took me home and stopped working. Together, we went to Bridgeport's welfare office, a squalid brick building near some of the town's many housing projects. We waited for hours to see the case worker, zapped by the pasty lighting and surrounded by depressed adults and screaming children. When we left, Anna Emerson had a check for almost $400 made out in her name. That and food stamps were supposed to last us the entire month.

At night, she wrapped me in a handmade patchwork quilt someone had sent her. Neither of us slept easily. I had recovered from the pneumonia but still struggled to breathe, and she sat by the bedside listening to me wheeze and gurgle. She thought about Jeff, who should have been there to share the work and worry. At every stage of the birth, she had pictured him alongside, lending support. Having a baby was supposed to give her new strength, but she had no idea how to care for a sick child in the underground. How could she pay for surgery to fix my leg? If she was arrested, where would I stay? She knew we couldn't get through this alone.

Somewhere, Anna and Ty would have to find help.

•••

At the beginning of 1976, when I remained just a twinkle in his eye, Jeff stood shivering in a phone booth. Without seeming too interested, he watched the yellow taxis trawling slowly down the main shopping strip in the Riverdale section of the Bronx. It was an old ladies' neighborhood, and normally Jeff would have been conspicuous. His hair was dark, and he had grown a mustache and dyed it brown. He did not look like a hippie anymore, but wore heavy jeans and work clothes. Over the years he had learned that no one ever looked twice at the help, so he posed as a laborer or a deliveryman and walked the streets in broad daylight.

During six years as a fugitive, he had conducted hundreds of these meetings. His contact would arrive at a particular spot and then walk a trajectory along a predetermined route. Jeff would watch and see that no one followed. He took these precautions each time even though the FBI no longer considered him a major threat. In January 1974, evidence of its own illegal wire-tapping and unsanctioned surveillance had forced the government to drop the conspiracy charges against Jeff and eleven others. Finding the Weather Fugitives, or "WeathFugs" as they were known inside the brand-new J. Edgar Hoover Building, was no longer a top priority. The FBI had spent millions of dollars on the search. Yet, after almost six years, agents had made only two arrests.

Outside in the street, Jeff watched as one of the taxis came to a stop and discharged a gray-haired lady with a prominent nose. She didn't look around but started walking. As if she had suddenly remembered something, she stopped in her tracks and doubled back. Most of this woman's adult life had been spent under the surveillance of the FBI and, like Jeff, she had learned to approach these meetings cautiously. She might spend an hour driving around, moving from bus to taxi before arriving.

Jeff watched her progress from across the street. Without seeming too interested, he examined the pedestrians walking behind her. When she spun around, he saw that none of them turned too. When she entered a Jewish deli, he waited to make sure no one else developed a sudden appetite. Satisfied that it was safe, he went and joined her table in the noisy restaurant. Annie ordered coffee, lit a Chesterfield, and got down to business. She was sixty-two, and he was twenty-eight. Two people could hardly have had more contrasting lives, yet when it came to politics, they found themselves in almost complete agreement.

They agreed, for instance, that times were hard. The country was gearing up to celebrate its bicentennial in July, but a recession, worse than any since before World War II, was ruining the patriotic mood. The movement had gone to pieces; the years of war had been like an adrenaline rush, and thousands of activists were left shaky and directionless when the buzz wore off. Abbie Hoffman was on the run from cocaine charges. Tom Hayden had turned respectable and was running for the U.S. Senate. Rennie Davis, another leading figure in the antiwar movement, had joined a maharishi cult.

In the current political climate, Jeff believed that the time for a revolutionary underground, if there ever had been such a time, was gone. He had recently proposed to put this belief into practice, creating a plan called "Inversion"—the complete reappearance of the Party and a return to the SDS style of mass protest. Jeff's proposals carried weight. He had been in the original Weather Bureau, and when the organization lost its sense of fun and changed the name to the Central Committee, he was a member of that. He had not been voted in and had no way to enforce his decisions. His authority had always been consensual, and the moment that others stopped following him, he would cease to be a leader. That moment was coming.

Never had the rank and file been so disgruntled. "Leadership," Weatherman David Gilbert wrote, "tended to become manipulative and commandist, while cadre tended to curry favor with leadership. Criticism/self-criticism was used to compete and maneuver for power rather than to build people." While the leaders made films and got into book publishing, the others were isolated and worked minimum-wage jobs to survive. Lenin had invented "democratic centralism," a model for a clandestine organization where only the leaders could contact the separate cells. Before the Weather Underground, his model had been used, with varying degrees of failure, in Moscow, Algiers, Havana, Saigon, and even Washington, D.C., by Eleanor's parents. In 1956, the man who fingered Arthur Stein to the House Committee on Un-American Activities had complained about the system as it had existed in the Communist Party. "It seemed to me," he told the row of congressmen, "that we were getting all centralism and no democracy in this particular unit."

Annie approved of the discipline. She took security precautions whenever she met with Eleanor or Jeff, but she had never believed in the underground strategy. In the 1950s, yes, when the witch hunt made it necessary, but not now. Could anyone look around America in 1976 and honestly say the Weather Underground Organization was still relevant? Annie had argued for mass organizing in 1932, she had argued for it in 1953, she had argued for it in 1969, and she was arguing for it now. She joined the Prairie Fire Organizing Committee, an above-ground support group for the fugitives, and pushed Jeff and Bill Ayers toward resurfacing.

When more than a dozen young radicals rented a house in Maine to serve as a cadre school, she and Chavy flew north to teach Marxism-Leninism to the new generation. The two women were unmistakable, but they took aliases anyway. Annie's name was Josephine, reminiscent of a certain dictator. Chavy, whose childhood polio forced her to wear heavy leg braces and walk with crutches, had transferred her allegiance from the Soviets to the Chinese and was known in the underground as Comrade Wu. Together, Josephine and Comrade Wu shared the lessons of almost fifty years of political activism that had begun when they met on a Brooklyn subway platform during the roaring twenties.

At first, Jeff had resented Annie's aggressive style, but he had long since accepted her as a coconspirator, his closest political ally in the organization. Sitting together at their plush booth in the crowded Bronx deli, with her cigarette smoke curling around them, they believed they were working on nothing less than the future of the left. They were planning a conference—Jeff called it the "Hard Times Conference"—that would gather all the broken shards of the movement and fuse them into a militant new party. Following the conference, Jeff would come in triumphant from the cold to claim a share of the leadership of the organization. After all, someone would have to take control, and he could think of no one more suited than a seasoned veteran of the notorious Weather Underground.

Annie stood behind a velvet-draped dais table at the University of Illinois in Chicago on the evening of January 30 and watched as the huge room filled to capacity and beyond. At her back hung a painted mural, reading: *"Los Tiempos Difíciles Son Tiempos De Lucha,"*—hard times are fighting times. So many people had come that the opening session of the Hard Times Conference was delayed to allow the overflow crowd to head to cafeterias where the proceedings were broadcast on closed-circuit TVs. Ten times as many people showed up for this than had participated in the previous mass event Jeff had organized, the Days of Rage.

"We have to develop a program for the working class as a whole in this period to fight the depression," Jennifer Dohrn, Bernardine's younger sister, told an audience that included attorney William Kunstler, who had defended members of the Chicago Eight, and Iberia Hampton, whose son Fred had been murdered by police in this same city during 1969, as well as representatives from the United Black Workers, Welfare Mothers for Justice, the Puerto Rican Socialist Party, the Republic of New Afrika, the American Indian Movement, and the Gray Panthers. Annie had emptied her Rolodex and called in her favors. She brought Chavy with her, of course, as well as SNCC leader Ella Baker and Thelma Hamilton, an activist for community control in the New York City public schools. Jeff and Eleanor flew to Chicago too. They could not attend the sessions in person, but the conference was broadcast live on Pacifica radio. They checked into a motel room and Jeff waited anxiously for reports, a director watching his play from the wings.

The large crowds had Annie feeling optimistic. But a reporter for the *Guardian* wrote, "The conference organizers were undoubtedly surprised to hear that a hastily convened 'Black Caucus' had prepared a major and sweeping criticism of the proceedings." The caucus wasn't there to be directed by anyone, especially honky radicals from whom no one had heard in years. In the closing session, delegates from the Republic of New Afrika held the floor for nearly an hour, chastising the conference and demanding that the whites assume a supportive role. "Black people are going to be the vanguard of the movement," one speaker announced, "and the working class will follow."

For Jeff, the conference was a disaster. His authority had become so tenuous that this one outburst, by a fringe and ultramilitant faction of the black liberation movement, was enough to break him and the rest of the Central Committee. On the West Coast, Clayton Van Lydegraf, the most militaristic leader within the Weather Underground, began organizing a coup. In 1970, he had been perfect for the role of Dr. Tim Leary's middle-aged fishing buddy; they had driven up the California coast together, arguing the entire way. He had opposed that action and deplored the direction that Annie and Jeff were taking the group. Under his leadership, the Weather Underground would make fewer films and more revolution.

When you depend so completely on a small group of people—trusting your liberty and even your life to them—you do not just shake hands and wish each other well when the time comes to separate. The split of the Weather Underground was going to be acrimonious and ugly.

During the spring and summer of 1976, Jeff continued making his rounds. He and Eleanor had bought a used telephone company van and built a bed in the back. They drove to the fringes of New York City—Orchard Beach and Sheepshead Bay—where the buildings thinned out and it was still possible to find some privacy. Everyone he met told him the same thing. People who had listened to him and followed his leadership for years now said, in so many words, "The black liberation struggle was everything we stood for. It was the whole reason I spent six years of my life underground. Your ego and identity got in the way of listening to what your comrades were saying and history is moving on without you."

Increasingly, his contacts simply stopped showing up for meetings. Formerly, no one would have come to New York City without Jeff knowing, but now he learned that Clayton Van Lydegraf was in town recruiting people to his side. To replace the Central Committee, he was establishing a Revolutionary Committee bent on armed struggle. All that was necessary to join was a complete denunciation of the old leadership. You couldn't talk to them or meet with them; it had to be a clean break. Van Lydegraf justified this treatment by listing the offenses committed by each of the disgraced leaders, including:

> Jeff Jones: Along with Ayers, main leader of the organization, developed opportunist lines over seven years. . . . To this day main rear base is yippie, Abby *[sic]* Hoffman types, most reactionary aspects of youth culture. . . . Conceived and led film and strategy for inversion. With Ayers seized position as military leader to control women, limit and eventually eliminate armed struggle. He has historically fought to do actions to counter criticism of his cowardly collaborationist political line.

These were the charges, and Van Lydegraf was the judge. "The consequences of this history," he wrote, "are the crimes of social imperialism; deadly, grave crimes committed against the women's movement, against revolutionary anti-imperialist politics and organization in the oppressor nation."

They were all expelled. It was simple to kick Annie out. She had gone meeting to meeting, knowing only when the next connection would take place. After Hard Times, her contact simply didn't show up, and she was cut off. Bill Ayers was out. Bernardine recorded a tape denouncing Jeff and herself, saying the Central Committee's aim had been, "nothing less than to establish itself, with its white and male supremacist politics as the leadership of the whole US revolutionary movement. Jeff Jones of the central committee initiated and led this strategy and the events I'm referring to." But soon she re-recanted and was also cast out.

Jeff, counterrevolutionary number one, was out. He had been a Weatherman for seven years and once, during a meeting with Abbie

Hoffman, had said, "All I want to do is smoke dope and make revolution." He had known the underground's effectiveness was over. His
former comrades had turned on him, and still, after all this, he would
have done almost anything to stay involved. But he never had an
opportunity to defend himself and still did not admit any mistake.

Eleanor's position was the most awkward. With Annie Stein for a
mother and Jeff Jones as a boyfriend, she was invariably associated
with the two most despised reactionaries in the movement. She had
gone along with them but had experienced the same doubts that she
now heard so many other people expressing. Jeff had wanted to start
a family, and, in August she got pregnant. That only made her feel
more trapped. While Jeff was cut off, she kept in touch with old allies
who had gone over to the Revolutionary Committee. They began to
whisper, telling her they knew she was on their side. If she wanted to
remain true to the movement, they told her, she must break with Jeff
and Annie. She had had the same thought. With some time alone,
away from the two powerful personalities, she could explore her
own feelings.

At the start of winter, she left the small apartment overlooking Van
Cortlandt Park and took the subway into Manhattan. She had a
heavy roll of quarters weighing down her pocket. Anonymous,
untraceable pay phone calls had allowed the underground to survive.
Everyone had their favorite phones, and Eleanor's were in New York
Hospital, a huge building with dozens of entrances and a maze of
passageways. She made her calls, and when she rang off, she had
agreed to take a few days away from Jeff, to meet with the new
organization and clear her head. Back at home, she told him that she
was going away for a while. Eleanor packed a bag and took a train to
Boston, where her friends welcomed her back within the pale.

It was supposed to be a weekend trip, but after a few days, she
called Jeff at a pay phone in a Howard Johnson's basement and told
him she was staying. He urged her to reconsider, to think about the
baby. Finally, she agreed to schedule another telephone call exactly
one month in the future.

In the meantime, Jeff was running out of money. His entire savings, a few dollars, fit comfortably inside his shoe. He hadn't held a real job since high school when he had folded shirts in a men's store in the San Fernando Valley. Since then, he had either worked for SDS or had been supported by the underground. Now he needed work. He drove to Albany in upstate New York, and dropped his bag off in a room at the YMCA. He spent a few days trying to find a job—applying as a short-order cook at a Denny's restaurant—but he had no résumé and no work experience. His ID cards were flimsy, and potential employers sensed that he was desperate and shifty.

He returned to the city, broke and defeated. Managing to borrow $100 from Maxwell Geismar, one of his few remaining friends, he used the money to rent an apartment across the river in Jersey City. He found a job in an industry that would hire anybody—he became a bicycle messenger. After a decade in one of America's most violent groups, this was by far the most dangerous thing, day in and day out, that he had ever done. He told the dispatcher that he wouldn't carry drugs and then spent weeks flying through Manhattan traffic and getting his pay in cash.

When the month expired and it was time for the phone call with Eleanor, Jeff felt sure she would relent. She had proven her point and taught him a little lesson. Now it was time for her to come home. But he was mistaken; she was enjoying her independence. He begged her to return and told her he had found an apartment in New Jersey. He asked that she at least tell him where she was living or agree to schedule another phone call, even if it was several months off.

"I'm not going to see you again," Eleanor said, and she hung up.

•••

Jeff was now a fugitive from the underground. Besides wasting away with worry for Eleanor and the baby, he realized that the denunciations of him were almost equivalent to a contract on his life. Someone from the new organization might try to make a name by finding the traitorous Jeff Jones and bumping him off the way Stalin had done Trotsky. It could be a total stranger he would never recognize in time, yet Jeff refused to flee. He had given Eleanor his address in Jersey City and he was determined to stay there until she came to find him.

He hadn't completely lost the instinct for self-preservation. He had his K-55 cat knife, a slim folding blade that the Motherfuckers had popularized in 1968. It had been used by the German army in World War II, and its handle was etched with a leaping black panther, which endeared it even more to the radicals. During 1969, when Jeff carried a revolver and shouted revolution at mass meetings, he had never traveled without one. When he went underground, he stopped carrying it. Now the cat knife was back. Neither his childhood as a Quaker nor his youth as a hippie had trained him how to use it, but when he slept, the blade was always within arm's reach.

After talking to Eleanor for the last time, Jeff didn't even make it to bed. Inside the front door of his apartment, he collapsed onto the floor and huddled with his knees pressed to his chest. He understood that it might be months or even years before he saw her. He was going to miss the birth of his son. When he woke up, after a freezing cold night, he was sick and feeble. But he had made a decision: he would put his life together but do nothing to jeopardize his chance of winning back his woman. He didn't know how to find her and couldn't risk a visit to Annie. He did have a tenuous link to her: Maxwell and Anne Geismar. He asked them if they were in touch with Eleanor, and though they didn't admit it, they didn't deny it either.

Max Geismar was the radical critic who first recognized Eldridge Cleaver's literary merits and had written the introduction to *Soul on Ice*. In a long career, he had argued politics and philosophy with some of the great intellectuals of the day and could tell about their jealousies, vanities, impotence, and alcoholism. Jeff and Eleanor had often gone together to the Geismars' beautiful colonial house in Harrison, New York, where Max would mix the drinks and dazzle them with stories. Now Jeff entrusted them with a key to his apartment and asked them to pass it on to Eleanor.

From a job placement office on Forty-Second Street, he was sent to work at M. J. Knoud, a Madison Avenue leather goods store where

Jackie Onassis bought her saddles. He held this job for almost six months, another security risk. His hair, reflecting his mood, was now jet black, and he dyed it every other week. Even in the middle of summer, he worked in long-sleeved shirts, buttoned at the wrists and collar to hide the blond hair on his arms and chest. On payday, he took a train to Harrison and left some money with the Geismars to hold for Eleanor and me. He also left a baby quilt he had made out of saddle wool samples from the shop.

In the evenings, he took aimless rambles through New York and Jersey City, always putting off the moment when it was time to go home. His apartment was almost bare. He had found a few pieces of furniture on the street, and his bed was a plywood board resting on four cinder blocks. For the first time in his life, smoking marijuana couldn't ease his nerves. Instead, it made him so paranoid that he was forced to stop. As an alternative, he sat dejectedly in the living room fighting to get a clear picture on his tiny black and white TV set.

His windows looked across the Hudson to the skyscrapers of mid-town Manhattan. At night, he was spellbound by low-hanging stars, unnaturally bright, that would stay still for almost half an hour and then suddenly vanish. Eventually he realized that his view was aligned with one of the runways at Kennedy Airport. He was watching not stars but transatlantic jets making their slow approach and dropping down behind the buildings to land. And that was it. For almost an entire year, he did nothing political, saw almost no one, but maintained his own holding pattern, waiting for clearance to return to his family.

I was three months old when some of Eleanor's work friends decided to take an impromptu trip into the city and invited her to tag along. It was hard for her to remember exactly why she had stormed off on her own, but it was easy to realize how much she missed having Jeff around. She had, as he suspected, met with Anne Geismar, where she took possession of the apartment key and almost a thousand dollars that Jeff had managed to save for her. I slept under the blanket every night of my life.

She decided to take that trip to New York.

It was dark when Eleanor's friends dropped her off in Greenwich

Village. I napped while she boarded a train and rode into Jersey City. It was past midnight when she stepped out of a taxi, approached Jeff's door, and stared at the row of buzzers.

Jeff had waited nearly a year for that doorbell to ring. When it finally did, he was sitting alone watching TV. The noise was metallic and startling. In all the months he had lived there, he had never once heard the sound. He opened the front window, leaned out until he could see Eleanor on the sidewalk below with an inert lump swathed in blankets and slung across her chest. He hurtled down the steps two and three at a time until he reached the second floor. There he paused to compose himself. He wondered what Eleanor was doing here. Was it a visit, an interview, or was she going to stay? He walked calmly down the last flight of stairs and opened the front door.

"Will you come up?" he asked, correct and reserved.

"Is that okay?"

"Please come up."

He led the way to the top floor and into his apartment. Eleanor disentangled me from my blankets and set me on his lap.

"His name is Thai," she said.

"Do you have a place to stay?" he asked.

"We want to stay here."

Jeff didn't have a crib, so he removed one of the drawers from his dresser, lined it with soft things, and put me in it to sleep. The next morning we woke up as a family.

•••

By January 1979, we had moved from Jersey City to a fifth-floor walkup at 321 Willow Avenue in Hoboken. Eleanor and Jeff were Jean and James Hayes. I was Timmy, although our Puerto Rican neighbors called me "TiTi." The only heat in the apartment came from the kitchen stove. All through that winter, we lived in the kitchen, huddled around the oven. The bathroom was so frigid that Jeff woke up at dawn each morning and ran hot water in the tub until the steam raised the room temperature above freezing.

The conditions were not healthy for a child who had already suffered one bout with pneumonia. I was allergic to dairy products, and so we went to Mott Street, in Chinatown, twice a week to buy fresh soy milk. I seemed to spend much of my time visiting various doctors, and, following each consultation, Jeff or Eleanor insisted on taking my medical records home with them. The documents were too precious to leave behind. Whenever we changed names, Jeff went to the public library and photocopied the pages, brushed white-out over my name, typed in a new one, and copied the sheet again.

The stone communist revolutionaries had become mommies and daddies—not just my parents but others too. Shortly after Jeff and Eleanor were reunited, they renewed their friendships with Bill Ayers and Bernardine Dohrn. We rode a Greyhound bus from New York City to Charleston, West Virginia, where they were waiting in a station wagon to pick us up. Bernardine and Bill also had a son, Zayd Osceola, who was just four days older than I was. While the adults smoothed over their recent differences—no one had gone through the splits of 1976 without having something to apologize for—Zayd and I sat on opposite ends of a blanket shaking our rattles at each other.

Salvaged friendships were the only remnants of the Weather Underground. Clayton Van Lydegraf had briefly lived up to his militant promise and launched a new campaign of bombings. His group was thoroughly infiltrated by FBI agents, and in November 1977, he and four other members of his Revolutionary Committee were arrested, convicted, and sent to prison in California. Mark Rudd turned himself in during 1977. In 1980, Cathlyn Wilkerson turned herself in to police and was sentenced to three years for her role in the townhouse explosion. In December of that year, Bernardine Dohrn and Bill Ayers also surfaced in Chicago.

Nine years had passed since Jeff had seen his dad. As a new father who had already been separated from his own son, he could guess at the pain and worry he had caused Albert. During one of their last visits, they had argued about Weatherman's violent tactics. Albert's words, "I would hope you yourself were hurt before you are able to hurt anyone else," had proved prophetic. During the years that followed, the underground had scrupulously avoided hurting anyone but themselves. Because of this record, and the fact that he was mostly through with the movement, Jeff believed it was time to return to Los Angeles. Besides, he had to tell Albert he was a grandfather.

Eleanor and I went to Penn Station to see him off on a cross-country train ride. When he arrived in Burbank, he waited in the parking lot for Albert to leave the Disney studio and head for home. His father came out into the evening, after a day's work splicing negatives, and there was his son. The two went to a Bob's Big Boy for dinner. They were both a decade older than they had been. Albert had recently remarried and had a happy family life for the first time since Millie left in 1966. As a Quaker, he had done draft counseling during the war, and the experience had soothed his opposition to Jeff's politics. "In combat some people take on the dangerous work. They go on point," Albert told his son, using a military metaphor. "The way I look at it, you guys were on point for the antiwar movement."

After the visit, Jeff, going by the name Jason Robert Russell, rode a Greyhound up the Pacific Coast. "My father is like I remember him," he wrote from a little town north of San Francisco, "only happy now because he is living with a very generous woman. He is good but he is also set in his ways. He convinced me that he placed my security above anything else and agreed to the terms of our meeting. . . . I see where I got my ego."

Millie lived in Eugene, Oregon, with her husband, Roger O'Donnell. She and Jeff had rarely been out of touch. A friend from her Quaker meeting agreed to act as go-between, and Jeff called this friend every month or two and scheduled a phone conversation with his mother. At the appointed time, Millie would sneak out of the house, without a word to her husband, and wait in the bus station for the telephone to ring.

It was April, and when Jeff had left New York, the weather had been miserable. In California, it was spring. "If I were seeing this scenery for the first time I would be delirious," he wrote. "As it is I am amazed at how green things can be and how blue the sky is." On April 24, he wrote back to us in the East.

It is beautiful here and it is . . . a remarkable trip but I never seem to get really overjoyed because I'm always thinking that I wish I was sharing it with you and T. His pictures evoke such a response in everyone who sees them. His spirit just comes charging through. This is probably the last letter I will send before his birthday so: Happy Birthday TiTi. You are a wonderful little person and a wonderful friend. Get ready to be Two and I will see you soon!

He was in Humboldt County now, where the marijuana industry was bringing in so much cash that tiny, rural restaurants posted signs reading, "We do not accept $100 bills." Jeff had always loved the pot culture, and now he did succumb to delirium. "The weed is another dimension," he wrote. "People around here casually make from $10,000 to $100,000 a year off their weed crop." He had been living well below the poverty line ever since his SDS days. He worked a full-time job just to pay rent and support his family. Anyone could grow marijuana plants. After all, nothing is heartier than a weed. Jeff was tempted by the idea of easy money, and when he boarded the train for his return trip, he had eight strong-looking sinsemilla seeds hidden away in his luggage.

Spring had reached New York by his arrival. He rolled a bamboo mat around the railings of our fire escape and planted the eight seeds in eight separate plastic pots. We lived on the top floor, so no one underneath us could see the garden. Eleanor complained, and he ignored her. He tinkered with fertilizing mixes until he had the perfect combination. Each evening, he came home from work and eagerly went out on the iron platform to see the progress. Soon his little babies were growing an inch a day. By the beginning of August, the plants had grown above the height of the railings and were visible to anyone with a keen or suspicious eye.

On Thursday, August 2, Jeff had the day off from work. He went to the store, and coming home around noon, parked his Ford station wagon a few blocks from the apartment. With a full grocery bag in each hand, he turned onto Willow Avenue. Two police cars were pulled up in front of the apartment house. They were parked haphazardly, and their doors were open, as if the officers had screamed up to the scene, jumped out of the vehicles, and run inside without a moment's pause. It was possible there were other criminals living at our address, so Jeff walked into the lobby to see what he could find out. In the long row of steel mailboxes one had been jimmied open—ours. That was all he needed to see, but as he made to leave, he ran into the building super, a friendly Cuban named José Garcia.

"Hay una problema?" Jeff asked. Is there a problem?

"Hay una problema con tus plantas," said Garcia. There is a problem with your plants.

Jeff turned then and walked briskly back down the street, still carrying his groceries. It was a hot day—over ninety degrees—and he wore sandals, shorts, and a T-shirt. These had just become all the clothes he owned in the world. We had lost everything: baby pictures and the blanket he'd quilted for me, a twelve-string Martin guitar made in 1967, my medical records and X-rays.

Jeff called Eleanor and learned she was lunching with her mother at Schrafft's on Fifth Avenue. He drove into Manhattan, feeling more afraid of Annie than of the Federal Bureau of Investigation. It would take hours before the police realized what they had stumbled on to. A Hoboken fire captain, making a routine inspection of the building's roof, had happened to look over the edge and spot the plants. When the police rushed in for their drug bust, they discovered signs of a radical hideout. Cops found two hidden cans of black powder and a briefcase filled with blank documents that could be used for forging IDs. In a wooden box, they discovered radical literature printed by the FALN, a Puerto Rican nationalist group.

When newspaper reporters arrived hours later, they saw "everything in disarray. Clothing, books, papers, photographs and furnishings were scattered about. Drawers had been pulled open and their contents dumped." Sticky black fingerprint-finding ink had been sprayed over all our possessions. Police told the newsmen that they had also discovered $500 under a loose shelf in a kitchen cabinet. There had been $1,200 there when Eleanor and Jeff left in the morning.

While Annie went to her bank to withdraw more than a thousand dollars for us to flee with, Jeff drove to pick me up from a day care center in Greenwich Village. He told the teachers that I wouldn't be coming back, and then we ditched the station wagon in a parking garage in midtown. When police finally found the car a month later, it would be ruined by the smell of the rotting groceries that had never quite made it to the refrigerator.

We rode an Amtrak to Connecticut—far enough, Jeff hoped, to get beyond the reach of New York City's tabloids, which he thought might print our photographs. Anticipating this exact situation, he and Eleanor had scouted a motel that was anonymous and close to the train station in New London. We would stay there until something came along to replace our story in the newspapers.

With no ID, Eleanor and Jeff started feeling romantic. In New York State, they could get a marriage license with only a baptismal certificate, which could be purchased at a stationery store; the marriage license could then be used to get a driver's license. They left me at a drop-in center and were married by a town clerk in the Catskills. After the ceremony, they snapped wedding pictures in a Woolworth's photo booth.

At any time in the previous five years, my parents could have resurfaced without facing any serious consequences. That option was now gone. The materials found in their apartment were suspicious enough that warrants were sent out on the charge of explosives possession. Eleanor had been living under assumed names since 1970; now, for the first time, she too was a fugitive.

•••

On a forty-degree morning in late October 1980, Jeff wore green shorts, a red bandanna, and a tank top. He stood on the Verrazano-Narrows Bridge between Staten Island and Brooklyn, shaking off the cold and limbering up before beginning the New York City marathon. He had been unable to register in the usual way, but a friend had pulled some strings with the organizers and entered him, under an alias, with the one group that was allowed as many participants as it wanted—the New York City Police Department running team.

He went on adrenaline and ran the fastest three miles of his life, then the fastest ten miles. At the halfway point, he was on pace to finish in under three hours. But he started flagging on the Queensboro Bridge, and by the time he ran by 138th Street, where I stood on the sidewalk cheering him like crazy, Jeff was taking more than eight minutes to complete each mile. Around 2:00 P.M., he passed under the line in Central Park. He had finished ahead of four-fifths of the runners, but was disappointed with his time of three hours and thirteen minutes.

I had watched my father with awe almost every morning for months as he returned home from a morning jog around the botanical gardens, slipped off his colorful running shoes and peeled away his sweaty socks. From his talk, I knew all about pacing and carbo loading, but I would never be a runner. When I was only a few weeks old, Eleanor had taken me to the Shriner's Hospital in Springfield, Massachusetts. There, a top specialist had told her that although the discrepancy between my legs was minor now, the difference would widen as I went through my growth spurts. In his opinion I would never learn how to walk, and he suggested amputating my left foot immediately so I could accustom myself to the prosthesis from an early age.

Eleanor sought a second opinion and then a third. She consulted New Age healers who looked at my left leg and, instead of wanting to chop it off, said, "This is a healthy limb, you should love it up." I had acupressure in a tiny shop in Chinatown and, later, acupuncture in one of the Black Liberation Army–funded health clinics in Harlem. Eleanor and Jeff burned incense in the evenings, letting the smoke tickle along my leg. Before I could wear any new pair of shoes, the left one first had to be sent to a repair shop and fitted with a rubber lift on the sole. Despite the doctor's warning, I learned to walk at the expected age, though I would always do so with a limp.

The underground was no place for a child, especially a sickly one who required constant visits to the doctors and whose medical records were in the hands of the FBI. Survival demanded abilities that children do not possess. As a toddler, I had a hundred opportunities a day to let a secret slip. As soon as I was old enough to understand anything, I understood that something was worrying my parents, and once I knew that, it was only a matter of time before I began talking about it to strangers.

It took a lot of explaining whenever we changed our apartment, let alone our names. They sat me down and said, "Our family is a little different from other families. We use lots of nicknames; sometimes we use one and sometimes we use another. Some people only know one of our names and others know all of them." Two names that I never heard spoken were Jeff and Eleanor. They tried to make it easy for me by sticking with the same sounds. My father was usually Jason, James, John, or Jake. My mother was Sally or Sarah. Somehow I never stopped to wonder at the situation. This was our family, and even if my parents admitted it was "a little different," I had nothing to compare it to.

There were other things for me to concentrate on. After the police raid in Hoboken, we spent a few months hiding out in the Catskills and then moved back into the City. We found an apartment in the Bronx that had a little room for me at the end of a long hallway. I was at a regular day care center, where all my friends called me Timmy. And there were these creatures called dinosaurs; they came in all shapes and sorts, and the matter seemed to require serious study. Our house was only a few blocks from the zoo, and though it had no dinosaurs, there were elephants.

One of our visits happened to be on the day when the zoo held wildlife races for children. The youngest kids were in the peanut division; their course was only a few hundred feet long. I wanted to join, and Eleanor and Jeff, though anxious and protective of me and my leg, had no way to prevent it. Twenty or thirty of us lined up at the start. I was three years old and one of the smallest entrants, but having listened to Jeff's talk about marathons, I knew a few tricks. When the whistle blew, kids started running in all directions. I headed straight for the finish. Lips pursed in determination, limping in my heavy shoe, focused on the approaching line, I won: the only runner who had taken the shortest route between two points.

Eleanor and Jeff had decided to have a second child, and by December 1980, she was seven months pregnant with my little sister.

We called her Coco, after a character from the movie *Fame*. Then on Christmas Eve, Eleanor felt painful stomach cramps. The next morning, she realized that she could no longer feel Coco kicking. In the emergency room at Albert Einstein College of Medicine, a young internist moved his stethoscope around her belly, looking in vain for a heartbeat. Eleanor had to wait a week before going into labor, and in the meantime strangers on the subway still came up to congratulate her and ask about the baby. When she and Jeff left for the hospital, they asked Annie to come stay with me in the Bronx. She brought some puzzle or game, and by the time my parents left, we were already engrossed in it. Coco was stillborn on January 1, 1981. Already the year was a bust, and it wasn't going to get better.

•••

Annie was the one grandparent I knew, but she was good propaganda for the rest: never did she come to visit without bringing a present. She made sure that the circuitous routes she took to meet us always brought her through at least one toy store. On lucky days, Eleanor and I met her at Macy's where I could play in the kids' department while they talked. Afterward, while I clutched some new gift, we would go for lunch in the basement cafeteria.

Annie believed I should cut out the mumbo-jumbo cures and see a doctor who operated on materialist principles. She contacted an old comrade from the 1930s, Dan Schwartz, who had become an administrator at Montefiore Medical Center in the Bronx. As a favor, Schwartz talked with his top pediatric orthopedist, Leonard Seimon, and told him that a family was coming to see him. They had some problems, Schwartz warned him, but were good people so he shouldn't ask too many personal questions. Dr. Seimon took X-rays and watched me walk up and down his corridor. The top of my femur, where it formed the hip joint, was deformed. It was, he said, a relatively mild case, but it required surgery. He would have to alter the shape of the bone by breaking it and then fixing it in a new position with a five-inch stainless steel clamp, which would stay in place for twelve months.

•

Annie would turn sixty-eight in March and she had never known exhaustion. For years she had kept a busy schedule. In the mornings, she woke up and clipped articles from the *New York Times,* which she then sorted and stowed away in files marked "RACE—confrontations," "China + U.S.," "Growth of Gangs," or "Soviet Education." Her apartment had been shrinking for years as the filing cabinets steadily encroached on the living space. In the afternoon, she might call her neighbor, Vicki Lawrence, and say, "Come on over—and bring ten sharpened pencils." Then Annie and Vicki, or Olivia Taylor, a school activist from East New York whom Annie had known since the mid-1960s, or whoever else was there that day, worked into the evening, pausing only for Chinese food. When she was done, Annie fixed herself a scotch and soda and savored an unfiltered Chesterfield. She had been a heavy smoker her entire adult life, always in the process of getting around to trying to quit. Lately, she had taken to keeping the packs in the mailbox in her building's lobby. Each time she wanted a smoke, she had to get dressed and ride the elevator down seven flights.

Annie had founded People Against Racism in Education, and after thirty years, was still trying to fix the inequities in the public school system. Her Marxist critique left her in little doubt about the true nature of the problem. "The average child in eighty-five percent of the Black and Puerto Rican schools," she had written in a 1971 issue of the *Harvard Education Review,* "is functionally illiterate after eight years of schooling in the richest city in the world. This is a massive accomplishment. It took the effort of 63,000 teachers, thousands more administrators, scholars, and social scientists, and the expenditure of billions of dollars to achieve."

She also sat on the board of the Puerto Rican Solidarity Committee and had spent a decade working for Puerto Rican independence. No goal was too small. When the landlords at Park West Village, the housing development where she had lived since 1963, tried to impose increased fees, Annie organized her neighbors and won the battle with the slogan, "Not a Cent Above the Rent." In fifty years, she had never missed a cause. Yet her goal of an equitable society was no closer. As the 1980s started, just the opposite was true.

Ronald Reagan had been elected president, and Annie recognized that the nation was cycling into another period of reaction. "Warm good wishes for the New Year," she wrote to friends in December 1980. "This business of living in interesting times is getting me down. I realize that in the transformation of the world from a capitalist to a socialist system, things are likely to get a bit troublesome. But do they have to get totally bizarre?"

In January, her energy suddenly vanished, and she checked into a hospital in the Bronx for tests. Doctors inserted a needle into her spine to look for cancer. Her friend Olivia came to visit and found her in a stiflingly hot room with several other patients. Annie was having trouble breathing and she looked so haggard, with her hair loose instead of in its usual neat bun, that at first Olivia hadn't recognized her. But she seemed to recover and was sent home. She told friends that the doctors had ruled out cancer and that she was her old self again. She finally quit smoking.

The next time Eleanor saw her mother—at an Upper East Side coffee shop—Annie was excitable, almost hyper. In her usual overbearing way, she was full of advice. My first major surgery was scheduled for early May, and Annie believed it would only worry me if I knew what to expect. It was the same parenting strategy she had used with Eleanor and Philip; for all the years of their childhood, she had kept from them the secret of their father's weak heart. About her own health, Annie seemed optimistic. The doctors were still doing tests, she said, but they didn't know what they were talking about. She was so positive that when Eleanor walked to the subway, she had no way of knowing that Annie was protecting her from the truth as well, and that she would never see her mother again.

As she often had before, Eleanor ignored her mother's advice, plying me with information about the procedure—a derotational osteotomy—that I was about to endure. She bought me Playmobil Emergency Room action figures and read *Curious George Goes to the Hospital* as a bedtime story. She explained the surgery in the gentlest terms possible, describing how doctors were going to go inside my leg and make it better. I still looked puzzled, and a few hours later, I asked how the doctors would make themselves small enough to fit inside my leg. She then showed me on my fuzzy green tyrannosaurus, taking a knife and making an incision in its plush left leg then sewing it up with a needle and thread. See? No problem.

I left day care for what was going to be a long absence. My schoolmates scribbled drawings on construction paper and collected them as a "Get Well Timmy" scrapbook. On May 8, 1981, we drove to the hospital early. I climbed onto the gurney, clutching my dinosaur, and the swinging doors shut my parents back in the waiting room. The anesthesiologist locked a rubbery mask over my mouth and the theater was dark before I counted ten. When I woke up three hours later, the steel clamp was in place on my bone, and I smelled like wet cement. I had a plaster cast running from my hips all the way down to the toes on my left foot. A previously active four-year-old, I would be bedridden for the next three months. To break the monotony, Jeff pulled me around the block in a red Radio Flyer wagon. No one told me that my grandmother was back in the hospital.

Annie's pain had increased until it hurt too much for her to leave her rooms. She could no longer digest Chinese food and survived exclusively on coffee ice cream, for which her admirers scoured the Upper West Side. Her stomach became distended, and she told her friends that she felt like she was "twenty months pregnant." She began to ask the same question over and over. Soon she admitted, "I'm just not myself anymore." Chavy spent most nights with her, and Annie lived at home for as long as she could stand it. But in the middle of a night in early May, the pain was too much and she called an ambulance.

When the crew arrived and told her to hurry up, Annie insisted on taking a final tour of her beloved apartment. She looked out of the windows at the park and the Empire State Building. Finally she agreed to leave. Refusing any help, she lifted herself onto the stretcher and was wheeled out and driven to New York Hospital. She was tested again for cancer, and this time, the doctors found it, active and voracious, in her lungs and liver. Giant new tumors appeared on her spine daily.

Eleanor was desperate to visit. She studied the hospital floor plan and learned that to have her radiation treatment, Annie was taken each day through underground tunnels to a different building. Eleanor considered disguising herself as a nurse and trying to make contact during one of these transfers. But one of the actual nurses had confided to Annie that there were FBI agents in the hospital watching her. Annie didn't want Eleanor to risk it. She made a decision that her daughter never could have, scribbling a barely legible note reading, "I break totally with our friends. Chavy has money." Eleanor couldn't visit, but they had ways of communicating. In particular, Annie wanted to hear about my surgery. Finally, she learned the good news—that I was fine. That day, her legs had at last grown too weak to support her. Relieved that I was safe, she looked down toward her feet and said, "I gave my legs to Thai."

After a long spell by the bedside, Eleanor's brother Philip left the hospital around midnight on May 13 and went to steal some sleep in the apartment on 100th Street. A few hours later, the phone woke him. It was the hospital: Annie was dead. He went back and sat in the room with her for a few hours before orderlies wheeled her away to the morgue.

Two hundred and fifty of her friends came to her memorial at the Riverside Chapel: comrades from the 1930s who were already old, young mothers from Brooklyn who were now grandmothers, and fighters who were still young and fresh. No one knew everyone; the ones whom no one knew were most likely government agents. Eleanor, who had never visited the hospital, sent a letter that was read aloud: "Being separated at this time must have been very painful for Annie; it certainly was for me. But Annie never wanted to give the government the satisfaction of a victory, no matter what the personal cost to herself. That was a decision my mother made early on, in the face of McCarthyism."

Joe Forer and Al Bernstein, from Washington, D.C., spoke about the movement to desegregate the lunch counters there. Olivia Taylor, Milton Galamison, and Ruth Messinger talked about the long campaign they had waged with New York's city schools. Finally the last speaker, Chavy, rose and walked with her crutches to the podium. She had been around constantly during Annie's final days. After Annie died, Chavy and Olivia were scheduled to go to her apartment and begin sorting her papers. Olivia got stuck on a train and arrived hours late. When she walked up Central Park West to the building, Chavy was still sitting outside, too sad to face the familiar rooms alone.

Now she told the mourners about the time "fifty-odd years ago in high school," when she and Annie had met on a subway platform in Brooklyn. "I was already in radical politics and Annie was not," Chavy said. "We had a big fight, and a month later she was convinced I was right. I cherish that memory because I think it's the last argument I ever won with her."

•••

One of Annie's final favors was to call Morty Stavis. He had been the attorney for the United Public Workers in the 1940s and since then had built a successful practice in New Jersey. After decades of schmoozing, there wasn't a judge or prosecutor in Hoboken or Jersey City whom Morty didn't count as a friend. In the old days, he had often been around the house in Brooklyn and remembered Eleanor as a little girl. Annie called him and said, "I'm giving you a charge. Take care of my daughter and make sure she comes to no harm." He took that charge seriously.

Eleanor and Jeff met with Stavis at a greasy diner near the piers, and he told them what to expect if they were going to turn themselves in. Once they opened up a line of communication with the FBI, he said, they would have to live their lives as if they might be arrested at any moment. No more radical literature lying around. No more friends at all hours. And, it went without saying, no more pot plants on the balcony.

They went right from the meeting to the stone building on narrow, tree-lined Decatur Avenue. They walked up the six flights of stairs to our apartment. Inside, they filled up garbage bags until the rooms were almost bare. Then they wiped down every surface with rubbing alcohol to eradicate all fingerprints.

My little room was left with just the bed and a pint-sized desk and chair. My Legos were also spared. My window looked out at the Empire State Building, and Jeff and I—mostly Jeff—had spent weeks building a model of the skyscraper that was taller than I was. By October 1981, I was finally out of my cast. A doctor had cut it away with scissors, freeing me to scratch the dry, ashen skin that had itched torturously for three months. When the leg was revealed, my first sight was the livid new scar running several inches down the outside of my thigh. With the surgery behind me, I was due a nice, long period of family normalcy.

Jeff was training for the marathon again and had never been in better shape. After each morning jog, he came home and logged his time in his black racing journal. He was running most miles in under six minutes, far faster than he would need if he was to achieve his goal of finishing the twenty-six miles in less than three hours. On October 20, with five days to go before the big race, he staggered back from a morning run and started dressing to go to work in Manhattan. He and Eleanor were both listening to the radio in their bedroom when the announcer flashed in with breaking news: a botched armored truck robbery in Rockland County, two police-men and a security guard dead, four unidentified people—two whites and two blacks—in custody. My parents looked at each other and had the exact same thought: I bet they're friends of ours.

"No matter how this unfolds," Jeff said to her, "our lives are not going to be the same." There was no explicit reason that the trail should lead to us and nothing we could do to avoid trouble. Jeff and Eleanor took me to school and then went to work. The story of the Brink's robbery developed throughout the day. The suspects' names were released, and that initial hunch had been correct: Kathy Boudin, Judy Clark, and David Gilbert were old, old friends.

Jeff's face, as well as Kathy and David's and Bernardine and Bill's, were in every newspaper. The old stories—about the townhouse explosion and the Days of Rage—were retold. The Joint Anti-Terrorism Task Force, a combination of FBI agents and New York City police, organized the most massive manhunt in state history to net everyone who might have been involved in the robbery. As a precaution, we left the apartment for a few days, but on Friday,

October 23, Jeff decided we could go back. Sunday morning was the marathon, and he had left his sneakers and his number at home.

Special Agent Larry Wack of the Federal Bureau of Investigation's New York field office hadn't been home in three days. It had been the busiest week of his career. He sped to the scene of ten apartments, and every new door he burst through revealed more leads: guns and ammunition, disguises, and, most unsettling, lists of prominent police officials and blueprints for station houses around the city. At night, Wack just lay down on the floor at the office and caught a few hours of sleep.

One of his first investigations, when he was still part of the Civil Rights Division based at FBI Headquarters in Washington, had been the 1969 Days of Rage in Chicago. He had been involved in the Weatherman case, off and on, ever since. His hair, which came down to the middle of his ears, was considered long in the Bureau, and he had recently grown a beard; instead of a suit and tie, he wore jeans and a leather jacket, but he was no hippie sympathizer. In his opinion the radicals were "ruthless, gutless revolutionaries hell bent on changing society to their way through the use of bombs, murder and violence." Much of the public seemed to think that the fugitives, by remaining at large for so many years, had made a mockery of him and his fellow agents. But Wack knew that sooner or later he would get his men. "Time," he would say, "is on our side."

In one of those secret apartments, or during an interrogation, Wack came upon our Bronx address. He drove up to Decatur Avenue and flashed some old photos to the building superintendent. Sure I know them, said the super, that's John and Sally Maynard. Then Wack told him who his tenants really were.

Jeff's wanted poster read, "JONES REPORTEDLY MAY RESIST ARREST, HAS BEEN ASSOCIATED WITH PERSONS WHO ADVOCATE USE OF EXPLOSIVES AND MAY HAVE ACQUIRED FIREARMS. CONSIDER DANGEROUS." Wack was dealing with him on those terms. He assembled a twelve-man SWAT team dressed in black and armed with M-16s. He himself carried only his standard .38 caliber revolver. He positioned his men on the fire escapes and in the stairwell on the sixth floor. Then, because he knew there was a child in the apartment, he made a suggestion to his superior.

"Look," Wack told his boss, "we got the place pretty well surrounded. If we have to wait 'em out, we'll wait 'em out, but let me call in there." It was always risky to give a suspect warning, but he insisted on trying. He usually got a melancholy feeling before an arrest. Some busts went smoothly, and some went to shit in about five seconds. He thought the phone call was the safest choice.

He placed it from the super's apartment, holding the receiver in one hand and his walkie-talkie in the other. After a few rings, Jeff answered. Wack told him the apartment was surrounded and that he should go and open the front door. Then, praying the batteries were working, he spoke into his walkie-talkie and warned his anxious men on the sixth floor landing that the door would open shortly. This done, he put down the phone and ran as fast as he could up to the scene. Jeff was in the corridor on his hands and knees when the four-year-old kid, for whom Wack had gone to such lengths already, bounded out of the apartment, and seeing his dad on his hands and knees, tried to climb onto his back, shouting, "Horsey! Horsey!" This kid thinks it's a god-damned game, Wack grumbled, and from then on the agents referred to this bust as the "Horsey Case."

When the agents first pounded on the door, Eleanor had shouted, "We've been negotiating. Call the FBI. They'll tell you."

"Lady," they yelled back, "We are the FBI."

The SWAT team was inhuman for the first minutes. The men, oddly proportioned with bullet-proof vests and visored helmets, looked like so many Darth Vaders. Each carried an automatic rifle. Having been to other safe houses where weapons were stored, they fully expected to confront armed radicals and were in fear for their lives. There were no pleasantries until every closet was checked, the beds unmade, and the dressers hurled open.

When the invaders were satisfied that this was a family apartment and there would be no fighting, the extreme tension vanished, and Eleanor started negotiating again. She was sitting in a rocking chair,

cuddling me on her lap. She started talking to the FBI agent about
me. She sat face to face with Wack, and all she could think was, "I
hope this man has children of his own." It was important, she told
him, for me to leave first. I should be spared seeing my parents taken
away from me. She also wanted to call a friend to get me. Wack
agreed on the condition that he make the actual phone call. This left
Eleanor and Jeff in the odd predicament of having to choose a
friend's name to give to the FBI. They settled on Harold Osborn, the
father of my best friend in day care. He lived on City Island and
could arrive quickly.

It was past midnight, and Harold Osborn, an emergency room doctor at North Central Bronx Hospital, was fast asleep when the telephone rang and Agent Wack came on the line to tell him he had a
quarter of an hour to come and pick me up. Minutes later he was on
the Pelham Parkway.

Wack had given him no details over the phone but Osborn had an
idea of what to expect. His son Jesse was in my class at Mosholu-
Montefiore day care center, and I had come over to his house on
City Island to play. He had given advice about my operation and
during the school year had slowly gotten to know our family. As a
progressive guy, he recognized my parents as fellow travelers. Then, as
things heated up around the Brink's robbery, he and his wife, Celia,
had met Eleanor and Jeff at a Mexican restaurant off the Sawmill
River Parkway. During the meal, Jeff had suddenly gone serious and
said, "There's something we need to tell you."

"Let me guess," Osborn said jokingly, "You're Mark Rudd and
Bernardine Dohrn."

"Close," said Jeff, and told them the story.

Now, Osborn swung off the parkway onto Bedford Avenue and
pulled up to our building. There were police vans, cruisers, and
unmarked cars. Flashing lights strobed the faces of a curious crowd
while policemen wound yellow crime scene tape across the front
entrance to the apartment house. Osborn identified himself to the
patrolmen and climbed the six flights to our apartment.

First, he saw Jeff, his hands cuffed behind his back. "How are you?" Jeff said, as if it was a social occasion. "Thanks for coming over." Osborn could feel the hostility and the nerves, even though the bust was more than an hour old. In the next room, I was sitting with Eleanor. I was not screaming or crying, just holding on tight. Eleanor told me to go with Osborn, and I seemed willing enough. He carried me downstairs to his car and strapped me in. He had been amazed, when he first learned the truth about our family, that I had never slipped or given a hint. Now, he watched me even more curiously. I was quiet and inward looking. On the drive home, Osborn said soothing things, and I seemed to accept them. When we got home, he unrolled a sleeping bag for me and spread it on the floor in his own bedroom. He didn't want to let me out of his sight.

After I was taken away, Agent Wack led Jeff and Eleanor downstairs and guided them into the back seat of a waiting agency car. As they sped down the FDR Drive toward jail, the FBI agent turned to Jeff, whom he had come to know through reading his files, and said, "Now you can put this behind you and get on with your life."

As I was finally going to sleep on the night of October 23, Albert Jones was driving home from a small gathering of the San Fernando Valley Friends Meeting. Over the years in Sylmar, some new shopping plazas had gone up and earthquakes had knocked some down, so little had changed. Tyler Street was still wide and quiet, and most houses on it had both a driveway and a garage.

At 10:00 P.M., Jeff called to say he was in the custody of the FBI. Albert must have been the happiest father ever to hear his son had been arrested. He had pictured—and then willed himself not to picture—all the violent ends Jeff might meet. During the previous decade, he had seen various radical groups wiped out in deadly gun battles, in fires and explosions. The images had haunted him, but now Jeff was safely behind bars, and Albert could complete the traditional Quaker task of arriving after troubles to patch things back together.

With only one small suitcase, he boarded an airplane to Newark, New Jersey. When he landed, he went directly to Morty Stavis's brownstone office on Hudson Street in Hoboken. Stavis caught

Albert up with events. His negotiations with the FBI before the arrest had stalled because they would not compromise enough to give Jeff only a one-year prison sentence. Now that Jeff was in custody, most of Stavis's leverage was gone. The police had cast a huge net following the robbery, and they had caught many kinds of fish in it. Stavis's strategy was to make Albert's son into a little fish, the kind that might qualify for the catch-and-release program. The seriousness of the recent crimes made the charge against Jeff—possessing a can of gunpowder—seem insignificant, and even the police admitted there was no link between him and the robbers. Morty's strategy was to separate Jeff and Eleanor from the Brink's investigation, get them from New York to New Jersey, and keep publicity to a minimum.

My parents spent their first night in general holding cells in the Tombs, Manhattan's decrepit and notorious downtown lock-up. At their arraignment, bail was set at $200,000 apiece; the figure was so high it implied a large degree of importance, and even worse for Stavis's plan, guilt. The prisoners were transferred to the Manhattan Correctional Center, a modern jail under federal jurisdiction. There, the other inmates agreed to forgo the football games and let Jeff watch the marathon on TV. On October 26, my parents were thrown together in the back of a police car. There were other cars before and behind them, as far as they could see. All had their lights and sirens on. The cops shut down the Holland Tunnel during the evening rush and—while Eleanor and Jeff held hands in the back seat—the huge motorcade sped under the Hudson River to the Garden State. This was not the way little fish were usually treated, but at least the suspects were now on Stavis's own grounds.

The next day, the lawyer led Albert into a Hudson County courtroom and guided him to a seat in the front row, directly behind the defendants' table. For bail purposes, Albert had emptied his account, withdrawing $10,000 from the bank. He had the ten crisp $1,000 bills in his inside jacket pocket, and every few minutes his hands involuntarily patted his chest to make sure the comforting bundle was still there. He was not wearing cowboy boots and a ten-gallon hat, but he had a western shirt and looked completely out of place. The room was crowded with reporters, and it seemed to him that every badge in the metropolitan area was there, shoving for space in front of the cameras.

The side doors opened. A uniformed officer appeared, followed by two manacled prisoners: Jeff Jones—aka Thomas Martin, Raymond Breman, Thomas Charles, Dennis Egerton, James N. Baker, Jonathan Logan, James Silva, James Martin, Joseph Navarro, James Hayes, John R. Hansen, Allen A. Hill—and Eleanor Stein—aka Jean Hayes, Jean Silva, Jean Martin, Clare Jordan, Ann C. Strauss, Anna Emerson, Marie Corey, Jean Russell.

When the hearing started, the prosecutor told the court that the charge of explosives possession carried a maximum penalty of ten years in prison. He admitted that no evidence linked the defendants to the Brink's robbery but said they were "subject to an ongoing investigation." Because of their pasts, he asked that bail for each be set at $200,000. Stavis said the sums were outrageous for such minor charges, and the judge compromised, setting Jeff's bail at $150,000 and Eleanor's at $100,000. They were both sent to Hudson County Jail. Eleanor would be released once she had posted bond, but Jeff was to remain inside so the FBI could continue their investigation.

Albert was pressed by reporters outside the courthouse. They asked him what it felt like not to see his son for eleven years and if he and Jeff had spoken in that time. Albert told them he had never known where his son was and had never wanted to know. But now he knew where Jeff was—the old County Jail—and he was going over to visit. As he climbed the stairs, he could hear the inmates clanging their bars and hooting catcalls at him. Jeff was on the top floor, at the end of a narrow municipal-green corridor. There were only single cells on this level, which was reserved for the prison's most dangerous criminals. The jailors considered Jeff such a hard case that they had emptied the rest of the floor and placed him alone in the farthest cell.

Albert hugged Jeff through the bars; keeping his expression cheerful, even as he winced to see his son imprisoned. Jeff was busy with details of his case; he needed money and documents and was trying to think like a lawyer. Albert agreed with everything he said; he was there to comfort and give confidence.

Eleanor was released that afternoon, and Chavy drove her and Albert to City Island to pick me up. Albert buckled his seat belt and breathed deep, calming breaths as Chavy lurched the car across the river and north on the highway. She was sixty-seven years old, and even though her legs were paralyzed, she still managed to drive around the frantic streets of New York City. Her car was equipped with levers that let her steer with the right hand and apply the gas and brakes with the left.

Eleanor had talked to the Osborns and knew what to expect. The child in this situation would feel suspicious and abandoned; he would defend himself by feigning aloofness or unconcern. When she arrived on City Island, I fit the pattern; I was stand-offish and disgruntled. Eleanor wanted to gather me up and tell me how much she needed forgiveness and love and the nod that meant the experience hadn't been too hurtful and that we could move on from this as a new family. But she couldn't say that. She had to relate as a child, so she asked about my week. Had I been going to school? What had I eaten for dinner? Were there any good toys to play with? We took a long walk alone together down Main Street and bought ice cream cones at the Black Whale. By the time, we were back from our stroll we were friends again; she was mom—whatever her name was—and I couldn't stay mad at her for long.

We went to Annie's old apartment. I had never been there, and Eleanor had kept away since March 7, 1970, the day after the townhouse explosion, when she had used her mother's rooms to disguise one of the survivors of the blast. Now she returned to the familiar building, the familiar elevator, the familiar hallway. A friend was waiting to hand her the key, and just holding it triggered another round of old sensations. Eleanor opened the door, and it was like walking into the Annie Stein museum. The photos and posters, and especially the files, were all intact.

It was a moment to respect, to soothe lingering ghosts, but Eleanor couldn't. Her four-year-old son was in a frenzy. Although we had made peace, I was still disturbed and showed it by shedding all clothing and running, screaming, through the apartment. Albert, though he appreciated the special case, had a different standard for child behavior. He didn't want to interfere, but in a quiet moment, he warned me, "If you don't listen to your mother you're going to get into trouble."

"Getting into trouble," said I, "is a little boy's job."

•••

Jeff was in jail—actually, it was three jails—for roughly two weeks. Then Albert spent his ten $1,000 bills to bail him out. Philip Stein put up his house as collateral for the rest. I had tried to visit my father and was turned away, but Eleanor, after she was released, was allowed in. She stood where Albert had been, in the corridor outside his cell, and Jeff got down on one knee and asked her, Eleanor Stein, to marry him, Jeffrey Jones. They had wed before but never with those names.

On December 11, 1981, a week before the sentencing, our small wedding party took the subway to Lower Manhattan. Only the desperate were married in the Municipal Building. A teenage Hispanic couple, the bride in her final trimester, was in line in front of us. Jeff was dressed in a gray sport coat. Eleanor carried a bouquet of daisies and wore the same pair of pants in which she had been arrested. As they walked down the steps of the building after the two-minute ceremony, I reached into a bag and showered them with organic brown rice.

At 9:00 A.M. on December 17, the respectably married couple returned, reluctantly, to New Jersey. They arrived at the County Administration Building on Newark Avenue and awaited their sentence. Jeff hoped that he wouldn't have to spend much more than a year in prison. Eleanor thought her penalty would be less but agonized over my response to losing my parents for a second time. Then Judge Gaulkin announced his decision. Jeff was sentenced to a year and a half of probation and six months of intense community service: he would work seven days a week as a volunteer until the time was up. All charges against Eleanor were dropped. Neither would spend another day in jail. Stavis had worked a miracle.

Millie had flown in from Oregon to be at the hearing. "Dear Morty," she wrote:

I'm using this familiar greeting, as I feel I know you as a close friend after meeting you at Jeffrey's sentencing in New Jersey, and knowing all you have done for him and therefore our whole family.

I really can't thank you enough. I have to pinch myself now and then to make sure I'm not dreaming, and that Jeff is a free man. We know he will need help from all of us to get through the next six months. For the first time in eleven years I was able to call him on the phone to say, "Merry Christmas."

•••

We lived in Annie's apartment. When Jeff returned from jail, I grabbed his hand and gave him the tour: it didn't take long to cover two rooms. Downstairs, there was a playground for residents, and, I pointed out to him, Central Park was right across the street. I didn't have a bedroom, but I commandeered a closet that once had been filled with files and built a fort. I was Thai now. On my first day back in class after the arrest, my teacher had made a little announcement. Timmy's back, she said, but now his name is Thai. Let's all sing a song for Thai. None of the other four-year-olds found this odd, but several of them thought it would be fun to change their names.

On weekends, Jeff fulfilled his community service requirements by volunteering at North General Hospital in East Harlem. On the weekdays, he worked as a school-bus driver at the Mosholu-Montefiore Daycare Center in the Bronx, which just happened to be the day care I attended. I had gone there before the arrest, and the teachers all knew us and wanted to help out.

From Monday to Friday for half a year, the clock-radio clicked on at 5:00 A.M. and Jeff got out of bed. He showered and shaved. After eleven years, these were the first mornings that weren't ruined by worry. During his time on the run, waking up had always carried the immediate realization of the tenuousness of his freedom. At best, he had imagined spending between five and ten years in prison. He marveled, during these mornings, at how well the family had managed to come through to the other side. Then he went into my room and woke me up.

It was still night when we left the building, walking hand in hand to the subway. A few taxis trawled unhopefully on Central Park West, and the street was so quiet we could hear the mechanical thud of the stoplights changing color.

The uptown local took us to 125th Street. Commuters lined up to go downtown, but on our side of the tracks, the platform was still deserted. The D Train to the Bronx was empty except for those, stretched out on the stiff seats, who had spent the night on board. We had a half-hour ride to the last station. For the first few months, winter months, it was still dark when we emerged from the train into the north Bronx. Jeff clocked in and picked up the key to one of the school's large vans. He strapped me in to the passenger seat, and for the next hour, we circled through Mosholu, Jerome Avenue, and Riverdale, gathering the students. Around a quarter to nine, in broad daylight, we returned to the school, and Jeff and I went off to class.

AFTERWORD

I N November 1979, Jeff's pot plants had drawn the attention of a Hoboken fire captain on a routine inspection. He had notified the police, and we had been forced to abandon the apartment, the plants, and all of our possessions. I had lost my X-rays and Eleanor her precious 1967 twelve-string Martin guitar.

After their arrest in the Bronx in October 1981, Eleanor and Jeff asked their lawyer, Morty Stavis, to get back our confiscated things. The *New York Times* had mentioned $500 in cash that the policemen found at the apartment, yet the police report of the incident didn't mention finding the money. In fact, there had been $1,200 in the apartment, hidden under a loose board in the kitchen cabinet, when Jeff left that morning to pick up groceries. But only $500 remained by the time reporters arrived. If they hadn't mentioned the sum in a news story, there would have been no record of any of the money. "On behalf of my clients," Stavis wrote, "I respectfully request that an accounting be made on this matter."

At the time, Jeff was serving his sentence by volunteering seven days a week while Eleanor, pregnant again, worked to support the family. A matter of $500 didn't seem so little. In March 1982, five months after their arrest, Eleanor and Jeff were back in a police station. The Hoboken police had agreed to return the goods. It was a tense and silent procession that led Eleanor and Jeff into a back room filled with cardboard boxes representing the worldly goods of Hudson County's criminals.

"Oh my God, look what's there," said Eleanor, squeezing Jeff's arm. On the counter was her guitar case. Next to it our things were divided into half a dozen boxes. My X-rays were there, tacky with fingerprint dust but still readable. The officer counted out five one hundred dollar bills, and Jeff signed for them in triplicate. He picked up the boxes, and Eleanor lifted up the case. Her heart fell. The Hoboken police had returned her guitar case, but they had kept the guitar.

•••

My brother was born on September 22, 1982. He looked just like his grandfather had as a baby and Eleanor named him Arthur. Considering that his extended family included not only Thai and Zayd but also Amilcar, Chesa, Malik, Haydee, Atariba, and Bear, he got off pretty lucky. But it didn't last. Arthur was too adult a name for a baby, and we put our heads together to find something better. All of us were crowded into Annie's one-bedroom apartment on Central Park West, and while we talked, a bluejay landed on our balcony.

"Let's call him Bluejay," I said, and so we have ever since.

•••

Eleanor was two-thirds of the way toward her law degree at Columbia Law School when she quit to make a revolution. After thirteen years, she was ready to return. Unfortunately, most of the administrators in 1982 had been administrators in 1969. For the faculty at the law school, the student revolts had been a shattering experience. A decade of revelations about Vietnam atrocities and government scandals had done nothing to soften their attitude toward any of the rebels, let alone Eleanor, who had been among the most notorious.

She went in for interviews with the rules committee. Prepared to answer for her years in the underground, Eleanor found that all the questions were about her activities as a student. Although no one doubted her academic abilities, her request to be reinstated was denied. A few weeks later, an envelope arrived anonymously at our apartment. Someone at the law school had sent the thick file of memoranda that the faculty had circulated concerning her case.

Spurned by Columbia, Eleanor turned to the newly founded City University of New York Law School at Queens College. She graduated in 1986, having taken only nineteen years to get her degree.

Back in upstate New York, she practices environmental and telecommunications law. She teaches both law school and undergraduate womens' studies and is part of a network of women working for peace. After years as a quilter, she picked up the paintbrush again.

•••

In 1986, Jeff finally traveled to Vietnam. Twenty years earlier, he had gone all the way to Cambodia, only to learn that heavy American bombing made it impossible to land in Hanoi. In the interval, Cambodia had changed its name to Kampuchea, and Saigon had become Ho Chi Minh City. But near Hanoi, many of the huge bomb craters still remained from the war.

Jeff stayed for three weeks. He met Kim Phuc, the young girl who became an international symbol of the war when a photographer captured an image of her fleeing down a street, her skin burning from a napalm attack. Jeff also visited the Tunnels of Cu Chi, a network of passageways buried deep beneath the surface, from which the Vietcong had directed their offensives. That was what it really meant to go underground.

With his charges behind him, Jeff became a reporter for the alternative media. In the mid-1980s he volunteered in the Nicaraguan coffee harvest and produced a book about the experience, *Brigadista, Harvest and War in Nicaragua*. After eight years as a reporter covering New York State government in Albany, Jeff returned to political activism as the communications director for Environmental Advocates of New York.

•••

Albert Jones lives in Las Vegas, Nevada, with his wife, Celeste. He rarely misses Quaker meeting on Sundays and still has the ornate spoon and silver loving cup that were commissioned for him by King Albert I of Belgium. When the *Antiques Road Show* came to the Las Vegas Convention Center, he gathered his treasures from a shelf in the closet and had them appraised. Apparently, the experts told him, they were loaded with sentimental value.

•••

Millie lives in Eugene, Oregon, with her third husband, Stanley Thompson. She recently stopped playing music in public but still gives violin lessons. She sends her son a Christmas card each year, a small pleasure that she was deprived of for more than a decade.

•••

Chavy celebrated her ninetieth birthday in April 2004. Her doctors tell her that childhood polio, though it weakened her legs, strengthened the rest of her. She lives on the Lower East Side of Manhattan, where once she ruled the Communist Party. She is still something of a menace, zipping around the sidewalks in her electric wheelchair, often taking aim at unsuspecting capitalist pedestrians.

She has outlived her friend Annie by more than twenty years. She was two years old when the czar was toppled and seventy-six when the Soviet Union was overthrown. She outlived that too.

•••

In the winter of 2003, I was alone in my parents' house in Albany, New York, when the doorbell rang. A tall man and a short man, both in suits, stood on the front porch. Before either of them spoke a word, I recognized who they were. When your family has been under suspicion for seventy years, you develop a kind of sixth sense when it comes to recognizing agents from the Federal Bureau of Investigation.

"Agent Shannon, FBI," said the short man, flashing me his identi-fication. I tried to remember what I was supposed to do in this situ-

ation. Should I answer questions, demand a lawyer, invite them in? What would Annie Stein have done?

"Is your father home?" Shannon asked.

"No," I answered. Whoops. Had I said too much?

"When do you expect him?"

"He'll be back in an hour," I said. Somehow the agent must have seen through my projection of cool nonchalance.

"Don't worry," he said. "He's not in any trouble." Then they walked down to an obviously rented car parked on the street. The tall one had never said a word during the entire interview.

I tried to call Jeff on his cell phone to tell him what had happened, and the thing started ringing right next to me. He'd left it at home. The old clandestine instincts weren't what they had been, I thought.

The agents returned later that night. They were investigating a bombing case from the early 1970s and had a few questions for an ex-Weatherman. Jeff told them to talk to his lawyer.

I was still recovering from the experience. It is an anxious thing to stand against a government, to face its agents, and to live under threat of its retribution.

NOTES

CHAPTER 1: COBBLESTONES

15 Two young women: This scene comes from interviews with Evelyn Wiener. "Heat Wave Booms Business at Coney," *New York Times*, July 30, 1929.

17 forty-three new graves: Judge, *Easter in Kishinev*, p. 72.

17 *Patricia* was one: Information on the Hamburg-American Line from the Ellis Island website, http://www.ellisisland.org

18 "I have not known such weather": "Big Wave Sweeps Liner," *New York Times*, Jan. 12, 1904.

19 "The borough enjoyed a spectacle of destruction": "10,000 See Firemen Fight Sea of Flame," *New York Times*, June 12, 1923.

19 a gloomy hoard of revolutionaries: "Reds Orderly Here in Parade in Rain," *New York Times*, May 2, 1932.

20 May Day had begun in America fifty years earlier: "May Day," *Student Review*, April 1932.

20 "Down with Socialism": "Reds Orderly Here in Parade in Rain," *New York Times*, May 2, 1932.

22 marcelled hair and V-neck sweaters: Hunter College Yearbook, 1931; *The Echo: Journal of Hunter College Archives*, 1995.

22 In a questionnaire given to Annie's class: "Of 750 Hunter Girls, Only 1 Plans to Wed," *New York Times*, Oct. 5, 1931.

22 the students handed Norman Thomas: "Thomas Wins in Hunter," *New York Times*, Nov. 7, 1932.

23 "Several members of the delegation were beaten": "Students Forcibly

Ejected from Kentucky Mine Area," *Hunter Bulletin,* April 11, 1932. "40 Students Leave on Harlan Inquiry," *New York Times,* March 24, 1932.

23 "Fight for the overthrow of the bosses' government": Writing in a typical Young Communist League pamphlet, from "Girl Radical Is Seized," *New York Times,* May 31, 1929.

23 "You are now celebrating the 15th Anniversary of the October Revolution": *Student Review,* Nov. 1935.

24 "The new student movement has crystallized": "An Appeal," *Student Review,* Oct. 1932.

24 they couldn't even find jobs in the factories themselves: Klehr, *Heyday of the American Communist Party,* chap. 9.

24 "The results are also good" Quoted in ibid., p. 193. This quote is from 1929.

24 "enemies of the working class": Quoted in Latham, *Communist Controversy,* p. 40. From the first issue of the *New Masses* in 1934.

25 sergeants were quietly trained in special street-fighting drills: "Cops in Secret May Day Drill," *Daily Worker,* April 30, 1933.

25 "More than 1,000 policemen will be on duty": "World Labor Plans May Day Parades; Police Guard Here," *New York Times,* May 1, 1933.

25 were mobilizing into two divisions: Description of the parade route and the organization of the divisions come from the *Daily Worker,* April 30, 1933.

26 a military review in Moscow: "Parade in Moscow Show of Strength," *New York Times,* May 2, 1933.

28 makeshift houses of Hooverville: Davis, *Great Day Coming,* p. 24.

28 rated at 150: From his FBI Files. The principal at Evander Childs High School provided Arthur's records to the agents.

28 "possessed ability well above average": FBI Files. This quote is from Professor Hotelling.

29 leaving copies of the *Worker:* Interviews with Evelyn Wiener, Jan. 2002.

30 "The boys and girls": "Students of 250 Colleges Gather in Capital," *Washington Post,* Dec. 12, 1933.

30 "slick-haired fraternity men": "Social Note: N.S.F.A.," *Student Review,* Feb. 1934.

31 met in a spired red-brick chapel: "National Student Convention Opens in Washington," *Daily Worker,* Dec. 28, 1933.

31 "The section of our program": Annie Steckler, "Three Conventions," *Student Review,* Feb. 1934.

31 "Early in the afternoon": "Students Wave Antiwar Flag at White House," *Washington Post,* Dec. 29, 1933.

32 "Let's not spend our energies": Annie Stein's FBI Files.

CHAPTER 2: L'ENFANT JONES

34 The King was finishing a tour: "Albert Acclaimed on 1919 Visit Here," *New York Times,* Feb. 18, 1934.

34 Albert was a keen outdoorsman: From Cammaerts, *Albert of Belgium*.

34 the souvenir postcard sights: "Each Moment a Delight: Scenic Beauties Vie in Yosemite National Park," *Overland Magazine,* June 1920.

35 "There has been another arrival": This and all the rest of the Jones family stories come from interviews with Albert Jones in Las Vegas, autumn 2002.

35 fall to his death: "King Albert Falls to Death Climbing Peak Near Namur," *New York Times,* Feb. 19, 1934.

35 subtle secrets of flapjack flipping: Sargent, *Yosemite's Famous Guests,* p. 25. Other details of the royal visit from "Queen's Charm Fails on a Mountain Lion," *New York Times,* Oct. 16, 1919. "Albert Sees the Big Trees," *New York Times,* Oct. 17, 1919. "Belgium Rulers Climb Trail to Yosemite Peak," *San Francisco Chronicle,* Oct. 16, 1919.

36 "low, rounded, bordering hills" From Cutler, *History of the State of Kansas.*

37 newly built $25,000 redbrick schoolhouse: Telephone interview with Cathy Haney, archivist for the Clay County Museum, Oct. 2002.

37 "with a bursting, rending, and crashing sound": Description of the *Maine* explosion by Captain Charles D. Sigsbee in Everett, *War with Spain and the Filipinos,* pp. 47–49.

37 "largely of farmers' sons": Kansas Adjutant General's Office, *Kansas Troops in the Volunteer Services of the United States in the Spanish and Philippine Wars,* p. 218.

38 far more dangerous place: "Camp Alger's Water Famine," *New York Times,* June 4, 1898. "Camp Alger's Bad Condition," *New York Times,* June 7, 1898. "Illness at Camp Alger," *New York Times,* Oct. 13, 1898.

38 desecrate some Confederate graves: "Desecration at Bull Run," *New York Times,* Aug. 12, 1898.

38 "had the exigencies of the service": Kansas Adjutant General's Office, *Kansas Troops,* p. 218.

39 instantly recognized as a greenhorn: Earnest King as told to Mahaffay, *Main Line,* p. 92.

40 towering minarets: 1924 photograph from the San Fernando Valley History Digital Library of California State University Northridge. Also, *Girard: A New Town in Southern California, in the San Fernando Valley,* a real estate pamphlet circulated by Victor Girard; and Cacioppo, *The History of Woodland Hills and Girard.*

41 "As King Albert stood against the invading Hun": "Heroic Ruler of the Belgians Cheered to the Echo as He Dines with the Men of S.F.," *San Francisco Chronicle,* Oct. 15, 1919.

42 new Los Angeles Stock Exchange: "Stock Mart Under Way," *Los Angeles Times,* Oct. 22, 1929. Also described in Leonard Leader's *Los Angeles and the Great Depression.*

44 "out of a job, able to work": Quoted in Leader.

45 "take an out-and-out stand for Christ": From the brochure for the Epworth League's Golden Jubilee, 1939.

45   "War has lost its glory": Quoted in Eller, *Conscientious Objectors and the Second World War,* p. 13.

48   Millie had grown up: Information about Millie's background comes from interviews conducted in her home in Eugene, Oregon, Thanksgiving 2002.

CHAPTER 3: *KONSPIRATSIA*

50   "In other world capitals . . .":"Cherry Blossom Time," *New York Times,* April 2, 1939.

50   President Roosevelt spent:"Capital Churches Filled," *New York Times,* April 10, 1939."75,000 Acclaim Miss Anderson; Easter Visitors Throng Capital," *Washington Post,* April 10, 1939.

51   Parks Department workers: Anderson, *My Lord, What a Morning.* Keiler, *Marian Anderson: A Singer's Journey.* "Concert and Opera," *New York Times,* April 9, 1939.

51   "Costumes were a Roman holiday":"75,000 Acclaim Miss Anderson; Easter Visitors Throng Capital," *Washington Post,* April 10, 1939.

52   "They stand almost in the shadow": Quoted in Keiler, *Marian Anderson,* p. 207. Other details about the Daughters of the American Revolution are also from Keiler.

53   the sun came out:"75,000 Acclaim Miss Anderson."

53   "irresponsible members": Quoted in Carroll, *The Odyssey of the Abraham Lincoln Brigade,* p. 60.

54   Roosevelt lifted the embargo:"Proclamation on Spain," *New York Times,* April 2, 1939.

54   "I had a feeling": Anderson, *My Lord, What a Morning,* p. 191.

54   "In attempting to congratulate":"75,000 Acclaim Miss Anderson."

55   Roosevelt's first five years: Latham, *The Communist Controversy in Washington,* p. 75.

56   first constitutional convention: *Proceedings of the First Constitutional Convention of the C.I.O.,* 1938, pp. 36–37.

57   "an imperialist war":This is Earl Browder in an interview in the *Daily Worker,* quoted in Klehr, *The Heyday of American Communism,* p. 390.

58   "Miss Perkins told me":This and all subsequent government memos come from Arthur Stein's FBI Files.

60   "Since I have been questioned": Arthur Stein's FBI Files.

61   "Members were told":This is from the testimony given by Louise Gerrard to FBI agents in her home in Miami. It is in Arthur's FBI Files.

61   "We would try to limit our knowledge": Davis, *Great Day Coming,* p. 69.

62   "Part of the evening": Louise Gerrard, from Arthur's FBI Files.

62   "I hadn't known": Gerrard from Arthur's FBI Files.

64   "state of *konspiratsia*": Weinstein, *The Haunted Wood,* p. 227.

65   "pledge ourselves to organize":"The Convention Launches UPWA-

CIO," *Public Record,* May 1946. *Public Record* is the monthly newspaper of the UPWA.

67 "the Communist bugaboo": Truman's feeling on communism comes from McCullough, *Truman,* pp. 550–553.

67 "A liberal is only a hop, skip": Lt. Col. Randolph of Military Intelligence, quoted in Caute, *The Great Fear,* p. 269.

68 "I don't think the people are concerned": Ibid., p. 275.

CHAPTER 4: THE OTHER CHEEK

70 "They were transported": *Minden Times,* June 5, 1942.

70 "After two weeks of discussion": "Crew Builds Shelves," *The Mono-Log,* July 1942.

72 R-Day, the day for registration: "Cream of Youth, from All Walks of Life, Sign Up," *San Francisco Chronicle,* Oct. 17, 1940. "16,000,000 to Enroll Today in First Peacetime Draft," *New York Times,* Oct. 16, 1940. "17,000,000 Register," *New York Times,* Oct. 20, 1940.

73 five years in prison: "Objectors to Service Advised to Register," *New York Times,* Oct. 10, 1940.

73 "We are sending": Quoted in Jervey, *The History of Methodism in Southern California.*

73 "in order to live in harmony": "Divinity Students Face Jail on Draft," *New York Times,* Oct. 13, 1940.

74 a gun battery near the Hollywood sign: "Hails Los Angeles for Air Defenses: Gen. Dewitt Praises Readiness of Anti-Aircraft Batteries 'to Meet Possible Enemy,'" *New York Times,* Feb. 27, 1942. "Los Angeles Undergoes Air Raid Alarm and Proves It Can Take It." *New York Times,* Feb. 26, 1942. "Los Angeles Wary on Blackout Toll," *New York Times,* Dec. 12, 1941.

76 "The summer work program": Albert Jones, "Bad Fire Season Expected by Mono," *Sage O'Pinon,* May 1944.

77 "You in the states": "Bloody Details Lurk in Mind," *Sage O'Pinon,* June 1944.

79 Second Lieutenant William E. Hunt: Details about the crash of the B-24 bomber come from the accident report compiled by Army Air Force investigators.

84 Baltimore's port been busier: "Through This Port: Life for Europe," *Baltimore Sun,* March 24, 1946.

84 his appointed vessel, the *Edward W. Burton:* Bunker, *Liberty Ships.*

85 A few minutes later, it was high tide: "Today's Almanac for Baltimore," *Baltimore Sun,* April 16, 1946.

87 more than a thousand war brides: "Queen Mary Ends Service for the U.S.," *New York Times,* May 11, 1946.

CHAPTER 5: THE COMMITTEES

91   "The heart of the comrade": "Moscow's Formal Announcement of
     Stalin's Death," *New York Times,* March 6, 1953.

91   "Amid the burst of bad manners": Stone, *The Haunted Fifties,* p. 50.

91   on the diplomatic headquarters: "Mourning Lines Drawn," *New York
     Times,* March 7, 1953.

93   "no property in a white section": Landis, *Segregation in Washington,* p. 30.

93   "The Confederacy, which was never able": Green, *The Secret City,* pp.
     278–279.

93   "Will Washington 'democrats' ": *Brief of Greater Washington Area Council of
     American Veterans Committee, Inc. Amicus Curiae,* 1952, Appendix A, p. 1.

94   "The rents are high": Quoted in Green, *Secret City,* p. 92.

95   "In our desire to make it quite clear": Artisan Productions to Mrs.
     Terrell, April 28, 1952, Mary Church Terrell Papers (MCTP).

95   "in the 1890s colored people": From a 1944 interview with the
     Pittsburgh Courier, quoted in Hine, *Black Women in United States History,* p.
     72.

95   "as a colored woman": Terrell, "What It Means to Be Colored in the
     Capital of the United States," *Independent,* Jan. 24, 1907.

95   Copies of the antidiscrimination laws: "District Lost Laws on Anti-
     Segregation Held Easily Available," *Washington Evening Star,* May 3, 1953.

96   "All Nazi laws": Landis, *Segregation in Washington,* p. 9.

96   "It is a foregone conclusion": Shapiro, "Eat Anywhere," pp. 12–13.

96   "We appreciate, of course": Stein to Terrell, Jan. 5, 1950, MCTP.

97   "four outstanding citizens": Shapiro, "Eat Anywhere," p. 21.

97   "We do not serve colored people here": From the affidavit of W. H.
     Jernagin, Jan. 1950, MCTP.

97   "Do you mean to tell me": From the affidavit of Mary Church Terrell,
     MCTP.

98   "place would be overrun": Caplan, "Eat Anywhere," p. 32.

98   "The solution of this particular problem": "Court Upholds Restaurant
     in Barring Negroes," *Washington Star,* July 11, 1950.

99   "a hide-bound Southerner": "Pickets Cost Biased Dime Store,"
     Washington Pittsburgh Courier, Dec. 30, 1950.

99   "Our boycott is going very well": Stein to Terrell, Dec. 5, 1950, MCTP.

99   "Committee members and community leaders": Stein, "A Woman Fights
     and . . . Jim Crow Bites the Dust."

100 Trenton Terrace: Caplan, "Trenton Terrace Remembered," p. 46.

101 "What white woman": *Pittsburgh Courier,* Sept. 13, 1952, quoted in
     Shapiro, "Eat Anywhere."

102 "We no more believe in that stuff": "Admits Display on Brotherhood
     Week Was Sham," *Washington Pittsburgh Courier,* April 18, 1951.

102 Josephine Baker: "Committee Says Picketing Costing Hechts Plenty,"
     Washington Pittsburgh Courier, Aug. 11, 1951.

103 "I sure hate to cross the picket line": "Hecht Picketing Now Under Way," *Washington Pittsburgh Courier,* July 28, 1951.

103 "They'll put up with us during December": Caplan, "Eat Anywhere!" p. 35. "Lunch Counter Is Now Open to All Patrons," *Washington Afro-American,* Jan. 19, 1952.

104 "frank declaration": From a Coordinating Committee leaflet, Feb. 1, 1953.

108 "A dark soft-spoken man": "Gorham Testifies to Communist Ties," *Washington Post,* Feb. 15, 1956.

112 "complete disillusionment": "University Acts to Oust Teacher," *New York Times,* Sept. 23, 1955.

112 "several hundred thousand former members": "Why No Fuss When a Helpful Ex-Red Professor Is Fired," *Saturday Evening Post,* Dec. 10, 1955.

116 "consistently directed toward the achievement": "Official Reports on the Expulsion of Communist Dominated Organizations from the CIO," CIO Publicity Department, publication no. 254, 1954, p. 34.

116 "the most devastating fifth column": Stone, *Haunted Fifties,* p. 223.

117 "You should adjourn this forever": Quoted in Belfrage, *The American Inquisition,* p. 253.

118 World Peace Appeal: Horne, *Black and Red,* p. 131.

CHAPTER 6: BREAKAWAY

121 He was in country: "President Visits G.I.'s in Vietnam in Surprise Trip," *New York Times,* Oct. 27, 1966.

121 During the past week: "Drop Is Reported in G.I. Casualties," *New York Times,* Oct. 21, 1966.

124 simply called The Farm: Details come from "Circle of Friends," unpublished recollections by Carol Kramer Hyland.

125 community events section of local newspapers: Jeff Jones, "Valley Model Legislature Delegates Pass 2 Laws," *Van Nuys News,* Feb. 12, 1963.

126 "walks 50 miles in one day": "Walking Craze: It Was Fun While It Lasted," *New York Times,* April 1, 1963.

128 "noisy but orderly": "Viet War Protest Here Bit Noisy But Orderly," *Cincinnati Enquirer,* Oct. 17, 1965.

129 the statement they produced: Gitlin, *The Sixties,* p. 110.

136 "talking with guys": "West Side Project," *New Left Notes,* July 24, 1967.

136 "Discussing the grinding meaninglessness": "Vice-President's Report," *New Left Notes,* Aug. 24, 1966.

138 4,000 homes whose inhabitants: "Thousands Reach Capital to Protest Vietnam War," *New York Times,* Oct. 21, 1967.

138 Women Strike for Peace: The list of organizations comes from Mailer, *The Armies of the Night.* p. 94.

141 "An SDS girl from Boston was dozing": "Power at the Pentagon," *New Left Notes,* Oct. 30, 1967.

141 "It is difficult to report publicly":"Everyone Is a Loser," *New York Times,* Oct. 23, 1967.

141 "Taste and decency had left the scene":"Blood Flows at Pentagon Rally," *Washington Post,* Oct. 22, 1967.

142 "A peace rally cannot become violent":"Peace Rally," *New York Times,* Oct. 20, 1967.

142 It was not, however, air-conditioned: Stone, "Where Communism Has Really Been Contained," in *In a Time of Torment,* p. 291.

142 "Phnom Penh was a beautiful city": Jeff wrote this in *Osawatomie,* the WUO's quarterly newsletter. These observations are from a short story he wrote under the pen name "Sparrow Hawk" about being the "only North American to become a short-order cook at a truck stop on the Ho Chi Minh trail." This is from the Autumn 1976 issue, p. 28.

143 "When two elephants are fighting":"Neutralist Cambodia," *New York Times,* Sept. 28, 1966.

CHAPTER 7: CLASS STRUGGLE

149 "To the gym, to the gym site!" Avorn, *Up Against the Ivy Wall,* p. 44.

150 "If they build the first story": Ibid., p. 21.

160 "friends from the 1930's": Raskin, J., *Out of the Whale,* p. 89.

162 "They send the Peace Corps to Nigeria":"Malcolm X Off to Smethwick," *Times* (London), Feb. 12, 1965.

164 Most of Eleanor's classmates: *Columbia Law School News,* May 13, 1968.

165 "There's a cop listening": Raskin, J., *Out of the Whale,* p. 98.

165 "Do you want to leave me?": Ibid., p. 102.

166 rumors of police action: Avorn, *Up Against the Ivy Wall,* pp. 181–199; "1,000 Police Act to Oust Students," *New York Times,* April 30, 1968. "CU Brings in Police to End Demonstration," *Columbia Spectator,* April 30, 1968.

CHAPTER 8: DAYS OF RAGE

174 "We now feel":"Haymarket Statue Bombed," *Chicago Tribune,* Oct. 7, 1969.

175 "You don't see any motherfucking students": Jacobs, *The Way the Wind Blew,* p. 196.

175 "We're going to trash": Bates, *Rads,* p. 137.

177 An orange glow: For the scene at the bonfire, see: Jacobs, *The Way the Wind Blew,* p. 200.

177 "I want you to know": Speech from "Weathermen Storm Chicago," *Berkeley Tribe,* Oct. 24–30, 1969. Jacobs, *The Way the Wind Blew,* p. 201.

178 "Judge Hoffman is up at the Drake": Jacobs, *The Way the Wind Blew,* p. 201.

181 "sitars for sale": *East Village Other,* Jan. 1–15, 1968.

181 "complete instructions for building strobes": *Rat Subterranean News,* March 1968.

181   Ninety-eight percent: *East Village Other,* Jan. 1–15, 1968.

182   "a group with a certain unprintable name": Hoffman, *Soon to Be a Major Motion Picture,* p. 123.

182   Jeff went to Times Square: "Damage in Riots Cost $45 Million," *New York Times,* April 13, 1969.

183   Lower East Side Red Squad: Details on the arrests come from an unpublished description written by John Sundstrom and correspondence with Terry Hanauer.

185   American troop level: "107 of Foe Killed in a 2-Day Battle," *New York Times,* Nov. 8, 1968.

185   Country Joe and the Fish: "Notes from a Yippizolean Era," *East Village Other,* Feb. 1968.

186   "Voted for every appropriation": "McCarthy's Voting Record," *New Left Notes,* May 13, 1968.

186   "Mayor Daley Welcomes You": The billboards are described in Royko, *Boss,* p. 183.

187   "a rabble rouser": Farber, *Chicago '68,* p. 139.

187   the people of Chicago: Ibid., p. 145.

189   On Sunday night: Ibid., p. 175. Farber quotes from a column in the weekend *Chicago's American; The Rat,* Sept. 9–16, 1968.

189   Outside, the police: Farber, *Chicago '68,* p. 187.

190   "Kill, kill, kill": Ibid., p. 200.

191   "Gestapo tactics on the streets": Hayden, *Reunion,* p. 320.

191   McCarthy spoke: McCarthy flip-flopped on his promise not to support the nominee, giving Humphrey a lukewarm endorsement in the final days of the campaign.

191   308 U.S. troops: Farber, *Chicago '68,* p. 205.

192   "a police riot": This conclusion was given in the Walker Report, released in December 1968. The report found "unrestrained and indiscriminate police violence on many occasions, particularly at night. That violence was made all the more shocking by the fact that it was often inflicted upon persons who had broken no law, disobeyed no order, made no threat."

192   Only 10 percent: Farber, *Chicago '68,* p. 206.

192   "Should talk less and drink more": Stern, *With the Weathermen,* p. 22.

193   "We've effectively shut down the college": "225 Radical Students Picket 8 Buildings," *New York Times,* March 26, 1969.

194   The SDS convention began: "S.D.S. Ousts PLP," *Guardian,* June 18, 1969.

199   *"The New York Times"*: Raskin, E., *The Bust Book,* p. 28.

201   "the action in Pittsburgh attacked imperialism": "Women's Militia," *New Left Notes,* Sept. 12, 1969.

201   "Packed a suitcase": Raskin, J., *Out of the Whale,* p. 117.

203   passed out free Popsicles: Ayers, *Fugitive Days.*

203   "You can jail a revolutionary": Foner, *The Black Panthers Speak,* p. 144.

204 "We believe that the Weathermen action": Fred Hampton's speech is in the documentary *Weather Underground*.

205 "What right has anyone to walk down the street": Daley's speech is from Emile de Antonio's film *Underground*.

206 "We're not going to be dealing in commandism": Foner, *The Black Panthers Speak,* p. 142.

206 Less than a week later: The *Times* reporter John Kifner was the first member of the mainstream press to expose the police account of the death of Fred Hampton. He visited the apartment, saw the forensic evidence for himself, and concluded that it had been a cold-blooded murder. "F.B.I., Before Raid, Gave Police Plan of Chicago Panther's Flat," *New York Times,* May 25, 1974. "Police in Chicago Slay 2 Panthers," *New York Times,* Dec. 5, 1969. "State's Attorney in Chicago Makes Photographs of Black Panther Apartment Available," *New York Times,* Dec. 12, 1969.

209 "He made people afraid": "Weatherman War Council," *Quicksilver Times,* Jan. 9–19, 1970.

CHAPTER 9: IN THE FOREST

210 "Hello. This is Bernardine Dohrn": Raskin, J., *The Weather Eye.* "A Radical 'Declaration' Warns of an Attack by Weathermen," *New York Times,* May 25, 1970. "Weathermessage," *Old Mole,* June 12, 1970.

211 Within a week: Sale, *S.D.S.,* p. 636.

211 "Raising people's hopes": "Notes to the Underground," *Berkeley Tribe,* June 12-19, 1970, quoted in Jacobs, *The Way the Wind Blew,* p.109.

211 "There is a bomb set to go off": Details of bombing at NYPD headquarters from "Bomb at Police Headquarters Injures 7 and Damages Offices," *New York Times,* June 10, 1970. Jacobs, *The Way the Wind Blew,* p. 109.

212 "The pigs in this country": "Anonymous Note Credits Weatherman with Bombing," *New York Times,* June 11, 1970.

212 "police investigation now going forward": "Mayor Vows 'Relentless' Drive to Track Down Police Bomber," *New York Times,* June 11, 1970.

212 "Convinced that only violence": "Bombs Blast a Message of Hate," *Life,* March 27, 1970. "Bombing: A Way of Protest and Death," *Time,* March 23, 1970. "Terrorism on the Left," *Newsweek,* March 23, 1970.

213 "What kind of person": This question was asked in a statement by Florida Congressman J. Herbert Burke, House Committee on the Judiciary, Hearings, *Explosives Control,* July 1970, p. 321.

213 "There is no real reason": The Ohio congressman is Chalmers P. Wylie. His "establishment" quote is in ibid., p. 308. The chart is in ibid., p. 85.

214 "Well-known New Leftists": FBI, *Annual Report, 1970,* quoted in Senate Committee on the Judiciary, report, *The Weather Underground,* 1975, p. 130.

214 The world-famous FBI laboratory: *The FBI Laboratory,* 1969. Also, Eleanor Stein's FBI Files.

215 "Intention to build a small": From FBI, *Annual Report, 1970,* quoted in 1975 Senate hearings, *The Weather Underground,* p. 67.

219 J.J. was a master propagandist: "The Last Radical," *Vancouver Magazine,* November 1998. *The Weather Underground,* report of Senate hearings, p. 75.

221 "I was able to practice": Rojas, *Tania,* p. 118.

221 "It has been said": Pomeroy, *The Forest,* p. 22.

221 "They have learned to survive": This quote is from the New Morning statement.

221 "He did for LSD": Tendler and May, *Brotherhood of Eternal Love from Flower Power to Hippie Mafia.* This quote is in the foreword.

222 The Weathermen were contacted: The details come from Leary, *Flashbacks,* chap. 34.

224 "He was disguised": "Tim's Here," *Berkeley Tribe,* Oct. 16–23, 1970.

224 "I escaped with the help": From *Weather Underground,* documentary by Sam Green and Bill Siegel, 2002.

224 Leary quickly alienated: Raskin, J., *Out of the Whale,* p. 166.

224 led investigators to the safe houses: "Tim Leary: Soul in Hock," *Rolling Stone,* Aug. 28, 1975.

227 "Last night we destroyed": "Letter Says Weathermen Blew Up Statue in Chicago," *New York Times,* Oct. 7, 1970.

228 During Thanksgiving Week: "U.S. War Deaths at 65 for Week," *New York Times,* Nov. 27, 1970.

231 "This building will blow up": "Where Capitol Bomb Exploded and Damaged Rooms," *New York Times,* March 2, 1971; and "Bomb in Capitol Causes Wide Damage," Jacobs, *The Way the Wind Blew,* p.128.

232 Weather bombs exploded: Jacobs, *The Way the Wind Blew,* p. 136. "Jackson an Enigma in Life and in Death," *New York Times,* Sept. 20, 1971.

232 "Two small bombs": Raskin, J., *Weather Eye,* p. 46.

232 a bomb exploded inside a women's bathroom: "Blast Occurs in Pentagon in the Air Force Section," *New York Times,* May 19, 1972. Jacobs, *The Way the Wind Blew,* p. 142.

232 "its people are irresponsible": Hitchens, *The Trial of Henry Kissinger,* p. 56. "I.T.T. Office Here Damaged by Bomb," *New York Times,* Sept. 29, 1973.

237 the word "PEACE": "'Peace' sign will flash in Times Square today," *New York Times,* Jan. 27, 1973.

238 "A half a million pieces of paper": This line is from Emile de Antonio's film *Underground.*

238 The original 5,000 copies: Jacobs, *The Way the Wind Blew,* p. 160.

239 de Antonio traveled: Lewis, *Emile de Antonio,* pp. 181–183.

CHAPTER 10: THE BUST

248 "Leadership,"Weatherman David Gilbert wrote": Gilbert, *S.D.S./WUO,*
     p. 21.
250 "HardTimes Conference": *Outlaws of America,* p. 24. "HardTimes at
     Chicago," *Guardian,* Feb. 11, 1976.
251 "The black liberation struggle":This is Eleanor's memory of the kind of
     conversations taking place during this period.
252 "Jeff Jones: Along with Ayers": *The Split of the Weather Underground
     Organization,* p. 31.
252 "The consequences of this history": Ibid., p. 27.
258 Clayton Van Lydegraf had briefly: Jacobs, *The Way the Wind Blew,* p. 181.
259 "My father is like":These letters were captured by the FBI a few months
     after they were written. An agent in the Portland, Oregon, area left them
     in a cardboard box in his garage, where they were discovered, more than
     twenty years later, by a reporter for the *Portland Tribune News.*
261 A Hoboken fire captain:The list of items, slightly different from the
     newspaper accounts, is taken from the official Hoboken police report. "A
     Bomb Factory Found in Jersey; Police Seeking 2," *NewYork Times,* Aug.
     4, 1979.
272 Special Agent Larry Wack: Information about retired special agent Larry
     Wack comes from telephone interviews and e-mails that he and I
     exchanged.

SOURCES

Abramovitch, Ilana, and Sean Galvin, eds. *Jews of Brooklyn*. Brandeis University Press, 2002.

Adamic, Louis, *Dynamite: A Century of Class Violence in America, 1830–1930*. Rebel Press, 1984.

Anderson, Marian. *My Lord, What a Morning*. University of Wisconsin Press, 1956.

Avorn, Jerry L. *Up Against the Ivy Wall*. Atheneum, 1969.

Ayers, Bill. *Fugitive Days: A Memoir*. Penguin Books, 2003.

Back, Adina. "Blacks, Jews and the Struggle to Integrate Brooklyn's Junior High School 258: A Cold War Story." *Journal of American Ethnic History*, Winter 2001.

Bates, Tom. *Rads: The 1970 Bombing of the Army Math Research Center at the University of Wisconsin and Its Aftermath*. HarperCollins, 1992.

Belfrage, Cedric. *The American Inquisition, 1945–1960: A Profile of the "McCarthy Era."* Thunder's Mouth Press, 1989.

Bernstein, Carl. *Loyalties: A Son's Memoir*. Simon & Schuster, 1989.

Bernstein, Irving. *Turbulent Years: A History of the American Worker, 1933–1941*. Houghton Mifflin, 1970.

Berube, Maurice, and Marilyn Gittell, eds. *Confrontation at Ocean Hill–Brownsville: The New York School Strikes of 1968*. Praeger, 1969.

Bunker, John Gorley. *Liberty Ships: The Ugly Ducklings of World War II*. Naval Institute Press, 1972.

Cacioppo, Richard. *The History of Woodland Hills and Girard*. White Stone, Inc., 1982.

Cammaerts, Emile. *Albert of Belgium: Defender of Right.* Macmillan, 1935.

Caplan, Marvin. "Eat Anywhere." *Washington History,* Spring 1989.

————. "Trenton Terrace Remembered." *Washington History,* Spring–Summer 1994.

Carroll, Peter N. *The Odyssey of the Abraham Lincoln Brigade.* Stanford University Press, 1994.

Castellucci, John. *The Big Dance: The Untold Story of Kathy Boudin and the Terrorist Family That Committed the Brink's Robbery Murders.* Dodd, Mead, 1986.

Caute, David. *The Great Fear: The Anti-Communist Purge Under Truman and Eisenhower.* Simon & Schuster, 1978.

Collier, Peter, and David Horowitz. *Destructive Generation: Second Thoughts About the '60s.* Summit Books, 1989.

Communism in the District of Columbia-Maryland Area. U.S. Congress, House. Committee on Un-American Activities. 82nd Cong. 1st sess. U.S. Government Printing Office, 1951.

Cutler, William G. *History of the State of Kansas.* A.T. Andreas, 1883.

Davis, Hope Hale. *Great Day Coming: A Memoir of the 1930s.* Steerforth Press, 1994.

Davitt, Michael. *Within the Pale: The True Story of Anti-Semitic Persecutions in Russia,* A. S. Barnes, 1903.

Dellinger, David. *From Yale to Jail: The Life Story of a Moral Dissenter.* Pantheon, 1993.

Eller, Cynthia. *Conscientious Objectors and the Second World War: Moral and Religious Arguments in Support of Pacifism.* Praeger, 1991.

Everett, Marshall, ed. *War with Spain and the Filipinos.* Book Publishers Union, 1899.

Explosives Control. U.S. Congress, House. Committee on the Judiciary. 91st Cong, 2nd sess. U.S. Government Printing Office, 1970.

Farber, David. *Chicago '68.* University of Chicago Press, 1988.

Fink, Gary, and Hugh Davis Graham, eds. *The Carter Presidency: Policy Changes in the Post-New Deal Era.* University Press of Kansas, 1998.

Foner, Philip, ed. *The Black Panthers Speak.* Da Capo Press, 1995.

Freedman, Samuel G. *The Inheritance: How Three Families and America Moved from Roosevelt to Reagan and Beyond.* Simon & Schuster, 1996.

Geismar, Maxwell. *Reluctant Radical: A Memoir.* Circumstantial Publications and the estate of Maxwell Geismar, 2002.

Gilbert, David. *S.D.S./WUO.* Arm the Spirit-Solidarity Press, 2002.

Gillies, Kevin. "The Last Radical." *Vancouver Magazine,* May 1998.

Gitlin, Todd. *The Sixties: Years of Hope, Days of Rage.* Bantam, 1987.

Glueck, Grace, and Paul Gardner. *Brooklyn: People and Places, Past and Present.* Harry N. Abrams, 1991.

Goodman, Walter. *The Committee: The Extraordinary Career of the House Committee on Un-American Activities.* Pelican Books, 1968.

Grathwohl, Larry. *Bringing Down America: An FBI Informer with the Weathermen.* Arlington House, 1976.

Green, Constance McLaughlin. *The Secret City: A History of Race Relations in the Nation's Capital.* Princeton University Press, 1967.

Harding, Mary Elizabeth. "Eleanor Nelson, Oliver Palmer and the Struggle to Organize the CIO in Washington D.C. 1937–1950." Unpublished doctoral dissertation,

Hayden, Tom. *Reunion: A Memoir.* Random House, 1988.

Hayes, John. *Red Scare or Red Menace? American Communism and Anti-Communism in the Cold War Era.* American Ways Series, 1996.

Hine, Darlene Clark, ed. *Black Women in United States History,* Vol. 13. Carlson Publishing Series, 1990.

Hitchens, Christopher. *The Trial of Henry Kissinger.* Verso, 2001.

Hoffman, Abbie. *Soon to Be a Major Motion Picture.* Putnam, 1980.

———. *Steal This Book.* Grove Press, 1971.

Horne, Gerald. *Black and Red: W.E.B. Du Bois and the Afro-American Response to the Cold War, 1944–1963.* SUNY Press, 1986.

Investigation of Communist Infiltration of Government—Part 1. U.S. Congress, House. Committee on Un-American Activities. 84th Cong., 1st sess. U.S. Government Printing Office, 1955.

Investigation of Communist Infiltration of Government—Part 3. U.S. Congress, House. Committee on Un-American Activities. 84th Cong., 2nd sess. U.S. Government Printing Office, 1956.

Investigation of Soviet Espionage—Part 2. U.S. Congress, House. Committee on Un-American Activities. 85th Cong. 2nd sess. U.S. Government Printing Office, 1958.

Jacobs, Harold. *Weatherman.* Ramparts Press, 1970.

Jacobs, Ron. *The Way the Wind Blew: A History of the Weather Underground.* Verso, 1997.

Jervey, Edward. *The History of Methodism in Southern California and Arizona.* Parthenon Press, 1960.

Judge, Edward H. *Easter in Kishinev: Anatomy of a Pogrom.* New York University Press, 1992.

Kansas. Adjutant General's Office. *Kansas Troops in the Volunteer Services of the United States in the Spanish and Philippine Wars, Mustered In Under the First and Second Calls of the President of the United States: May 19–October 28, 1899.* 1900.

Kessler, Ronald. *The Bureau: The Secret History of the FBI.* St. Martin's Press, 2002.

Keiler, Allan. *Marian Anderson: A Singer's Journey.* Scribner, 2000.

Keim, Albert N. *The CPS Story: An Illustrated History of Civilian Public Service.* Good Books, 1990.

Kidd, Alan. *Manchester.* Keele University Press, 1996.

Klehr, Harvey. *The Heyday of American Communism.* Basic Books, 1984.

Klehr, Harvey, John Earl Haynes, and Kyrill M. Anderson. *The Soviet World of American Communism*. Yale University Press, 1998.

Kunen, James. *The Strawberry Statement*. Random House, 1968.

Landis, Kenesaw M. *Segregation in Washington*. A Report of the National Committee on Segregation in the Nation's Capital, 1948.

Latham, Earl. *The Communist Controversy in Washington: From the New Deal to McCarthy*. Harvard University Press, 1966.

Leader, Leonard. *Los Angeles and the Great Depression*. Garland, 1991.

Leary, Timothy. *Flashbacks: An Autobiography*. Tarcher, 1983.

Lerner, Jonathan. "I Was a Terrorist." *Washington Post Magazine,* Feb. 24, 2002.

Lewis, Randolph. *Emile de Antonio: Radical Filmmaker in Cold War America*. University of Wisconsin Press, 2000.

Louchheim, Katie, ed. *The Making of the New Deal: The Insiders Speak*. Harvard University Press, 1983.

Mahaffay, Robert. *Main Line: Fifty Years of Railroading with the Southern Pacific*. Doubleday, 1948.

Mailer, Norman. *The Armies of the Night: History as a Novel, The Novel as History*. New American Library, 1968.

McCullough, David. *Truman*. Simon & Schuster, 1992.

McElvaine, Robert S. *The Great Depression: America, 1929–1941*. Times Books, 1993.

Meeropol, Robert. *An Execution in the Family: One Son's Journey*. St. Martin's Press, 2003.

Miller, James. *"Democracy Is in the Streets": From Port Huron to the Siege of Chicago*. Touchstone, 1987.

Mishler, Paul. *Raising Reds: The Young Pioneers, Radical Summer Camps, and Communist Culture in the United States*. Columbia University Press, 1999.

"Official Reports on the Expulsion of Communist Dominated Organizations from the CIO." CIO Publicity Department, publication no. 254, 1954.

O'Sullivan, John, and Alan M. Meckler, *The Draft and Its Enemies: A Documentary History*. University of Illinois Press, 1974.

Pomeroy, William. *The Forest*. International Publishers, 1963.

Raskin, Eleanor, et al. *The Bust Book: What to Do Until the Lawyer Comes*. Grove Press, 1970.

Raskin, Jonah. *For the Hell of It: The Life and Times of Abbie Hoffman*. University of California Press, 1996.

———. *Out of the Whale: Growing Up in the American Left*. Links Books, 1974.

———. Ed. *The Weather Eye: Communiqués from the Weather Underground*. Union Square Press, 1974.

Ravitch, Diane. *The Great School Wars. New York City, 1805–1973*. Basic Books, 1974.

Roderick, Kevin. *The San Fernando Valley: America's Suburb*. Los Angeles Times Books, 2001.

Rojas, Marta, and Mirta Rodriguez Calderon, eds. *Tania: The Unforgettable Guerrilla*. Random House, 1971.

Royko, Mike. *Boss: Richard J. Daley of Chicago*. Plume Books, 1971.

Sale, Kirkpatrick. *S.D.S.* Vintage Books, 1974.

Sargent, Shirley. *Yosemite's Famous Guests,* Flying Spur Press, 1970.

———. *Yosemite and Its Innkeepers*. Flying Spur Press, 1975.

Schissel, Lillian, ed. *Conscience in America: A Documentary History of Conscientious Objection in America*. Dutton, 1968.

Schrecker, Ellen W. *No Ivory Tower: McCarthyism and the Universities*. Oxford University Press, 1986.

Shapiro, Linn. "Eat Anywhere: A History of the Coordinating Committee for the Enforcement of the D.C. Anti-Discrimination Laws." Graduate seminar paper. 1989.

The Split of the Weather Underground Organization. John Brown Book Club, 1977.

Starr, Kevin. *Endangered Dreams: The Great Depression in California*. Oxford University Press, 1996.

———. *Material Dreams: Southern California Through the 1920s*. Oxford University Press, 1990.

Stein, Annie. "A Woman Fights and . . . Jim Crow Bites the Dust." *March of Labor Magazine,* July 1954.

———. "Strategies for Failure." *Harvard Educational Review,* May 1971.

Stern, Susan. *With the Weathermen: The Personal Journey of a Revolutionary Woman*. Doubleday, 1975.

Stone, I. F. *The Haunted Fifties and a Glance at the Startling Sixties*. Random House, 1963.

———. *Polemics and Prophecies, 1967–1970*. Little, Brown. 1989.

———. *In a Time of Torment, 1961–1967*. Little, Brown, 1989.

Subversive Control of the United Public Workers of America. U.S. Congress, Senate. Subcommittee to Investigate the Administration of the Internal Security Act and Other Internal Security Laws of the Committee on the Judiciary. 82nd Cong. 1st sess. U.S. Government Printing Office, 1952.

Sundstrom, John. "Conspiracy to Kill Police." Unpublished recollections.

Swanson, Bert E. *School Integration Controversies in New York City: A Pilot Study*. Institute for Community Studies, Sarah Lawrence College, 1965.

Taylor, Clarence. *Knocking at Our Own Door: Milton A. Galamison and the Struggle to Integrate New York City Schools*. Columbia University Press, 1997.

Tendler, Stewart, and David May. *Brotherhood of Eternal Love from Flower Power to Hippie Mafia: The Story of the LSD Counterculture*. Panther Books, 1984.

Terrell, Mary Church. "What It Means to Be Colored in the Capital of the United States." *Independent,* Jan. 24, 1907.

———. *A Colored Woman in a White Woman's World*. National Association of Colored Women's Clubs, 1968.

Thomas, Hugh. *The Spanish Civil War.* Harper and Row. 1961.

Walker, Daniel. *Rights in Conflict: Convention Week in Chicago, August 25–29, 1968: A Report*. Dutton, 1968.

The Weather Underground. U.S. Congress, Senate. Subcommittee to Investigate the Administration of the Internal Security Act and Other Internal Security Laws of the Committee on the Judiciary. 94th Cong. 1st sess. U.S. Government Printing Office, 1975.

Weinstein, Allen. *The Haunted Wood: Soviet Espionage in America. The Stalin Era*. Random House, 1999.

Wells, Tom. *The War Within: America's Battle over Vietnam*. University of California Press, 1994.

Wicker, Tom. *A Time to Die*. New York Times Books, 1975.

Wilson, Edmund. *The American Earthquake*. Da Capo Press, 1996.

———. *The Fifties*. Farrar Straus & Giroux, 1986.

Woodbridge, George. *UNRRA: The History of the United Nations Relief and Rehabilitation Administration. Volume 2*. Columbia University Press, 1950.

Zieger, Robert H. *The C.I.O., 1935–1955*. University of North Carolina Press, 1995.

ACKNOWLEDGMENTS

M Y parents and I struck a deal two years ago when I began to interview them for this book: they could refuse to answer any questions that might get people into trouble, but at the same time everything they did tell me would be—to the best of their memory—accurate. Eleanor and Jeff, I believe you stuck to this deal throughout the process. For that I thank you.

Albert, Millie, and Chavy revived a world that existed for me only in faded photos and jumpy black-and-white films. Your memories of events going back seventy and even eighty years were remarkably alive and vivid to the point of tiny detail. It was an inspiration to hear your stories. Thank you.

To Bluejay, Zayd Dohrn, Rachel DeWoskin, Jonah Hoyle, Margaret Black, and Daphne Sashin, for the red ink on several drafts. To Tom Meredith and Amilcar Dohrn-Melendez, for an air mattress on the floor in Santa Monica. To Harry Kellerman, for the library card and password. To Michael and Eleanore Kennedy, Jane Hirschmann, Michael Ratner, Patrick Brown. Thank you.

To those I interviewed: Harry Magdoff, Victor Rabinowitz, Philip Stein and Carole Armel, Vicki Lawrence, Anne Geismar, Olivia Taylor, Bob Reilly and Barbara Schneider, Pat and Joe Walter, Ellen

Belton, Ruth Marcus, Peggy Fuchs Singer, Bernardine Dohrn, Bill Ayers, Cathlyn Wilkerson, Brian Flanagan, Stew Albert, Jonah Raskin, Jonny Lerner, Jamie Willett, Clark Kissinger, John Sundstrom, Creek Hanauer, Walter Teague, Rick Ayers, Harold Osborn, Jennifer Dohrn, Leonard Seimon, Jeannie Darling and Harry Bailey, Eric Jones, Julie Keechler, Celeste Jones. Thank you.

To Special Agent Larry Wack, thank you for taking the time to make that phone call.

Thanks to Elizabeth Stein, my editor at Free Press, and Maris Kreizman, Edith Lewis, and Beverly Miller; Anna Ghosh, my agent; and Samuel G. Freedman and the Columbia Journalism School book class.

INDEX

Adler, Sol, 65
Albert, Stew, 224
Albert I, King of Belgium, 34–36, 41, 286
Algeria, 224
Alien Sedition Act, 68
Allende, Salvador, 232–233
American Communist Party. *See* Communist Party (U.S.)
American Friends Service Committee, 83, 88, 138
American Indian Movement, 250
American League for Peace and Democracy, 57
American Peace Mobilization, 57, 59
American People's Mobilization, 59
American University, 112
Anderson, Marian, 51, 52, 54
Angkor Wat, 144
Anti-Discrimination Laws of 1872 and 1873, 90, 92, 93, 96–104
Antioch College, 9, 120, 127, 128, 131, 220
Apartheid boycott, 148

Aptheker, Herbert, 131
Arens, Dick, 108–109, 113–115, 118
Ashley, Karin, 174
Associated Press, 212
Atomic bomb, 82, 115
Ayers, Bill, 10, 172, 174, 197, 212, 214, 219, 223, 226, 227, 229, 240, 249, 252, 258, 271

B-24 Liberator, 79–81
Baker, Ella, 250
Baker, Josephine, 102
Bakuninites, 20
Baldwin, James, 160
Barnard College, 158–161
Battle of Algiers, The (film), 220
Bay of Pigs, 171
Beatles, the, 146
Beatty, Warren, 240
Becker, Sylvester, 97–98, 104–105
Belmondo, Jean-Paul, 159
Bentley, Elizabeth, 64, 111
Berlin Agreement of 1945, 96
Bernstein, Al, 56, 68, 156, 157, 269

Black Panthers, 196, 199, 202–207, 213, 231
Blaster's Handbook, 230
Bolsheviks, 23
Boudin, Kathy, 5, 198, 212, 240, 271
Boudin, Leonard, 154
Breathless (film), 159
Breslin, Jimmy, 141–142, 228
Bridgeport, Connecticut, 244–245
Brigadista, Harvest and War in Nicaragua (Jones), 285
Brink's robbery, 271, 276, 277
Brooks, Mel, 240
Brotherhood of Eternal Love, 222, 225
Browder, Earl, 64
Brown, H. Rap, 150, 211
Brown, Helen Wentworth, 48, 49
Brown, John, 239
Bunche, Ralph, 153
Bust Book, The: What to Do Until the Lawyer Comes (Stein, Boudin, Reichbach, and Glick), 198–199

Cabral, Amílcar, 220
Cadbury, Henry, 88
Cambodia, 4, 11, 142–144, 207, 211
Cam Ranh Bay, 121
Carmichael, Stokely, 151
Castro, Fidel, 154–155, 208
Central Intelligence Agency (CIA), 143, 171, 233
Chambers, Whittaker, 64, 111
Chase Manhattan Bank, 232
Chicago, Illinois, 10, 20. *See also* Haymarket Square
Days of Rage in, 10, 12, 173–180, 212–213, 250, 271
Democratic National Convention in, 10, 173, 174, 177, 185–192, 205, 242
Chicago Coliseum, 192, 194

Chicago Eight, 177, 201, 212, 250
Chicago Police Sergeants Association, 174
Chicago Tribune, 173, 176
Chile, 11, 232–233
Christian Century, 45–46
Churchill, Winston, 66
CIA. *See* Central Intelligence Agency (CIA)
CIO. *See* Congress of Labor Organizations (CIO)
City College of New York, 20, 22, 136
City University of New York Law School, 285
Civilian Public Service Camp #37, Coleville, California, 70–71, 76–78, 83
Civil rights, 90, 92–94, 96–105, 153, 269
Civil rights movement, 127
Civil War, U.S., 94
Clark, Judy, 271
Clay, Henry, 36
Clay Center, Kansas, 36–39
Cleaver, Eldridge, 211, 224, 255
Cold War, 107
Coleman, Ornette, 182
Columbia University, 20, 28, 29, 136, 146, 148, 201, 284–285
student uprising at, 149–152, 163–168, 189, 190
Commission on Loyalty, 67
Committee to Aid the National Liberation Front, 139
Communist Manifesto, The (Marx and Engels), 161
Communist Party (U.S.), 15, 20, 23, 32, 55, 60–65, 195
Daily Worker, 21, 25, 29, 61
front organizations, 57, 59
House Committee on Un-American Activities (HUAC)

and, 67, 98, 100, 106–119
May Days. *See* May Days
membership, 24
race issue and, 94
Stalin's death and, 91–92
Concentration camps, 86
Congress of Labor Organizations
    (CIO), 56, 115–116, 118
Congress of Racial Equality
    (CORE), 138
Conrad Hilton Hotel, Chicago, 189
Conscientious objectors, 69–84
Constitution Hall, Washington, D.C.,
    52, 53
Coordinating Committee for the
    Enforcement of the D.C.
    Anti-Discrimination Laws of
    1872 and 1873, 90, 92, 93,
    96–104
Country Joe and the Fish, 185
Cowley, Malcolm, 24
Cronkite, Walter, 205
Cuba, 154, 169–172
Czechoslovakia, 91

Daily Worker, 21, 25, 29, 61
Daley, Richard J., 186–192, 205
Daughters of the American
    Revolution, 52
Davis, Jefferson, 160
Davis, Rennie, 248
Days of Rage (1969), 10, 12,
    173–180, 212–213, 250, 271
de Antonio, Emile, 239–241
Declaration of a State of War,
    210–211, 214, 220
Delaware Indians, 36
Delgado, Marion, 178
Dellinger, David, 73, 137, 185
Democratic National Convention
    (1968), 10, 173, 174, 177,
    185–192, 205, 242
Democratic Party, 21, 66, 120

Dewey, Thomas, 67
Disney, Walt, 124
Disneyland, 124
Disney Scholarship, 135
"Dixie" (Foster), 153
Dixon, Mary E., 102
Dohrn, Bernardine, 169, 172, 174,
    197, 204, 205, 210, 212, 240,
    258, 271
    expelled from Weathermen, 252
    Leary escape and, 223, 224
    national meeting in Mendocino,
        218, 219
    underground life of, 214, 215,
        225–227, 229
Dohrn, Jennifer, 250
Dohrn, Zayd Osceola, 258
Doors, the, 181
Dos Passos, John, 24
Douglass, Frederick, 94, 95
Douglass, Lewis, 94
Draft cards, burning, 131, 140
Drake Hotel, Chicago, 178, 179
Dreiser, Theodore, 24
Du Bois, W.E.B., 158
Du Bois Clubs, 138
Dylan, Bob, 127, 174, 185, 229

Eastland, James, 110
East Village Other (newspaper), 181
Edward W. Burton (relief ship), 84–87
Eightieth Congress, 66
Eisenhower, Dwight, 68, 94, 148
Ellsberg, Daniel, 240–241
Engels, Friedrich, 161, 162
Environmental Advocates of New
    York, 285
Epworth League, 45, 46
Erasmus Hall High School, Flatbush,
    155
Executive Order 9835 (Loyalty
    Order), 67–68
Ex-Servicemen's League, 25

Fair Play for Cuba Committee, 154
Farm, The, 124–126
Federal Bureau of Investigation
    (FBI), 5, 90, 91, 206, 240, 241
  arrest of Jeff Jones and Eleanor
      Stein, 1–2, 272–276
  Communist Party and, 62, 63
  Loyalty Order and, 67
  Security Index of, 66
  Stein, Annie and Arthur and, 8,
      13–14, 32, 58–60, 66, 67, 100,
      110, 154, 162–163
  Weathermen, hunt for, 13,
      213–214, 224, 227, 247, 272
  Wiener, Evelyn (Chavy) and, 63
Federal Emergency Relief, 55
Fifth Amendment to the
    Constitution, 114, 115, 118
Fillmore East, New York, 181, 192
Finland, 91
Fire!, 202
Fordham University, 136
Forer, Joseph, 98, 269
Foster, Stephen, 153
Foster, William Z., 20
Franco, Francisco, 53, 54
Frapolly, Bill, 176
Freddie and the Dreamers, 162
Freiheit, 21
Friedman, Robert, 239
Fuchs, Herbert, 111–114
Fugs, the, 139
Fullerton, Norma J., 231
Funicello, Annette, 124

Galamison, Milton, 269
Gang That Couldn't Shoot Straight, The
    (Breslin), 228
Garfield, James, 95
Gaulkin, Judge, 279
Geismar, Anne, 255, 256
Geismar, Maxwell, 254–256
Gerrard, Louise, 62–63

Giap, Vo Nguyen, 221
Gilbert, David, 248, 271
Girard, California, 40, 42, 44, 75, 125
Gitlin, Todd, 131
Glick, Brian, 198
Godard, Jean-Luc, 159
Gold, Teddy, 11
Golden Rule, 47
Goldman, Emma, 21
Gorham, James E., 108–109, 111,
    113, 114, 249
Grapes of Wrath, The (Steinbeck), 46
Gray Panthers, 250
Great Depression, 20, 21, 24, 43–45,
    55, 122, 129
Greeley, Horace, 94
Guadalcanal, 78
Guernica, 53
Guevara, (Ernesto) Che, 151, 154,
    177, 208, 220
Guthrie, Arlo, 185

Haber, Al, 128, 131
Haight-Ashbury, San Francisco, 180
Hamburg-American Line, 17
Hamilton, Thelma, 250
Hampton, Fred, 203–209, 231, 250
Hampton, Iberia, 250
Hanauer, Terry, 183, 184
Hard Times Conference, 250–251
Harlan County, Kentucky, 22
Harvard Education Review, 266
Hatch Act of 1939, 58, 61
Havana, Cuba, 169–172
Havens, Richie, 181
Hayden, Tom, 128, 131, 132, 143,
    177–178, 187, 248
Haymarket Square, Chicago
  bombing of police statue (1969),
      173
  bombing of police statue (1970),
      227
  riot of 1886, 20, 173

Hearst, Patty, 220–221
Hecht, Samuel, 102
Hecht's department store,
    Washington, D.C., 102–103
Hell's Angels, 128, 203
Hendrix, Jimi, 181, 224
Herman's Hermits, 162
Hershey, Lewis B., 71
Hiroshima, 82
Hiss, Alger, 111
Hitler, Adolf, 53, 57, 96
Ho Chi Minh, 199, 208, 232, 242
Ho Chi Minh Trail, 170
Hoffman, Abbie, 177–178, 181, 187,
    248, 252–253
Hoffman, Julius, 177, 178, 213
Hollies, the, 162
Hoover, Herbert, 22
Hoover, J. Edgar, 58, 60, 64–68, 116,
    213
House Committee on Un-American
    Activities (HUAC), 67, 98,
    100, 106–119, 124, 154
Howard University, 31, 92
HUAC. *See* House Committee on
    Un-American Activities
    (HUAC)
Huk guerrillas, 221
Humphrey, Hubert, 186, 188, 189,
    191, 192
Hungary, 91
Hunt, William E., 79–81
Hunter College, 21–23, 31

Ickes, Harold, 52
International Association of Theater
    and Stage Employees, 188
International Control Commission,
    143
International Day of Labor (1933),
    26
International Days of Protest (1965),
    128, 133

International Telephone and
    Telegraph (ITT), 232, 233
In the Year of the Pig (documentary),
    239
Isolationism, 57

Jackson, George, 231–232
Jackson State University, 211
Jacobs, John (J.J.), 174, 212, 217–220
Japanese-Americans, 66, 74, 78
Jefferson, Thomas, 68
Jefferson Airplane, 181
Jewish Daily Forward, 20, 21
Johnson, Lyndon, 121, 142, 184–186
Jones, Albert Leopold, 14, 40–49,
    120, 132, 133, 142
    birth of, 35–36
    birth of son Jeff, 89
    as conscientious objector, 12,
        69–84, 124, 136
    father (Malcolm) and, 69, 72
    FBI and, 241
    as film technician, 123–124
    Jeff, relationship with, 12–13, 122,
        123, 144–145, 188, 218,
        241–243, 258–259, 275–277
    later life of, 286
    marriage of, 123, 134–135, 145
    as Quaker, 83, 123–125, 133, 259
    with UNRRA, 83–87
Jones, Bluejay, 284
Jones, Celeste, 286
Jones, Eric, 123, 134–135
Jones, Jeffrey Carl, 120–121
    at Antioch College, 9, 127–128,
        131, 220
    arrests of, 1–2, 179–180, 183, 194,
        205, 206, 272–277, 283
    birth of, 89
    birth of Thai, 89
    in Cambodia, 142–144, 212
    childhood and adolescence of, 9,
        123–127

Jones, Jeffrey Carl *(cont.)*
  Columbia uprising and, 164
  Days of Rage and, 10, 174–180,
    205, 212–213, 250
  at Democratic National
    Convention, 185–186,
    188–191, 242
  draft status of, 136
  Eleanor Stein, relationship with,
    234–235, 245, 246, 253–263,
    279
  end of Vietnam War and, 237
  expelled from Weathermen,
    252–254
  father (Albert), relationship with,
    12–13, 122, 123, 144–145, 188,
    218, 241–243, 258–259,
    275–277
  Hard Times Conference and,
    250–251
  as interorganizational secretary of
    Weathermen, 197, 202, 203
  joins SDS, 128, 130–132
  Leary prison escape and, 222–224
  march on Pentagon and, 138–141
  national meeting in Mendocino,
    218–220
  as parent, 257–259, 263–264,
    270–271, 280–281
  pen name of, 239
  pot-growing by, 261–262, 283
  as regional director of SDS in
    New York, 135–137, 180–184
  at SDS national convention
    (1969), 194, 197
  sentencing of, 279–280
  Stein, Annie and, 235–236,
    247–250
  underground life of, 10, 11, 13,
    209, 214–217, 221, 225–230,
    233–234
  Underground and, 240–243
  in Vietnam, 285

  at War Council, Flint, Michigan,
    207, 209
Jones, Julie, 12, 134–135
Jones, Malcolm Barton, 33–46, 69,
    72, 125
Jones, Millie, 12, 69–71, 74, 75,
    77–79, 82–84, 87–89, 122–123,
    259, 279–280
  birth of son Jeff, 89
  later life of, 286
  marriage of, 123, 133–135, 144
Jones, Mina Christine Tande. *See*
    Tande, Christine
Joplin, Janis, 181

Kapital, Das (Marx), 16
Kasserine Pass, 78
Kennedy, Jackie, 144, 256
Kennedy, John F., 126, 159
Kennedy, Robert F., 185, 186
Kent State University, 211
Khmer Rouge, 143
Khrushchev, Nikita, 107
King, Martin Luther, Jr., 158, 231
  assassination of, 148, 182
  Daley on, 187
Kirk, Grayson, 151
Kishinev, Ukraine, 17
Kissinger, C. Clark, 130
Kissinger, Henry, 232
Korean War, 124, 137
KPFK radio station, 210
Kresge's, Washington, D.C., 99–100,
    102
Ku Klux Klan, 127
Kunstler, William, 250

Lafayette, Marquis de, 231
La Guardia, Fiorello, 68
Lampson, Mary, 240
Laos, 11, 230–231
Lawrence, Vicki, 266
League for Industrial Democracy, 30,

31, 57, 129
Leary, Rosemary, 224
Leary, Timothy, 221–225, 251
Lee, Frank, 39
Lee, Robert E., 160
Lenin, V.I., 8, 151, 160, 236, 249
Leninists, 57
Leopold III, King of Belgium, 35, 49
Lerner, Jonny, 122, 181, 208
Liberated Guardian, 211
Liberation News Service, 210
Library of Congress, 109
Life magazine, 212
Lincoln, Abraham, 51, 52, 54
Lincoln Park, Chicago, 176–178,
    187, 189
Lindsay, John, 181, 212
London, Jack, 30
Long, Gerry, 174
Los Angeles Community College, 47
Los Angeles Stock Exchange, 42
Lundy's Restaurant, Brooklyn, 239
Lynd, Staughton, 131

Machtinger, Howie, 174
Madison Square Garden, New York,
    53
Maine (battleship), 37
Malcolm X, 151, 162, 231
Malick, Terence, 240
Manson, Charles, 207–209
Mao Tse-tung, 236, 238
Marian Anderson Citizens'
    Committee, 52
Marighella, Carlos, 220
Marijuana, 181, 261–262, 283
Marine and Transport Workers
    Union, 25
Marx, Karl, 16, 160, 161, 195, 236
Marxists, 20
Max, Steve, 131
May Days, 57
    1931, 20

1932, 19–21
1933, 25–27
Mayflower Hotel, New York City, 6
Mazritch, Poland, 28
McCarran, Pat, 110
McCarran-Walter Immigration Act
    of 1952, 108
McCarthy, Eugene, 185, 186, 191
McCarthy, Joseph, 107, 110
McCarthy Kids, 185, 188
McKim, Mead & White, 148
McKinley, William, 37, 38
McNamara, Robert, 139
Meeropol, Robert, 131
Mellen, Jim, 174
Mendocino, California, 218–220
Mensheviks, 20
Messinger, Ruth, 269
Methodist Peace Commission, 47
Meyer, Carl, 48
Meyer, Mildred, 47–49
Miguel Ascunçe (merchant ship), 171,
    172
Military Art of People's War, The (Giap),
    221
Millhouse: A White Comedy (docu-
    mentary), 239
Missouri Compromise, 36
Mobilization Committee to End the
    War in Vietnam, 185
Monkees, the, 185
Mooney, Tom, 27
Morea, Ben, 137, 182, 192
Mussolini, Benito, 27, 53
Myers, Judge, 98

National Brotherhood Week (1951),
    102
National Federation for
    Constitutional Liberties, 57
National Lawyers Guild, 138, 147
National Liberation Front, 144, 169,
    170, 175, 185

National Recovery Administration, 55, 113
National Student Federation, 29–30
National Student League, 22–24, 30–32, 55, 57
NBC (National Broadcasting Corporation), 51, 53
Neuman, Tom, 182
New Deal, 45, 55–56, 64, 66, 68
New Left Notes (Students for a Democratic Society), 136, 141, 178, 185, 186, 193, 194, 196, 198, 200, 202
New Masses, 24
New Morning Statement, 228–230, 236
New Paltz, New York, 235
New Republic, 68
New York City police, 166–168, 183–184, 211–212, 262, 271
New York Daily News, 121
New York Times, 19, 50, 68, 122, 141–143, 193, 199, 210–212, 233, 283
New York University, 20, 136
Nhu, Madame, 159
Nicholas II, Czar, 15, 17
Nicholson, Jack, 240
Nixon, Richard, 188, 192, 211, 228, 230–233, 237, 239, 243
NKVD, 64
North Africa, 78
North Sea, 86
"North Star, The" (E. Stein), 155
North Vietnamese, 131, 142–144, 169–172

Ochs, Phil, 138, 185
O'Donnell, Roger, 123, 134–135, 259
Oglesby, Carl, 128, 131
Old Mole, 211
Osawatomie, 239

Osborn, Celia, 274, 278
Osborn, Harold, 274–275, 278
Osborn, Jesse, 274
Oughton, Diana, 11

Pacifism, 45–47, 49, 71–73, 82, 136, 145
Parent Teacher Association, 153
Patricia (steamer), 17
Pawnee Indians, 36
Pearl Harbor, 59, 72
Pentagon, march on (1967), 10, 137–141, 163, 189, 190
Pentagon Papers, 241
People Against Racism in Education, 266
Pepsi Cola, 232
Perkins, Frances, 58
Perlo, Victor, 64, 111
Peter, Paul and Mary, 138
Philippines, 221
Phnom Penh, Cambodia, 142–143
Phuc, Kim, 285
Pittsburgh, Pennsylvania, 199–201
Pius XII, Pope, 50, 54
Point of Order (documentary), 239
Poland, 57, 86–88, 91
Pomeroy, William, 221
Port Huron Statement, 129, 130, 194–195, 236
Prairie Fire: The Politics of Anti-Imperialism, 238–239
Prairie Fire Organizing Committee, 249
Presidential elections
    1932, 22
    1948, 67
    1964, 121
    1968, 185, 186, 188
Progressive Labor Party, 104, 196–198, 204
Protestant peace movement, 45
Proudhonistes, 20

Psychedelic drugs, 181, 221, 222, 224
Public Works Administration, 55
Puerto Rican Socialist Party, 250

Quakers, 12, 71, 83, 88, 123–125, 133

Rabinowitz, Victor, 107, 116–117
Raskin, Eleanor E. *See* Stein, Eleanor
E.
Raskin, Jonah, 146, 147, 159–163,
165, 199, 201, 224
Rat (newspaper), 181, 182
Reagan, Ronald, 269
Red Dragon Print Collective, 238
Red Scare, 67
Reed, John, 30, 129
Reessing, Captain, 18
Reichbach, Gus, 149, 167, 198
Rein, David, 98
Republican Party, 21, 45, 66, 67
Republic of New Afrika, 250, 251
Reserve Officer Training Corps
(ROTC), 22, 31
Reston, James, 141
Ribicoff, Abraham, 191
Robbins, Terry, 11, 174, 204–205,
217
Robeson, Paul, 56, 117
Roger Wagner Chorale, 122, 123,
134–135
Rolling Thunder missions, 143
Romania, 91
Romny, Ukraine, 16, 17
Roosevelt, Eleanor, 50, 52, 68
Roosevelt, Franklin Delano, 30, 50,
51, 53, 54, 115
death of, 66
election of 1932 and, 22
New Deal of, 45, 55
organized labor and, 57–58
World War II and, 63, 72
Roosevelt, Theodore, 46, 126
Rosenberg, Ethel, 90–91, 105, 131

Rosenberg, Julius, 90–91, 105, 131
Rubin, Jerry, 187
Rudd, Mark, 10, 148, 172, 174, 197,
212, 214, 258
Rustin, Bayard, 158

Sacramento Office of California
Prisons, 232
St. Marks Place, New York, 181–184
Salisbury, Harrison, 143
San Francisco, California, 10, 11, 180,
219, 225–226
San Francisco Department of
Corrections, 232
San Juan Hill, battle of, 38, 46
Saturday Evening Post, 112
Schwartz, Dan, 265
Scottsboro Boys, 27
SDS. *See* Students for a Democratic
Society (SDS)
Seale, Bobby, 213
Securities and Exchange
Commission (SEC), 109
Seeger, Pete, 117
Segregation in Washington, 94
Seimon, Leonard, 265
Selective Service, 72–73, 82, 83, 136,
237
Senate Committee on Government
Operations, 110
Senate Judiciary Committee, 110,
116
Senate Permanent Subcommittee on
Investigations, 110
Senate Subcommittee on
Monopolistic Practices, 109
Senate Subcommittee to Investigate
the Administration of the
Internal Security Act, 110
Sicily, 78
Sihanouk, Prince Norodom, 143
Sinclair, Upton, 30, 129
Sipser, Weinstock and Weinman, 133

Sly and the Family Stone, 209
Smash Monogamy movement, 208
Socialists, 20, 26, 57, 120, 122
Soledad Brother (Jackson), 231
Soul on Ice (Cleaver), 255
South Africa, 148
Southern Christian Leadership
    Conference (SCLC), 138
Southern Pacific Railroad, 71
Soviet Union, 23, 26, 27, 53, 57, 59,
    63–64, 91–94, 107, 129, 158,
    286
Spanish American War, 37–38, 46
Spanish Civil War, 53–54
Stalin, Joseph, 23, 26, 57, 91–92, 107,
    254
Stalingrad, 78
Stalinists, 57
State, U.S. Department of, 111, 131
Stavis, Morty, 270, 275–277,
    279–280, 283
Steckler, Annie. See Stein, Annie
    Steckler
Steckler, Bessie Volozhinsky, 16, 18,
    27
Steckler, Frieda, 18, 27
Steckler, Philip, 16–19, 27, 269
Steckler, Sylvia, 18, 27–28
Stein, Annie Steckler, 7–8, 16, 18, 19,
    21–25, 27–32, 56, 62, 152, 154,
    195
  birth of children, 65, 66
  civil rights work of, 90, 92–94,
    96–105, 153, 269
  Columbia uprising and, 166, 167
  daughter Eleanor and, 147–148,
    155, 157–160, 162, 167, 168,
    198, 267, 269, 278
  death of, 269
  death of Arthur and, 157
  expelled from Communist Party,
    158
  expelled from Weathermen, 252

  FBI and, 8, 13–14, 32, 100, 110,
    162–163
  as grandmother, 265, 269
  Hard Times Conference and, 250
  Jones, Jeff and, 235–236, 247–250
  later life of, 266–269
  at Marian Anderson concert,
    51–55
  marriage of, 29
  at Pentagon protest, 139, 163
Stein, Arthur, 8, 28, 91, 100, 152, 195
  appearance before House
    Committee on Un-American
    Activities (HUAC), 106–115,
    117–119, 154, 249
  Communist Party and, 60–65
  Cuban revolution of 1959 and,
    154
  death of, 156–157
  FBI and, 58–60, 66, 67, 110, 154
  health of, 55, 56, 65, 104, 154, 267
  labor politics and, 56, 58, 65–68,
    104, 110, 115–118
  at Marian Anderson concert,
    51–55
  marriage of, 29
Stein, Charles, 28
Stein, Eleanor E., 3–9, 14, 239, 250
  action in Pittsburgh, 199–201
  arrests of, 1–2, 167–168, 200,
    272–277, 283
  birth of, 66
  birth of Bluejay, 284
  birth of Thai, 244–247
  Bust Book by, 198–199
  childhood of, 101, 104–106, 119,
    152–158, 267
  at Columbia University, 146–152,
    193, 201, 284–285
  Columbia uprising and, 163–168
  education of, 146, 155, 158, 160,
    161, 163, 285
  father (Arthur), relationship with,

154, 155, 157
Jeff, relationship with, 234–235,
    245, 246, 253–263, 279
in Manchester, 146, 161–163
marriage to Jeff Jones, 279
marriage to Jonah Raskin, 146,
    160, 199, 201
at Mendocino national meeting,
    219
mother (Annie), relationship with,
    147–148, 155, 157–160, 162,
    167, 168, 198, 267, 269, 278
as parent, 257–259, 263–265,
    267–269, 270–271, 278
at Pentagon protest, 139, 163
at SDS national convention
    (1969), 193, 194, 196, 197
sentencing of, 279
stillborn daughter, 264–265
style of, 146–148
trip to Havana, 169–172
with Weathermen, 197–199, 201,
    219, 228, 229
Stein, Frederick L., 35
Stein, Philip, 279
    birth of, 65
    childhood of, 101, 104, 105, 119,
        267
Stein, Sadie Gordon, 28, 156
Steinbeck, John, 46
Stock market crash (1929), 42
Stone, I.F., 91
Story of Zoya and Shura, The, 152
Student Non-Violent Coordinating
    Committee (SNCC), 138
Student Review (magazine), 24, 31
Students for a Democratic Society
    (SDS), 5, 9, 10, 30, 181. *See also*
    Jones, Jeffrey Carl; Weathermen
Antioch chapter of, 127, 128, 130
Black Panthers and, 204–206
Columbia chapter of, 148–150,
    193
Columbia uprising and, 163–168
Democratic National Convention
    and, 185–187, 189–191
divisions within, 172, 173, 196,
    197, 215
founders of, 129–130
Madison chapter of, 175–176
march on Pentagon, 138–141
membership numbers, 131, 136,
    193
national convention (1965),
    130–131
national convention (1967),
    137–142
national convention (1969),
    192–194, 196–198, 204
New Left Notes, 136, 141, 178,
    185, 186, 193, 194, 196, 198,
    200, 202
officers, 197
Port Huron Statement, 129, 130,
    194–195, 236
trip to Havana, 169–172
Sundstrom, John, 182–184
Symbionese Liberation Army, 221

Tande, Christine, 35–36, 39–41,
    43–45, 69, 125
Tania: The Unforgettable Guerrilla,
    220–221
Tappis, Steve, 174
Tate, Sharon, 208
Taylor, Olivia, 266, 267, 269, 270
Terrell, Mary Church, 90, 93–99,
    101, 103–106, 153
Terrell, Robert, 95
Tet Offensive, 170, 185
Thai, Nguyen, 170–172
Thirty-Fourth Bomber Group,
    Seventh Bomber Squadron,
    79–81
Thomas, Norman, 22
Thompson, Stanley, 286

Thompson's Restaurant, Washington,
　　D.C., 97–98, 102, 104–105
Till, Emmett, 153
Toms, John, 80–81
Tonkin Gulf resolution, 186
Tonopah, Nevada, 79–80
Treasury, U.S. Department of the,
　　213
Trotsky, Leon, 254
Trotskyites, 57
Trud (newspaper), 93
Truman, Harry, 65, 67, 68, 94, 105,
　　110, 115
Tunnels of Cu Chi, 285
Twentieth Soviet Party Congress,
　　107

Ukraine, 16–17
Underground (film), 239–241
Union Square, New York, 19–21, 25,
　　26, 53
Union Theological Seminary, New
　　York, 73
United Black Workers, 250
United Federal Workers of America,
　　56, 58, 115
United Front, 57
United Nations Relief and
　　Rehabilitation Administration
　　(UNRRA), 83–87
United Public Workers of America
　　(UPWA), 65–68, 104, 110,
　　115–118, 270
University of Manchester, 161
Up Against the Wall Motherfuckers,
　　182–184, 192, 255

Van Lydegraf, Clayton, 223, 251, 252,
　　258
Velvet Underground, 181
Vietnam War, 12, 120, 128, 136, 144,
　　163, 170, 185
　　Americans in Hanoi, 131, 143

Cambodian incursion, 4, 207, 211
　　casualties, 121, 185, 191–192,
　　228–229, 242
　　end of, 237, 242, 244
　　escalation of air war, 228, 232
　　Johnson's visit, 121
　　Laos, invasion of, 230–231
　　peace talks, 232
　　protest march on Pentagon, 10,
　　137–141, 163, 189, 190
　　Vietnamization policy, 228, 231
Von Steuben, Baron, 231

Wack, Lawrence, 1, 272–275
Walt Disney Company, 123–134, 241
Walter, Francis E., 107–110, 117–119
War Council, Flint, Michigan (1970),
　　207–209, 211
Warhol, Andy, 181
War Production Board, 59, 60, 64
Washington, George, 231
Washington Afro-American, 104
Washington Board of Trade, 30
Washington Courier, 101
Washington Evening Star, 93
Washington Federation Civic
　　Association, 102
Washington Post, 30, 31, 51–52, 54,
　　102, 108, 141–142
Washington Real Estate Board, 93
Washington Times-Herald, 52
Watergate, 243
Watts riots, 182
Weathermen (Weather
　　Underground), 4, 10, 13. *See
　　also* Jones, Jeffrey Carl
　　Days of Rage, 173–179
　　Declaration of a State of War,
　　210–211, 214; 220
　　expulsions from, 252–254
　　Leary prison escape and, 222–225
　　in Madison, Wisconsin, 175–176
　　name changes, 229, 238

National Action, 202, 206

national convention (1969), 197–198

national meeting in Mendocino, 218–220

New Morning Statement, 228–230, 236

War Council, Flint, Michigan, 207–209

West Eleventh Street townhouse explosion and, 4–5, 7, 11, 14, 210, 212, 217, 229, 258, 271

"You Don't Need a Weatherman to Know Which Way the Wind Blows," 174, 194–195

Webb, Lee, 131

Welfare Mothers for Justice, 250

West Eleventh Street townhouse explosion (1970), 4–5, 7, 11, 14, 210, 212, 217, 229, 258, 271

Westmoreland, William, 121

Wexler, Haskell, 240

What Is to Be Done? (Lenin), 8

Who, The, 181

Wiener, Evelyn (Chavy), 26, 28, 56, 64, 160, 249, 278

  Communist Party and, 15–16, 21, 25, 63, 152, 153, 158

  FBI and, 63

  later life of, 286

Stein, Annie and, 16, 55, 268–270

Wilkerson, Cathlyn, 5, 8–9, 137, 142, 212, 240, 258

Wilkerson, James, 210

Willett, Bill, 176, 202–203, 208

Women's movement, 229, 252

Women Strike for Peace, 138

Woodstock, 207, 208, 224, 235

Works Progress Administration (WPA), 45, 56, 59, 62, 64, 109, 112

World Peace Appeal, 118

World Trade Center, New York, 133

World War I, 34, 48

World War II, 12, 49, 50, 57, 59, 63, 66, 69–70, 72, 74, 77, 78, 82, 83, 124

Wright, Richard, 160

Yippies, 181, 185, 187

Yosemite National Park, 33–35

"You Don't Need a Weatherman to Know Which Way the Wind Blows," 174, 194–195

Young Communist League, 16, 24, 32

Young Lords, 199

Young Pioneers, 15

Zengakuren league, 137

About the Author

THAI JONES used multiple aliases before he reached the age of four. In 1981, heavily armed agents of the Federal Bureau of Investigation and New York Police Department swept into his family's New York apartment and arrested his parents, fugitive leaders of the radical Weather Underground. Jones has since worked as a reporter for *Newsday* and is a graduate of Columbia University's School of Journalism. He lives in Albany, New York.